Praise for *Nothing Is Wasted*

We serve a God who never wastes anything—because everyone and everything is valuable in His eyes. Davey Blackburn is a walking, talking illustration of how God can bring light out of incredible darkness. You may not understand everything you're going through right now, but the message behind *Nothing Is Wasted* will challenge you to keep putting one foot in front of the other.

—**Dave Ramsey,** *bestselling author and nationally syndicated radio show host*

Davey Blackburn's story is one of the most heartbreaking, yet faith-building, stories I've ever encountered. If you are hurting from a betrayal, grieving a loss, or struggling to overcome a deep wound, Davey's book *Nothing Is Wasted* is for you.

—**Craig Groeschel,** *pastor of Life.Church, and bestselling author*

For my friend Davey Blackburn, "the valley of the shadow of death" is more than a line from a psalm. It's a permanent part of his story. The murder of his wife, Amanda Blackburn, sent shockwaves through a local community and the community of faith. In *Nothing Is Wasted*, Davey tells his story—their story. But at some level, it is or will be our story. In the end, it's a story of hope and redemption.

—**Andy Stanley,** *pastor of Northpoint Church and bestselling author*

Moving. Hope-filled. Faith-building. Scripture tells us that suffering is the refiner's fire God purposes for the purification of our faith. Davey Blackburn is walking through that fire, and his made-like-gold faith is evident in the way he's stewarding his story. If you've ever wondered what your Father's plan is for your pain, *Nothing Is Wasted* will help you anchor in His promises and trust His purposes.

—**Louie Giglio,** *pastor of Passion City Church, founder of Passion Conferences, and bestselling author*

God is in the business of taking what the Enemy intends for evil and using it for His purpose and for our destiny. I am grateful for stories like Davey's that remind us of that truth and fill us with hope no matter what unexpected challenges we face.

—**Christine Caine,** *founder of A21 and Propel Women*

Davey's story of love and loss with his sweet wife, Amanda, is touching, devastating, and God-glorifying all at the same time. If you're questioning the Lord in the midst of your own pain, *Nothing Is Wasted* will help you find healing and trust that God is good even if our circumstances aren't.

—**Lysa TerKeurst,** New York Times *bestselling author and president of Proverbs 31 Ministries*

Every single one of us at some point will come face-to-face with circumstances we perceive to be "impossible." In this book Davey walks us through his journey of how he found himself in that exact situation—but what seemed impossible to get through was actually transformed into a miraculous story as Jesus didn't deliver Davey from the storm, but rather through the storm. As you read the pages that follow, you will be not only encouraged but also equipped to walk through your "impossible" circumstances, knowing with confidence that Jesus will see you through.

—**Perry Noble,** *pastor and author of* Unleash *and* Overwhelmed

I've known Davey and his family for some time. I watched him as a college student, passionate about reaching the student-athletes surrounding him. I mentored him as he and Amanda cut their teeth in ministry at NewSpring Church. I stood by them as they planted Resonate Church in Indianapolis. And I've walked with Davey as he's endured the loss of his precious bride. In *Nothing Is Wasted* you'll experience a story of love, calling, loss, heartache, hurt, forgiveness, and fear at a gut-wrenching level. But more importantly you'll also experience the faith, hope, peace, resolve, strength, and courage our God is willing to give anyone walking through trial. Regardless of what situation you currently find yourself in, this book is for you—an inspiration and guide to faith in the midst of fire.

—**Kevin Myers,** *senior pastor of 12Stone Church in Atlanta and author of* Home Run

Davey Blackburn is a courageous person of faith who has found strength from God in the midst of unspeakable pain. He offers powerful encouragement for all of us in difficult seasons and points the way forward in faith and hope.

—**Jud Wilhite,** *pastor of Central Church in Las Vegas*

In *Nothing Is Wasted*, Davey Blackburn tells an incredible and emotional journey of overcoming. The tragedy Davey faced was unthinkable. His strength in the face of heartbreak and his unyielding faith in God will inspire and give hope to so many.

—**Roma Downey,** *actor, producer, and president of LightWorkers Media*

Few people these days are willing to be transparent in the midst of a trial. Even fewer are willing to openly explore issues as sensitive as trauma, forgiveness, and race relations. As someone who is passionate about racial reconciliation, I admire how Davey seeks to build bridges in an age where many are driving division. His journey is sure to prompt an introspective look into your own heart and bring a fresh perspective to your pain.

—**Miles McPherson,** *pastor of The Rock Church in San Diego, motivational speaker, and former NFL football player*

I remember sitting across the table from Davey when we were interviewing him for our ministry team at NewSpring Church. As I heard him talk, I knew with all confidence that God had great plans in store for him. I, of course, had no idea how that journey would unfold. No one should have to experience what Davey has. Yet, even in the face of tragedy and pain, it's evident that God's goodness and mercy still prevail. Be inspired by this incredible story.

—**Tony Morgan,** *founder and lead strategist of The Unstuck Group*

Davey Blackburn is a great friend and brother. His life's journey has taken him through the valley of unimaginable tragedy to the heights of healing and hope. This book recounts every step. If you have ever questioned the purpose in the pain of life, Davey's book *Nothing Is Wasted* is for you.

—**Brad Cooper,** *pastor, NewSpring Church*

When I met Davey, it was not how you'd want to meet anyone. He's now had a little time to heal and process, but I met him right after the death of his wife. When I heard about what happened, I remember thinking about my own wife and my daughters, who were around Amanda's age. I wondered if I would have been able to stand back up and proclaim the goodness of God after such a tragedy. Then I met Davey. I could already sense that a power greater than his own was at work. I believe in that power. I preach that power, but I've never had to rely on it like this. *Nothing Is Wasted* is a book that you should read for yourself and then pass on to people in your life who question their faith for whatever reason. While an educational degree might give you some credibility when it comes to explaining God, nothing comes close to having a story of your own. Davey has a story, and if he can say God is good—then God is good!

—**Dr. Tim Harlow,** *senior pastor, Parkview Christian Church in Orland Park, Illinois, and author of* What Made Jesus Mad?

I hate clichés. Even more, I hate psychobabble. Let me assure you that *Nothing Is Wasted* is neither. It is gut-wrenching truth that testifies to the fact that our God is very near, very involved, really does care, and works both upstream and downstream. This book reassures us that this is true when you can see it and when you can neither see it, feel it, nor sense it in the moment of utter despair and pain. This story is a testimony of hope and goodness in the darkest of times. It's the real deal! How can I say that? Because I personally took professional care of Davey shortly after this tragedy. *Nothing Is Wasted* is a must-read for anyone who wants to live well in spite of...

—**Dr. John M. Walker,** *president and chief psychologist, Blessing Ranch Ministries*

I honestly wasn't prepared for the emotional journey that this book took me on. God used every excruciating detail and impeccably timed revelation to remind me that His plan for our lives is far beyond our understanding. And although the events that happened in Davey's life were tragic, this book does so much more than recount a tragedy. Davey's unflinching and vulnerable telling of his journey serves as a road map to restoration and to

God's provision for all of us. I believe that for all the pain that was endured, there is infinite wisdom and blessing for any and all who come across this story. It will most certainly leave you encouraged and determined to trust Him through any valley you might find yourself in.

—**Bear Rinehart,** *songwriter and lead singer of NEEDTOBREATHE*

It is unimaginable to me the horror that Davey Blackburn and his family had to face as told in this book. Even harder to understand may be a faith so unshakable that it could lead them to such a powerful lesson about trusting God. If the difficulties you are going through have convinced you the only fruit of those hard times is sadness, read this. Now.

—**Walt Aldridge,** *songwriter and coauthor of* I Loved Her First

I've never met Davey Blackburn. He and I are connected only by my prior knowledge of his story, and his appreciation of a wedding song I wrote years ago. But when his editor gave me a copy of this book, she could not have known the bitterness I have been grappling with this past year. Though nowhere near the degree of loss Davey suffered, I felt the bond of understanding and encouragement from a fellow life traveler. This book is a journey through the joy of things beginning, the maddening pain of things ending, and the courage of life continuing. It is both heartbreaking and heart-lifting, and so becomes a confidently centered message of hope to anyone struggling with great loss.

—**Elliott Park,** *songwriter and coauthor of* I Loved Her First

NOTHING IS WASTED

A TRUE STORY OF HOPE, FORGIVENESS, AND FINDING PURPOSE IN PAIN

DAVEY BLACKBURN

Forefront
BOOKS

Published by Forefront Books, Nashville, Tennessee.
Distributed by Simon & Schuster.

Library of Congress Control Number: 2024907759

Print ISBN: 978-1-63763-327-4
E-book ISBN: 978-1-63763-328-1

Cover Design by Tara Vanhooser
Interior Design by Bill Kersey, KerseyGraphics

Author is represented by Ambassador Literary, Nashville, Tennessee.

Printed in the United States of America

For Amanda Grace
You taught me to love, to lead, and
to leave a beautiful legacy.
Thank you for running hard after Jesus and
loving Weston and me so well in the process.
With all my heart . . .

CONTENTS

FOREWORD

IN THE NINETEENTH CENTURY, BISON WERE SLAUGHTERED ACROSS North America almost to the point of extinction. The worst and most appalling killings occurred when rail companies allowed paying customers to shoot buffalo from the windows of moving trains for fun, mowing them down by the thousands. It is appalling to think of the corpses of these magnificent beasts that once roamed the prairies and plains left behind to rot on the ground so senselessly.

Juxtaposed to this is the approach of the Native Americans who also killed the buffalo, but they did so not for fun, but for a purpose. They killed only enough to feed their families; and out of sincere respect for the life they'd taken, they left nothing behind after the hunt. In addition to the meat and hides they procured, they also made leather strings for their bows, glue out of the hooves, and even used dried dung for fires. Blood was still shed and the buffalo was still dead, but it was all for a purpose.

My first encounter with Davey and Amanda Blackburn was while they were heading to Chicago on a train and I was on the other side of the country. As the Blackburns shared iPhone headphones, split between their ears the way Lady and the Tramp shared pasta, they listened to me speak about my own journey and discovered that where His children and suffering are concerned, God has the mindset of a Native American hunter—nothing is wasted. Davey had earlier listened to this message alone and had decided to bring the *Through the Eyes of a Lion* podcast on this day trip to share with his wife. Like bison hide, hair, and hooves being harvested and put to use, God skillfully took a great pain my family had walked through and turned it into something beautiful and helpful as He prepared Davey and Amanda for the days to come.

I found out about their day on the train as one hears most things these days, on social media. Thanks, Twitter. Learning about the Blackburns and our connection made my heart soar and sink at the same time. In the days and months following Amanda's murder, I joined countless others who stand in awe, watching courage be personified and Jesus be glorified again and again through Davey's boldness and honesty in response to unfathomable pain. He has taken a principle I believe in and have found instrumental in handling suffering—running toward the roar—and has lived it out to an unimaginable degree.

It makes me tremble with anticipation knowing that the book you hold in your hands is destined for the same glorious purpose as the podcast they listened to that day on the train. No matter what the future holds for you, God wants to use the precious words on these pages to help you train for the trial you are not yet in. What God has entrusted to my friend Davey is sure to buoy your heart and tether it to a heavenly anchor that will keep you steadfast and immovable no matter what life sends your way.

Levi Lusko
Whitefish, Montana

INTRODUCTION

I'VE ALWAYS WANTED TO WRITE A BOOK. BOOKS HAVE HAD A profound impact on my spiritual and intellectual formation throughout my childhood and on into my adulthood. My dad is a pastor, and while I grew up, my mom and dad would bring me along to all of their get-togethers, board meetings, and Sunday service rehearsals. My mom, always concerned with my early development, would stick a book in my hands rather than a Game Boy. I learned how to tune out the hum of adult conversation and put myself in the plot of whatever happened to be in front of my eyes at the time—The Hardy Boys, The Chronicles of Narnia, *Little House on the Prairie.*

I always wanted to write a book. But this is the book I never wanted to write. Nor could I have ever fathomed I would *have* to write. No one imagines stepping into a story like this.

In my mind, my story would read a bit differently. Tenacious twenty-five-year-old maverick moves to Indianapolis with his wife to start a church. After a few years their church explodes to a membership of a few thousand people. Leaders everywhere clamor to find out how they did it. Read the tale, discover the secret sauce, and hear lessons learned along the way as they took this little group of four people and willed it into a movement that turned a city upside down.

At least that's how I dreamed it would go. I thought God would use my talent and tenacity to grow something that would influence the world. And then I'd write about it. But what I'm discovering is that God usually generates more impact from your

15

brokenness than from your talent (I talk more about this later, so I'm getting ahead of myself).

Immediately after Amanda was killed, some very influential people reached out to care for me, encourage me, and walk with me. One of those influential people was Bob Goff, the author of *Love Does*. One evening in December after Amanda passed, Bob invited me to an event he was speaking at in Chicago. I made the three-hour drive up from Indy, and we shared a plate of sushi before his gig. I was on the verge of tears the entire dinner as this author—who has impacted hundreds of thousands, if not millions—took a couple of hours to love on me individually and personally.

At the end of our dinner, Bob gave me one of the best pieces of advice I could have ever received as a writer. He said, "Davey, you need to be writing down everything you're feeling right now. You're going to have the opportunity to help a lot of people, but before you can help them, you have to connect with them. There are a lot of hurting people in this world, and they need to know what you're feeling and how you're processing through your pain."

A couple of months later Bob invited me to fly out to Anaheim, California, to hang out with him and a couple hundred other folks for one of his "Living Room" events. One night during that week, he invited all eight of the event presenters and musicians to join him at Club 33, one of the most exclusive cigar clubs in the entire world located in the middle of Disneyland.

I sat on a couch socializing with a few of the presenters when from across the room a woman waltzed over and plopped down on the couch across from me. I can't remember if she introduced herself or not before she cut straight to the point. "Are you going to write a book?" she asked.

I told her I had certainly thought about it but had decided I would wait for a few years, until I was completely healed from this whole thing—whatever that means. I'll never forget what she told me. It went something like this:

"Davey, the Lord has put His hand on this story unlike anything I've ever seen. People are connecting with Amanda's life from all over the globe and clamoring to hear more. I think you should tell your story while it's fresh and while you can portray the raw emotion of what you're living in every day. I'd love to be of some help in the process if I could. I coach writers on how to take their project from infancy to fruition."

A couple of months later I hired this woman, Ally Fallon, to be my writing coach. I don't think I could have walked through this process without her. Even the *idea* of writing can be so daunting it paralyzes you. Most people don't know where to begin. Ally helped me put the process into bite-size steps and craft a flow to the book that would tell the story in a way readers could engage with. After one day with her, the entire book was outlined, and we started down a road that would arguably bring more healing to me than to any one of my readers.

When I finally sat down to write *Nothing Is Wasted*, I knew there were things the Lord had been teaching me, new perspectives He had begun to show me. Since most pastor books I had read were of a self-help nature, I figured that's how my book would flesh itself out as well. I assumed I would take the things I had been learning and the messages I had been preaching since losing Amanda, compile them, and that would be my book.

But when I began writing in that style, it felt sterile. It lacked depth. It almost felt as if I were telling you—the reader—how you should walk through tragedy. Like I was now the expert on it.

The reality is I'm not.

The past two years have not been about me demonstrating expertise on trudging through the valley of the shadow of death.

I'm not some virtuoso on the subject. On the contrary, I'm a victim—a victim of God's grace. *He's* carried me. *He's* taught me. *He's* loved me. *He's* walked with me. *He's* healed me.

So I scrapped it. All of it. And I started over.

I sat down at my kitchen table one Friday morning and began writing out the story. In detail. Everything. Beginning with the morning I walked in to find Amanda. There were several moments when I had to get up and walk away—my heart pounding, my head swimming, my ears hot, my breathing heavy—just remembering how I felt in those moments kneeling beside my beautiful bride waiting for the paramedics, convinced this wasn't really happening.

I finished chapter 1 that day and sent it over to Ally. I told her I didn't know if it was appropriate to be this raw in a book and that if she didn't think I should submit it to my publishers, I was fine with it. I told her just writing it all down had brought more healing to me than almost anything else I'd experienced since Amanda passed. I had written that chapter in a way that the reader could walk this journey with me—inside my head— discovering things as I discovered them.

To my surprise, Ally told me she loved it and she thought that publishers would too. So I kept writing.

Page by page, chapter by chapter, everything seemed to flow, like some supernatural force was taking over my fingers and doing all the typing for me. In the initial manuscript I didn't once experience the infamous writer's block. My mind was clear, my creativity free, and my focus crisp. And only the Lord is to get the credit for it. This project quickly turned into a labor of love, like a final love letter to my beautiful bride.

As the story laid itself out, something profound happened—I began to heal even more. The *entire* story slowly came into focus. Before, I saw merely bits and pieces, excerpts and clips, but now

I was beginning to see this beautiful canvas, a tapestry of God's redeeming story emerging through my tragedy.

I began to realize that I am not the author of this book. I didn't come up with this story. God did. He's the author. I'm merely the reporter. I'm the journalist showing you the goodness of God during the little part my family has played in His grand narrative. He's the author and perfecter of our life and faith. As you read this book, I don't want you to think that I'm someone special; rather, I want you to say, "Wow, God is a really good God. And if He can do that for Davey in the midst of his pain, He can do that for me in the midst of mine."

I must warn you. What you're about to read is very raw and transparent. I realize I'm taking a huge risk by being as vulnerable as I am here. I realize I'm opening myself up to even more scrutiny and criticism. But I also realize that many people face the same feelings I've felt. If even one person is moved, touched, healed, or brought closer to Jesus because of my transparency and brokenness in these pages, it's worth all the scrutiny I may endure.

Amanda used to always joke around with me that the real litmus test on whether or not I had written a good book was if *she* could sit down and read it. She wasn't much of a reader outside of her regular morning Bible reading. If she read a book all the way through, I knew it was because it had captured her heart and imagination. Oh, how I wish she could read this one. Not many people have a book written about their love story, their life, and their legacy. Amanda undoubtedly deserved it.

In the pages to follow, my prayer is—and I know Amanda's prayer would be—that you find hope in the midst of your trial, joy in the midst of your sorrow, purpose in the midst of your pain, and a good Father in the midst of your circumstance—a Father who never wastes our pain but brings strength and new beginnings.

PART 1

WHEN TRAGEDY STRIKES

1

DREAM TO A NIGHTMARE

It was supposed to be a normal Tuesday. My wife, Amanda, and I had spent the last four years laboring tirelessly to get a church plant off the ground in the city of Indianapolis. Preaching and pastoring people occupied Sunday mornings, meetings filled up Sunday afternoons, and follow-up appointments ranged all day on Mondays, which ended with our late-night leadership meetings. By the time Tuesdays rolled around, I looked forward to an early morning workout, getting started on the next Sunday's message, and kicking back for a quiet evening at home with Amanda and our fifteen-month-old son, Weston.

This Tuesday I was even more excited than normal to spend time with Amanda because we had recently found out she was pregnant. She wasn't far along yet, but Amanda was convinced the baby was a girl, and I could already envision the four of us together as a growing family. We had planned to put up Christmas decorations and continue a discussion on baby names we had started the weekend before. Amanda had mentioned the name Everette (Evie) Grace if it was a girl. After only a couple of days of mulling it over, I was already dreaming about daddy/daughter dates with little Evie.

As usual, I woke up around 4:30 a.m., spent time reading my Bible, grabbed my gym bag, and headed down to the fitness center. I left the house frustrated that I was running a little behind from what I had planned and that I hadn't thought to pack a change of clothes so I could shower at the gym. Showering there meant I could save time by going straight to the coffee shop and drinking a cup of joe; calling my best friend, Kenneth Wagner; and getting an early start on message prep for the next Sunday. As someone who loves productivity and forward progress, I typically packed each moment of the workday full. Plus I wanted to wrap up sooner rather than later on this particular day so I could get on to a cozy and festive evening with Amanda.

Oh well, I'll just run back home, shower after my phone call, and hop over to the nearest Starbucks.

It was 7 a.m., and I had started on my lat pull-downs and upright rows when Kenneth called.

"Hey, dude! You good to start our convo?"

"Absolutely, bro! As long as you're okay with me finishing up my workout while we chat."

I grinned slightly, thinking how annoying it must be for him to hear me breathing in his ear with every rep. But hey, if this was going to maximize my work time so I could get home even sooner, I would do whatever it took. Headphones in place, I began our normal Tuesday conversation.

Kenneth and I had been best friends since our time playing baseball at Southern Wesleyan University. I remember meeting him at freshmen orientation and immediately thinking of him as a brother from another mother. We soon discovered we had much in common—interests, personality, dreams, ambitions, and best of all, before we had ever met, we both answered a call to full-time ministry during the same message at the same youth conference in Charlotte, North Carolina.

He and I soon became inseparable and remained that way through college. I was there when he met Sherry, who is now his wife. I was the one who often drove him around as we discussed how their relationship was developing. I was there to snap pictures when he proposed to her in front of Wrigley Field in Chicago before a Cubs game. I was in their wedding. He was the first person I told about Amanda after meeting her on a blind date over fall break. During college, while Amanda was at school in Florida, Kenneth, Sherry, and I would go on what we called "Davey Dates." These were double dates without Amanda. Often we'd call her and tell her how much we wished she were sitting with us at Starbucks in Clemson. He was my leaning post when Amanda gave me up for forty days of Lent (that's a whole different story, which I'll explain later). He was one of the first people I called when I proposed to Amanda, and he stood by me on our wedding day. With him alone I had shared my hopes and dreams of building a church that would turn a major metropolitan city upside down for Jesus, of growing old with Amanda, and of raising a family who made a dramatic impact in the world for God's kingdom.

Amanda and I trusted Kenneth and Sherry unequivocally. When we first made the decision to move to Indianapolis to plant Resonate Church, they were two of the first people we asked to join us. They felt called to remain in Delaware, and we celebrated with them when they made the decision to start their own church in the heart of Dover. Kenneth and Sherry became our biggest cheerleaders through what would be, up to that point, the toughest four years of our lives.

Even from a distance, every Tuesday morning we would talk about whatever came to our minds: victories, defeats, stresses, marriage, pastoring, people pressures, church planting, financial struggles, and most recently, parenting.

That morning, after finishing up my sets in the gym, I jumped back in the car and began driving home. While I drove,

Kenneth and I chatted about the amazing success and growth he was seeing at United Church, his two-month-old church plant.

I pulled back into the driveway of my house around 7:40 a.m. and paused there. Our Tuesday morning conversations had become such a routine that Amanda had asked me to finish them outside. Weston would sleep, without fail, from 8:00 p.m. to 8:00 a.m., and the 7:00 a.m. to 8:00 a.m. hour was the only time Amanda had space to herself to read her Bible, talk to Jesus, journal, and gather her thoughts for the day. On a few occasions I had barged back into the house at 7:30, only to accidentally wake Weston and interrupt her alone time.

So I paced in the driveway, talking on the phone, waiting for the time when I knew it would be safe to go inside. From the little window of the front door I could see the door to Weston's room. An open door was always the indicator it was safe to enter. This occurred at 8:00 a.m. on the dot every Tuesday. But not this Tuesday. The door was still closed.

At 8:05, I peered through the window again, and Weston's door was still shut. No problem. I would take a couple more minutes and wrap up this call.

At 8:10, still no sign to come in. At 8:15, nothing.

"Hey man, I probably better go," I finally said to Kenneth. "I have a lot of work to do today and should get a start on it. Love ya, dude."

I hung up the phone, opened the front door, and walked in.

Nothing could have prepared me for the scene I stepped into—or just how, exactly, my life was about to change.

You don't realize how fast your life can be turned upside down without any notice. But in just one moment, it's possible for everything to go from normal to tragic. And this was that moment for me.

When I stepped through the doorway, there was Amanda, my bride, my beauty, my love, lying face down next to the fireplace. My heart stopped. I froze.

"Babe? You okay?"

No response.

"Sweetheart? Amanda Grace?!"

Still nothing.

"Amanda!!?"

My headphones and car keys both fell from my hands and crashed against the floor in the entryway. I flew down the two steps that led from our doorway to the living room and straight to Amanda's side.

Immediately, everything began moving lightning fast and in slow motion at the same time. My heart pounded, my mind began to swim. All my senses became suddenly heightened, crystal clear, and at the same time I felt like I was wading through a muddied blur.

"Jesus, no. Jesus, no. This can't be happening!"

The words escaped my lips without my permission. I dropped to my knees beside her, noticing the pool of blood surrounding her head. I moved to turn her over. *Maybe I could wake her up,* I thought to myself. My mind raced to figure out what could be happening, how she could have possibly ended up here, like that. During pregnancy, she would often get lightheaded and have to sit down. Maybe a dizzy spell had overtaken her, she fell and hit her head, and I could somehow wake her from it.

But when I turned her over, I gasped. Blood covered her mouth and nose. Now on her back, breathing suddenly became an intense struggle for her. I quickly turned her back over and returned her head to the position I originally found her in. It was then I felt the blood matting the hair on the back of her head. Not knowing what to do, I just kept my hand there. I desperately scanned the room for something I could get to stop the bleeding, at the same time refusing to leave her side.

"Amanda, baby, can you hear me?! Wake up, sweetheart!"

Oh, Jesus. I shouldn't have turned her over.

I reached for my phone, my fingers shaking. Blood now smeared over my thumb made it almost impossible to swipe the screen and unlock it. After what seemed like a hundred attempts, I finally got it open, and as quickly as I could, dialed 911.

It wasn't until after I spoke with the 911 operator that panic began to set in. *Had I made sense? Was I coherent? Did I give them the right address? Why are they not here yet? What could be taking them so long? The operator didn't seem as urgent as this situation certainly calls for!*

It was probably only a couple of minutes but it felt like an eternity. I knelt there as questions about the scene I had just entered frantically swarmed in my head. My mind began taking snapshots of what I was seeing scattered around me.

What happened here? Why are her clothes off? Did she get out of the shower and get lightheaded? Did she fall? Did the decorative wall ladder that was now on the ground fall on her? What could explain her head bleeding and the cuts on her back? Why is her wallet on the floor, and credit cards strewn all over the ground? What was she trying to purchase this early in the morning? Did something go horribly wrong with the pregnancy? Oh dear God, I'm sure we've lost the baby! If we can get Amanda to the hospital she's going to be okay. She has to be okay. This kind of thing isn't supposed to happen to us. We're going to get through this. We have *to get through this!*

Then suddenly, *Where's Weston!?*

In the shock of the situation I had completely forgotten about Weston! His door was still shut upstairs. He was okay, right? Almost on cue I heard the squeaking of his vintage crib and soft coos coming from upstairs. "Dah dah dah dah, oooohh."

Of course he was okay. Why wouldn't he be? Since the door was still closed, it didn't appear Amanda had even made it up to his room yet. My attention quickly switched back to my beautiful bride, struggling for her life in front of me.

"You're going to be okay, babe. Stay with me. Help is coming. Keep breathing! Stay with me!"

I remained fixed by her side listening to her labored breaths, and felt more and more helpless and alone with every passing moment. I had to call someone! The paramedics weren't there yet, and although I was calling out to Jesus, He didn't seem to be responding. I felt like there had to be *someone* who could just fix this situation for me right now! I picked up my phone, now smeared with blood, and touched my dad's name on speed dial.

"Hey buddy."

"Dad!" I could barely get words out of my mouth. "I need you to pray. I just found Amanda on our living room floor. She's unconscious; I don't know what's wrong. Just pray. Please, Dad, pray!"

I hung up before my dad could even respond. Hearing his voice still didn't seem to ease the helplessness and despair that was quickly enveloping me. I turned my focus back to Amanda.

Just then, I heard the faint scream of sirens from the ambulance coming up the street. I pulled my blood-soaked hand from Amanda's head and instinctively darted for the front door that was still wide open from when I came in, back when life was still normal. When it was a *normal* Tuesday morning. When I was expecting to find Amanda in her normal spot on the couch, sipping her cup of coffee—Weston on her lap with his sippy cup drinking his morning milk.

Now looming questions filled my mind: What on earth is happening? Would Amanda be okay? Would we ever have a normal Tuesday again?

As I reached the street to meet the paramedics, the thought occurred to me: *Should I have just left her in there? She's all alone now!* I couldn't think straight. Nothing made sense to me anymore. I just knew she needed help, and I knew the people parking the emergency vehicle were the only ones who could.

"Please hurry! She's breathing but it seems very labored! Hurry please!"

The EMTs couldn't move fast enough for me. Didn't they understand what was happening? My wife was unconscious in our house with blood all around her!

Once the EMTs finally entered the house, everything seemed to swirl around me. Lightheadedness began to set in. *What did he just ask me? I can't think right now. This can't be real.*

They very quickly got Amanda on a stretcher attached to a ventilator and lifted into the back of the ambulance.

"Which hospital do you want her to go to?" the paramedic who looked in charge asked me.

"Huh? Wha . . . ? Hospital? I don't care!! Just get her somewhere fast and bring her back to me!!"

I grabbed Weston and his milk and we jumped in the car to follow them. The next thing I knew, I was in a private hospital waiting room, sweating, shaking, freezing, clutching Weston, and telling him, "Everything's going to be okay, buddy. We're going to be okay. It's okay." The only thing was, I wasn't sure I believed myself.

I'm not sure how long we sat there before investigators entered the room.

"Mr. Blackburn? We need to ask you a few questions."

A little dazed and confused as to why policemen were there, I looked up at the two men.

"Okay, yeah. Absolutely. How is Amanda? Is she going to be okay?"

"The doctors are getting her taken care of right now."

They proceeded with their questions, many of which made me wonder what they had to do with her and the pregnancy. I felt my mind slipping away from their inquiries to her face after I had turned her over on the living room floor. Her precious lips had been swollen and bloodied.

At that moment, my mind flashed to the first time I ever noticed her lips. We had just been set up on a blind date, spent an incredible evening together at a concert, and were now sitting at a Steak 'n Shake in Grand Rapids, Michigan. I couldn't understand why this senior in high school had me so smitten already. It was only a couple of hours into our first meeting and I was already taken by her.

Up to that point, I had almost given up on the dating scene. I was frustrated that I hadn't met a girl who was truly and primarily passionate about Jesus. One who didn't place her identity in *who* she dated, or *that* she was dating. One who didn't play games. Most girls I had met seemed more in love with the *idea* of love rather than being grounded in God's love and building her identity from that. I was exhausted by the girls who, out of deep-rooted insecurity, constantly asserted their presence in social settings to get guys to notice them.

Now, here was this gorgeous blond, somewhat quiet, reserved, and yet confident in who she was, sitting across from me, sipping on a strawberry milkshake. She seemed principled, sanguine, and mysterious. I couldn't help but want to dig deeper.

"Milkshake drinking contest. *Ready, Go!*" I blurted out, struggling to figure out a way to get past my butterflies and have a little fun with this girl.

We began slurping from each of our shakes. Her lips closed over the straw amid a flirtatious smile. Earlier, I'd learned from a friend that Amanda had never kissed a boy. In fact, she'd made a pact with her sister, Amber, that she wouldn't until she was engaged to be married. Those beautiful, pure lips had never been touched by anyone! She glanced up from her shake and looked into my eyes. I saw my opportunity to cheat my way to victory. I made a goofy face at her that caused her to break away from her straw and laugh, milkshake spewing from her mouth and nose.

She grabbed a napkin and wiped up her mess while I sucked down the final remnants of my shake. Winner! As I came up for air she looked at me with this huge smile and said, "That wasn't fair ... but it was cute."

I could look at that smile for the rest of my life, I remember thinking. I believed I might be the one to put a ring on her finger and kiss those lips for the first time.

"Thank you, son. The doctors will be in to see you in a moment." The investigator's voice snapped me back to reality. Had I answered any of their questions? What had they even asked? I wasn't sure.

"Um ... Yeah. Absolutely. Thank you," I said.

They left and the door closed behind them, leaving me alone again with my spinning, swirling thoughts and all my fears about what had happened to Amanda and what was going to happen with Weston and me.

Within minutes, the door opened again to three doctors, all in blue scrubs, and one donning a white lab coat. They made their way across the small room, and before they could take the open seats next to me I rose from my chair to meet them halfway.

"Doctor, how is she?! Is she going to be okay? What about the baby?"

"Mr. Blackburn." I sensed a strange hesitation in his voice. "Can we sit, please?"

"Sure ... What is it? She's going to be okay, right?"

"Mr. Blackburn, we've done everything we can right now. It looks very serious. We discovered three bullet wounds in Amanda. One in her arm, a flesh wound on her back, and the last one in her head. The third bullet is still lodged behind her eye."

My heart dropped to my stomach and my body began to shake again. I wanted to throw up. I put my hand over my mouth and felt my eyes get wide. I could feel the skin stretching on my face as I pulled my hands down. I couldn't believe it. Bullet wounds?

"Wha ... ? What happened?"

"It seems there was an invasion in your home this morning and Amanda was caught in the middle of it."

All of a sudden my mind began to recall the snapshots it had taken not an hour earlier. The credit cards. The purse emptied out over the counter. The cut on her back. The ladder that had fallen from the wall. The blood matted on her head.

"Well, she was still breathing, so she's going to be okay, right? You can get the bullet out can't you?" I could feel myself panicking. "You have to do something?!"

"At this point, Mr. Blackburn, we can't do anything. We're waiting for the swelling to go down in her brain, and unless it does, there's nothing more we can do."

Immediately a wave of nausea hit me, followed by a burst of confusion and helplessness. I clutched my chest with one hand, and with Weston still in my other arm, I began taking deep breaths. I suddenly felt as if the room were suffocating me, the hands of a slow tidal wave of darkness slithering up my chest and closing off my mouth from gasping for air. I felt my eyes widen, my face surged with heat, and the room began to spin. I was weightless, like my body was tumbling through space. The ceiling and the floor had no distinction, and I couldn't decipher which way was up and which way was down. And then, what happened next, I can't fully explain. Maybe it was shock. Maybe it was faith. It was probably some weird combination of the two. But for just a moment, the riptide of panic broke and I was just moving with the current.

I grabbed the doctor's hand and said, "Can I pray with you, Doctor?" Everyone in the room looked up somewhat confused.

"Umm. Sure," the one sitting next to me responded.

I could tell none of these doctors were accustomed to this. I don't think they'd ever had a patient's spouse grab their hands before, the way I was—so tightly it probably hurt—and force them to pray. But I didn't care. I already knew God was doing something big. I knew that nothing happened without purpose and that God was going to use Amanda's suffering, and ours, in a big way.

But I didn't even know the half of it.

That's when a memory came back to me, in a flash. It was just a few months earlier, in August, when it was still warm outside. I went on a long walk with Amanda, and we were reflecting on how well things seemed to be going at our church. We were finally seeing traction and growth. She looked at me and said, "Davey, things seem too easy right now. There's no way this can last. I feel like we're about to walk into a tough season soon."

My wife was always right about these things. She had a strong sense of intuition and discernment. She was such a woman of faith, such a fighter. And as my mind returned to the doctor's report, I was sure she was going to pull through this.

So I held that doctor's hands like they were my lifeline, and I began praying. As I did, I pictured a revival sweeping through the halls of that hospital.

"Lord, we don't know what to do right now," I began. "But You're the Great Physician. You can heal with the snap of a finger. I pray that You would begin to heal Amanda. Cause the swelling to subside. Rebuild brain matter as we speak. Give the doctors wisdom to know what to do every step of the way. I know there are people in this hospital who don't know You. I pray that You would perform such a powerful miracle here that everyone in this hospital puts their faith in You. Sweep a revival across this hospital. We know You can do this. Amen."

As I stood there, I leaned on my faith, convinced God was going to heal my Amanda. I had such *reassurance* that she was going to be okay and that we were all going to be reunited as a family. But if faith is the confidence that what we hope for will actually happen, the assurance of what we cannot see, my faith still had some growing to do. There were so many things I could not yet see.

What do we do about faith when the thing we hope for doesn't happen? What are we supposed to do when we pray— in great faith—and God doesn't answer the way we want Him to? Standing there in that hospital waiting room, I wasn't asking myself any of those questions. I didn't know I needed to. Not yet anyway.

2

OUR WEAPON
AGAINST WORRY

WESTON AND I WERE ONCE AGAIN ALONE IN THE HOSPITAL WAITING room. Every so often a nurse or attendant would come in and offer us a glass of water or some crackers. But I mostly just sat and shivered. My entire body was locked in shaking tension, my arms crossed to cradle my stomach. I felt outside of myself, as though I were watching the two of us from above the room. This couldn't be happening. It was some strange dream and soon I'd wake up. My whole mind was numb except for two looming questions: Is Amanda okay? And when can I see her?

Amanda's sister, Amber, was the first to arrive at the hospital, followed quickly by Derek and Ashley, our two best friends on staff with us at the church. The night before, Amber happened to be staying at her grandparents' house, which was three hours closer to this hospital than where she lived. She and Amanda had spent the entire previous day together, carting all the kids— Amber's as well as Weston—from one activity to another and enjoying time as sisters.

The two were closer than I've ever seen sisters be—they were the *best* of friends. Amber always spontaneous and winsome, riding the emotional highs and lows of life, and Amanda always grounded, methodical, and straightforward—the perfect complement to one another.

I honestly couldn't believe it when eight years before they both agreed to a double wedding.

Gavin, my now brother-in-law, was one of my best friends in college. As fellow athletes at Southern Wesleyan University, we lived directly down the hall from each other in the same dorm. To be honest, we didn't get the best first impressions of each other. He saw me as the loud kid who carried his guitar around everywhere to impress freshman girls. I thought of him as the guy who bought his friendships, since he had taken a couple of my buddies out for a steak dinner one Sunday night and paid for everything. But over time we realized that, for all our differences, we had a shared passion in wanting our lives to count by doing something great for Jesus. We became the best of friends.

Gavin and I would always joke that we needed to go down the road to Clemson University and meet two girls who were best friends and loved Jesus so he and I could double-date and hang out all the time. Then, toward the end of our freshman year, he rekindled a relationship with Amber—his former high school sweetheart.

At that point I gave up on the idea of Gavin and me dating close friends, until the beginning of our sophomore year when he approached me with an idea. "Bro, I don't know why I haven't thought about this, but you should meet Amber's sister. I saw her again this summer and she's really grown up, she's gorgeous, she comes from a great family, and I could see you guys hitting it off! She would be perfect for you!"

"What do you mean she's 'grown up'?" I remember only one of Gavin's comments jumping out at me. "How old is she exactly?"

"Well, she's a senior in high school, but I'm telling you, dude, she's really mature for her age. And she is outrageously passionate about Jesus."

"Not a chance, Gavin. I can't date a high schooler. I'd never be able to live that down from the guys on the baseball team. Plus the whole long-distance thing never works. Besides, I give you and Amber two more months and you'll be a thing of the past."

Despite my reluctance, there was something about the way Gavin described this girl and her family that intrigued me. Then he showed me a couple of pictures and convinced me to go home with him to Elkhart, Indiana, over the upcoming fall break to meet her. And I was smitten—Amanda and I spent the entire week together. I called my mom that week and told her I had met the girl of my dreams.

She replied, "The Davey I know makes levelheaded decisions. Who is this girl and what has she done with my son?"

After almost two years of long-distance dating, we were all four nearing graduation—Gavin, Amber, and I with four-year degrees and Amanda with an associate's. I knew by this point I wanted to marry Amanda, and Gavin had already decided Amber was his soulmate. We weren't too sure, however, what their dad was going to say about two weddings happening in the same summer.

Gavin beat me to the punch and asked for Amber's hand in marriage in May 2007. So when I asked their dad for permission to propose to Amanda, he gave me his blessing and some conditions—either wait another year or convince the girls to do a double wedding.

Soon after my conversation with her dad, I planned a scavenger hunt around Indianapolis. My whole family was in Indy for my cousin's wedding, and Amanda had driven three hours from Elkhart to be my plus-one. Each stop of this scavenger hunt represented a pivotal moment in our relationship and revealed a cheesy, romantic clue to the next location. The hunt culminated in a gondola ride in a downtown canal. My guitar just happened to be in the boat. When the gondolier stopped at the spot I had predetermined, I sat her down and sang a song I'd written that ended with "will you marry me?" I pulled out a half-carat, princess-cut diamond ring, got down on one knee, and proposed.

She said yes, and we both cried, hugged ... oh, and I kissed her for the first time ... then I broke to her the news of her dad's stipulation. "So I guess we'll have to wait six months or so longer than we originally wanted," I said.

"No we won't! Amber and I *want* to do a double wedding! We both think it would be a blast! What a fun event with all our family and closest friends! Plus, you and Gavin are so close! You guys wouldn't mind, right?!"

I couldn't believe it! What girl would share her special day with someone else? The wedding day is the one instance where it's acceptable for all the focus to be on the bride, and this girl wants to share the spotlight? The selflessness of that decision made me love Amanda all the more—but this was Amanda, always willing and ready to redirect the spotlight, to take the focus off herself and give up what she wanted for the sake of those around her.

This was my favorite quality about her. And it's also the greatest lesson she ever taught me, the most beautiful legacy a person could leave.

Amber was steadily there for the major events of Amanda's life. The two were inseparable. They walked down the aisle together, on either arm of their dad. Amber was the only person other than me that Amanda wanted in the hospital room when she was giving birth to Weston.

Amber was with Amanda when her pregnancy test was positive and she discovered we were having baby number two. And now Amber and I found ourselves once again at the hospital with Amanda. Only this time instead of welcoming another baby into our family like we had planned, we sat there shocked and distraught over the looming possibility that we'd be saying goodbye to both Evie *and* Amanda.

"Mr. Blackburn. If you're ready, you can go back and see Amanda now." A nurse's voice interrupted my thoughts. "We have her on a ventilator, and she is somewhat stabilized. I just need to warn you she probably isn't going to look like herself. She's pretty beat-up."

"Um … yeah. I definitely want to … I mean I think I'm ready."

Something about the reality of seeing my beautiful bride in a hospital bed, unconscious and hooked up to a ventilator, terrified me and caused my stomach to clench. I looked at Amber. "You're going with me, right?"

I knew Amber had been in situations like this before. As a nurse for the past seven years, she was proficient and comfortable in hospital settings. When I saw her face go as white as a sheet, however, I knew this was not going to be a typical stroll down a hospital hallway for her. Suddenly her experience no longer provided the security blanket I was hoping for.

I left Weston in the waiting room with Derek and Ashley, who were arranging someone to pick him up and watch him the rest of the day. I didn't know what I was about to see when I walked into Amanda's room but I was sure I didn't want Weston having that image burned into his memory. Amber and I followed the nurse back to the Intensive Care Unit room. With every step forward it seemed like my heart was trying to grab my whole body and get it to run as fast as it could in the opposite direction.

This whole thing can't be happening! I was convinced that when we got to her room, Amanda would be sitting up in her bed sipping some water through a straw and smiling at us. Surely we'll all sit around sighing in relief that we just narrowly missed a dangerously close call.

We entered the room and all these thoughts quickly dissipated like a morning mist burned away by a scorching hot sun. There was Amanda, slightly propped up in the hospital bed, eyes shut, a breathing tube in her mouth and bandages wrapped around her head. Her right eye was puffy and bruised, remnants of dried blood still caked under her nose.

I sank into the seat on the right side of her bed, overwhelmed by all the gadgets and machines she was connected to. Numbers, beeps, monitors, gauges, all of which spoke a foreign language to me on the true condition of my best friend. Again, a sickening helpless feeling slid over me. I grabbed Amanda's hand, now swollen from all the fluids they were pumping into her body.

"Come on, baby. Give me a sign you're still here with us." I gently squeezed her hand like I always had, expecting the familiar response of a warm, reciprocating squeeze. Nothing.

Immediately my mind flashed back to the first time I held her hand—the first time any boy had held her hand.

It was a little over two months after we began dating. I was visiting her for a week over Christmas break. She had planned a ski trip an hour into Michigan for the two of us for the day. We drove up in a little 1997 Civic. She and her siblings had driven this car since high school, her dad gave it to us when we got married, and I still have it in my garage. I can't bring myself to part with it and all the nostalgia that lives inside its doors.

Amanda and I had spent that entire day frolicking around the ski slopes. Having grown up in the South doing only lake sports, I barely knew what snow *was*, let alone how to navigate the white landscape with boards attached to my feet. She, on the other hand, was this cute snow bunny who had learned grace on the slopes during family trips to California and Colorado.

She thoroughly enjoyed giggling at me slipping around like Bambi on the bunny hill all afternoon. Although I was terrible at it, I saw it as an incredible opportunity to hold her hand for the first time—that is, if I could keep my balance long enough not to drag both of us into a powdered wipeout.

Every time I thought I had mustered up the courage to grab her hand, I would chicken out. Several times that afternoon I had started to reach for it, but the timing never seemed quite right. Now we were driving back to her house, the heat thawing out our feet below the dash. It was late in the evening, and I was in the driver's seat of the Civic, kicking myself for not having had more guts.

In the middle of a conversation, I looked over at her hands. In one, she was holding the package of Sour Patch Kids we were sharing, and in the other, a road atlas to get us home (this was before smartphones and Google Maps). But I wasn't going to let these two trifles keep me from my goal. So I held my hand out toward her over the middle console.

She looked at it ... and put the atlas in my hand.

"No. That's not what I want." I peered into her eyes with a playful smirk.

So she handed me two Sour Patch Kids.

"Ha ha! No! I want to hold your hand!"

"Oh!" She giggled and her face flushed.

She slipped her hand in, each finger interlocking with mine. It felt so right. It felt like home. My heart skipped a couple of beats and I grinned at her. No words were necessary. We both knew this was perfect.

Now I sat in this ICU room, holding her hand and wondering how many more times I would be able to, thinking to myself how many more times I would have reached out to grab her hand had I known my last opportunity would come so soon.

For the first time, my emotions caught up to my shock, and tears began streaming down my face. And then they came, uncontrollably, like a torrent, a rush of pain and grief erupting from my chest and squeezing out every corner of my mouth and eyes. I sobbed right there over her hospital bed. I clutched her hand and sobbed.

"I'm so sorry, baby! I'm so sorry! I can't believe I wasn't there! I'm so sorry I wasn't there! I'm so sorry you had to go through this! I'm so sorry!!"

After a few moments I managed to gain control and I looked up at Amber. Tears streamed down her face as well. She clutched Amanda's hand on the other side of the bed. We were seated in the exact same positions on opposite sides of Amanda's hospital bed and holding the exact same hands we had fifteen months before when Amanda gave birth to Weston.

"She's going to make it, Davey. It's going to be okay. She's going to be okay. She has to be okay."

Amber and I are both notoriously optimistic, so this is what we kept telling ourselves as we sat next to Amanda's near life-less body, even though, deep inside, we still weren't sure we believed it.

Just then a doctor walked into the room. "There are other family members and friends here, Mr. Blackburn."

Between Amber, Derek, and Ashley, the phone tree had been activated. Everyone was receiving word of what had happened.

My parents, as quickly as they could, drove eight hours to Indy. Amanda's parents, Phil and Robin, and her brother, James, and his wife, Angela, were all in California on vacation at the time and took the first flight they could from Sacramento. Over the next several hours, family and friends swarmed the Intensive Care Unit. One by one they entered, and each time I hugged them, I witnessed them react to the situation—some quiet and somber, others convulsing with sobs. With each hug it triggered more tears in me. After about eight hours of this—which seemed both like an eternity and only a few minutes—I didn't think I had any tears left in my body.

I honestly can't remember much of the events in the hospital during the next twenty-four hours. Everything seemed a blur to me. People coming, people lingering, people going. Doctors checking on vitals and levels. All the while I sat there holding Amanda's hand and watching the numbers on the machines, hoping to see some sign that swelling was going down in her brain so the doctors could do something about the bullet in her head and bring her back to us.

In all the movement around her room, I remained stationary next to Amanda, holding tightly to her hand.

Come on, babe. Come back to us, please.

Every once in a while her hand would twitch and I'd jump to my feet in a shot of adrenaline and hope.

She's going to wake up!

Amber noticed me doing this a couple of times. She reluctantly told me this twitching was a natural response to brain trauma. I slinked back into my seat and stared at Amanda's closed eyes, silently coaxing her to come back to us.

At one point I watched a tiny tear part from the corner of Amanda's right eye and trickle down her cheek. I took my thumb and wiped it away, remembering all the times she and I shed tears together and I'd wipe hers in that same motion. I secretly feared this would be her last tear she'd ever cry before standing in front of Jesus.

He will wipe every tear from their eyes—I wasn't sure if that verse brought me comfort or terror in this moment.

Just then Todd and Lori, a couple from our church, walked in the room. They each hugged me, and Lori handed me a Bible, looked me in the eyes, and said with resolve and conviction, "Davey. Remember what you preached this Sunday? You prayed, 'Lord, we don't know what to do, but our eyes are on You.' God used you on Sunday to prepare everyone's hearts for this moment. We must keep our eyes on Jesus in the midst of feeling out of control."

She was right. I had completely forgotten about this, or hadn't made the connection. But the previous Sunday, I had preached a message from 2 Chronicles 20. The second book of Chronicles is an account of a king of Judah named Jehoshaphat. He was a God-fearing king who had found himself in a grave predicament.

The Bible describes a "great multitude" of enemy forces coming against him. He was altogether outnumbered. There was very little chance of victory. On Sunday, I had talked about how Jehoshaphat must have felt watching that army advance toward him—completely out of control, frustrated, defeated before he had even started. Eventually he would be victorious in the battle, but his path to victory was unconventional to say the least.

Jehoshaphat loved God, but his love for God did not prevent him from facing this trial. It wasn't an instant guarantee to his success. You see, the misconception in Christianity is that if we're following Jesus, we'll be spared from any kind of hardship or trouble. We sometimes act as though life with Jesus will always be easy—that our victory over hardships is guaranteed. While Jesus *did* guarantee we'd have ultimate victory in life through

His death and resurrection, He didn't guarantee we'd see victory in each little battle. He certainly didn't guarantee life would be easy but just the opposite: Jesus Himself said, "In this world you will have *trouble*. But take heart! I have overcome the world" (John 16:33 NIV, emphasis mine).

What I quickly discovered in that hospital room was that I was completely out of control and desperate for an act of God. But in my sermon, I asked, "What happens when our prayers of desperation aren't answered the way we want? Is our faith shaken?" I thought I knew the answer on Sunday; now I had to think again.

What makes Jehoshaphat's story even more interesting is he was famous for making military allies. He was very strategic in hedging himself against enemy attacks and ensuring that if he were attacked he would have allied troops from other nations at his disposal. On this occasion, however, none of his allies came to his aide. The force coming against him was too great. His allies didn't hold up under the pressure.

That Sunday I asked our congregation how many of us were "making allies" for ourselves in life. Hedging ourselves with things we *think* will stave off the difficult times—a nest egg, career advancement, an elevated status—only to discover that when the pressure rises in our lives, when tragedy strikes, these allies are insufficient to provide protection.

In the hospital that day I was grateful to have godly friends and family—true earthly allies—come to my side and point me to the only one who is all sufficient to carry us during difficult times—Jesus.

We—myself included—often neglect to spend time building our faith muscle in the good times, so when the bad times hit, our faith is anemic and there is nothing for us to draw from. Faith is built by reading and meditating on God's Word. But when we don't get in God's Word on a daily basis, when we don't read it regularly, we deplete ourselves of faith. Amanda lived out the daily discipline of getting in God's Word and, more importantly, letting God's Word get into *her*. She never stopped searching for what God had to say, or pursuing her relationship with Jesus, no matter what was going on in our lives, good or bad. Because of this, God's Word would pour out of Amanda when life's pressures squeezed her.

As I sat holding my Amanda's hand, I thought about how easy it is, when bad times strike, to lose faith and confidence that God is in control. In that moment I wished I had her confident, calming voice in my ear to remind me to remain faith filled.

There are times when life doesn't make sense, and like us, Jehoshaphat found himself in one of those situations. The story in 2 Chronicles says when he got the report of the enemies coming, he "was afraid," but instead of slinking away in fear, he "set his face to seek the LORD." Like how a sponge when squeezed produces what it has already soaked up, Jehoshaphat in his squeezing moment yielded a trust in God that had been forged over years of following His Word.

There was a moment where I scanned the friends and family surrounding Amanda in the hospital. My grandfather stood at the foot of her bed—a man who had given his life to mission work in Haiti and who lost his wife to ovarian cancer at an early age. My cousin leaned against the doorway. She had miscarried her baby just a year before. Amanda's grandparents stood at the side of her bed. Amanda and I used to sit with them for hours and listen to their stories of God's provision during their years of itinerant preaching ministry. Both our parents—pastors who had spent their lives serving Jesus by serving others—stood beside me. My eyes bounced from one person to the next. If Jesus said faith like a mustard seed could move mountains, you could bottle up the faith represented in that one room and it would shake planets. And yet this moment had rendered us all terrified.

I've heard it said before that courage isn't the absence of fear, but it's acting in the midst of fear. Jehoshaphat, although afraid, prayed to God and then commanded the whole nation to do the same. They declared, "We do not know what to do, but our eyes are on you" (2 Chronicles 20:12 ESV). This is exactly what Lori was reminding me of in that hospital room. When we find ourselves in situations that are completely overwhelming and out of our control, the only thing we can do is put our eyes on Jesus and draw from our faith and trust in Him.

While Jehoshaphat and the people prayed, God answered them and assured them He would save them from calamity. His only stipulation was that they had to trust Him and follow what He commanded them to do, no matter how ridiculous it seemed.

The next morning, Jehoshaphat summoned all the people. What he told them to do next made absolutely no sense. He told them, "God said we need to put the musicians and worshippers on the front line of the battle! They're going to lead the way for us!"

What?!

I can just imagine the reaction of the people. The warriors must have been miffed, not to mention terrified, at how this was going to help them in the battle. *What is this!? Has Jehoshaphat gone crazy!? I don't care what the King of Pop did in "Thriller"! This is real life! How are we going to subdue the enemy with music!?*

Not to mention the musicians, who must have been *terrified*. I can imagine a trombonist jabbing his slider back and forth, trying to figure out how his instrument was going to help him fend off the enemy on the front lines of battle. That's how I felt that day in the hospital, terrified—wondering what on earth God was doing and how He was going to get us out of this mess. The enemy forces of worry were charging full speed, and it took everything within me not to fall in defeat.

Sometimes God's strategy to defeat an enemy doesn't make *any* sense. In fact, sometimes it seems downright ridiculous to our finite, limited understanding. But despite it not making sense, the people of Judah obeyed God. They put the worshippers out on the front lines.

Second Chronicles 20:22 (ESV) says, "And when they began to sing and praise, the LORD set an ambush against [the enemy forces]." What God was teaching them, and what I was attempting to teach my congregation that Sunday, was that the best weapon we have against worry is *worship*! Somehow when you worship in the midst of your overwhelming situation, no matter how grave, it takes your eyes off your problem and puts them on your Provider. It takes your focus on the situation and puts it on your Savior. When you lift up praise in the midst of your circumstance, your view of God is greater than any stress over your situation. As in Jehoshaphat's day, God is still truly the only one powerful enough to handle our greatest tragedies.

So when Lori handed me that Bible and told me to keep my eyes on Jesus, something resonated inside me—a courage deep within my soul that was outside my own ability to muster up. I looked at everyone standing in that room around Amanda's hospital bed and then looked at Derek, our worship pastor.

"We need to sing," I said to him. "Can you lead us?"

I'll never forget that moment for as long as I live. In that tiny hospital room, thirty or forty of our closest friends and family gathered in close around that hospital bed and lifted up our hearts and voices. We stood beside our precious Amanda. A community of people Amanda spent her life serving was now lifting her up in her final hours. Even while her life slipped away, we felt a fresh presence of God fill the room with a new warmth— the same God who gave Amanda life, who gave all of us life, who gave *His* life so that we could have life and hope for all of eternity. A chorus of voices resounded through the hospital hallways.

Great is Thy faithfulness, O God my Father,
There is no shadow of turning with Thee,
Thou changest not, Thy compassions, they fail not,
As Thou hast been, Thou forever will be.
Great is Thy faithfulness!
Great is Thy faithfulness!
Morning by morning new mercies I see.
All I have needed Thy hand hath provided,
Great is Thy faithfulness, Lord, unto me!

Later, the doctors and nurses would tell us that moment was the most powerful thing they'd ever experienced. They witnessed a group of people who had spent years—decades even—training for a trial they never knew they would face and that was now being squeezed . . . and what came out was worship.

When peace like a river, attendeth my way
When sorrows like sea billows roll
Whatever my lot, Thou has taught me to say
It is well, it is well, with my soul

One of the songs we sang stuck out to me more than all of them. I later found this song written in Amanda's last prayer journal entry.

She wrote the entry the Monday morning after my 2 Chronicles 20 message and the day before she was shot. It read,

Turn your eyes upon Jesus
Look full in His wonderful face

And the things of this world will grow strangely dim
In the light of His glory and grace
What an amazing Sunday yesterday. Truly filled my heart to
see so many people in Your church. Learning, growing, meeting
You and taking next steps. Thank you for letting me get to see all
of this with my own eyes
I love you, Lord. Glory and praise to You.

After probably an hour of singing and sobbing together, we prayed over Amanda—this girl who, we'd later discover in her journals, had prayed for each one of us in our own times of need. We prayed that God would heal her but that if He chose to take her home to heaven He would give us peace and strength to walk through the next season without her. As the voices subsided and the prayers faded that evening, a blanket of peace covered that hospital room and our hearts. We had waged war on the Enemy. We had worshipped away the worry. We had placed our trust and hope in an almighty God.

Evening began to slip away, and Amber and I found ourselves once again alone in Amanda's room, still waiting to hear from the doctors what the next step would be, still anticipating brain scan tests to return positive, and still praying for a miracle. But something was different now. There was a sense of peace. There was a sense of hope. That no matter what happened we would be okay.

I pulled out my phone and opened up the Pandora Radio app. I wasn't sure if Amanda was aware of anything that was going on around her. I wasn't sure if she could hear us, but I knew if she could, she would want to listen to Elevation Worship.

She used to listen to Elevation Worship every time she'd go for a run. I'd catch her stretching in the driveway singing the songs after spending three miles talking to Jesus between strides and breaths. Nothing used to melt my heart quicker than watching and hearing her worship. In church, she used to raise her right hand when a song really touched her, and as soon as she would, tears would fill my eyes. I'd have to stop singing to regain composure.

I loved to watch her worship her Savior.

In that moment, I wasn't sure if she was in the room worshipping with us or if she was already worshipping at the feet of Jesus, but I knew she would want to worship to Elevation. So I tuned it to Elevation's Pandora station.

What happened next would leave me breathless and would establish an anchor to ground our family in the midst of this tragedy. In the random shuffle of songs, a very familiar melody interrupted the silence first. It was the song "Nothing Is Wasted."

You know my every need
You see my poverty
You are enough for me, Jesus
You gave the blind man sight
You raised the dead to life
You've done the same for me, Jesus
You are loving, You are wise
There is nothing in my life You cannot revive
You are loving, You are wise
There is nothing too hard for our God
Your word inside of me
My strength, my everything
My hope will always be Jesus
Your breath inside my lungs
You're worthy of my trust
You will forever be Jesus
Nothing is wasted
You work all things for good

Nothing is wasted
Your promise remains
Forever You reign[1]

I couldn't believe it. It seemed too providential to be coincidental. Of all songs that could have played, this one was first?

In that moment the Lord reached straight into my soul and met me in the profoundest of ways. Even in that cold hospital room holding Amanda's hand I felt the warmth of His gentle whisper, *Son, none of this will be wasted. I assure you. I work all things together for the good of those who love Me and who are called according to My purposes. I won't waste your pain. I won't waste Amanda's pain. With Me, nothing is wasted.*

3

A CALLING WITH A COST

BEEP. BEEP. BEEP. THE MONITORS ECHOED OMINOUSLY THROUGHOUT the room. The occasional buzz gave warning that fluid bags needed to be refilled and IV packs needed changing. The nurse walked in, checked the screens, pressed a few buttons, forced a smile in my direction, and walked out. My eyes were dry and bloodshot. I wasn't sure when I last ate. The nurses had come through the hallway and softened the lighting to evening mode. Everything was quiet and dim.

There was conversation happening outside the room. I could see my aunt—a doctor herself—through the window talking with one of the nurses. They would occasionally look over at me— their faces grim and somber. I felt like everyone was keeping something from me, like I wasn't receiving the full scope of the information.

How was this happening? How did we even get here? I sat and wondered. They say in traumatic moments you begin to see your whole life flash in front of you. In this lonely hospital room, next to my bride, I sat in a daze, staring at the ventilator over her face, watching her chest rise and fall—in a much quicker rhythm than a few hours before.

How did we get here? I kept wondering. My mind began to slip and my thoughts began following the series of pivotal events that had led me to this moment—the events that would eventually lead us to move to Indianapolis in the first place to start a church.

I grew up as a pastor's kid in Birmingham, Alabama. Most pastor's kids, "PKs" as they're often called, grow up either extremely rebellious or religious—and in either case, acting like they have it all together. I was the latter. I never had a major rebellious season in life, but through middle school and high school I certainly wasn't one to speak out about my faith. I was a good student, a good kid, a good athlete, and good at blending into a group. People knew I was a pastor's kid. They knew I didn't get into much trouble, and they knew I was involved in church. But that was the extent of my faith. I was much more serious about school and sports than I was about my relationship with Jesus.

Ever since I can remember, church was not just part of my life, it *was* my life—by default. I enjoyed church when I was a kid, but as I entered high school, other things began competing for my attention—girls, sports, school, and the social scene. Up to the end of high school, I had only experienced my dad's small traditional church of a hundred and fifty people or so. There were some great people in that church who really invested a lot of time and focus on me, perhaps thinking I might follow in Dad's footsteps, but becoming a pastor was by far the last career I intended to pursue. From the time I was twelve I had my eyes set on being an orthopedic surgeon, and I justified what was really a desire to make money with the veneer of helping people.

All that would change my senior year of high school when my family moved to a larger church in Tuscaloosa. I got highly involved in the youth group, and, in late December of that year, we attended a Wesleyan youth conference.

During one of the conference worship services, something completely unexpected happened. I was sitting in my seat as the program began, surrounded by ten thousand other teenagers, watching the Reverend Earl Wilson—this gray-haired elderly man—gingerly approach the podium. He frankly looked like he could keel over and die at any minute. It amused me that this guy thought he could actually connect with me, an eighteen-year-old with my whole life ahead of me. At the time I didn't understand the value of faith being transferred from one generation to the next.

He leaned into the microphone and announced he was going to talk to us about answering a "call to full-time ministry." That was the moment I decided to completely check out. I didn't need to hear this message. I was already settled on what I wanted to do with my life: play Division I collegiate baseball, study medicine to become an orthopedic surgeon, and make a bunch of money. I didn't want to put my family through the ministry life.

My family had moved to a different city five times since I was born, and the most recent time was just before I was about to start my senior year of high school. This move forced me to completely start over in sports, school, and relationships—everything that was valuable to me at the time. Even though my senior year would eventually turn out to be one of the best years of my life, I couldn't see what God was trying to do in me while in the midst of it. There was no way I was going to uproot my family like this to answer some call from God. Full-time ministry? No thank you.

Up to that point, I had responded to Jesus and received salvation, the forgiveness of sins He made available by His work on the cross, but I was under the false assumption that following Jesus daily merely meant being a good person. While I knew I'd never be perfect, I figured if I conducted myself respectably, did my best at what I put my efforts to, and was genuinely nice to people, Jesus would let me live out the life I had designed for myself.

So I sat in that auditorium in Charlotte, doodling in my notebook and passing notes to my friends next to me. This was pre-smartphone days. No iPhones, no Samsung Galaxy S7s blowing up in your hand. This was even before the day of the Razr, so I distracted myself with the only means I had available throughout the entire message—pen and paper.

At the end of his message, Pastor Wilson asked everyone to bow their heads and close their eyes. As a polite southern pastor's kid, I obliged, scooting forward in my chair and bowing my head. "If you feel called to walk away from *your* plans and give your life to full-time ministry, I want you to stand up, step out of your row, and walk to the back of the auditorium." Immediately I felt this sensation I'd never experienced before. A heat almost like tiny bolts of lightning began firing through my veins, my heart started racing, and involuntarily I stood up and stepped out of my aisle. Before I realized what was happening, I was halfway to the back of the auditorium.

What am I doing?! I'm not supposed to do ministry. That's the last thing I want to do with my life. My mind was racing. But at that same moment, I felt this rush of peace come over me like I'd never felt before, and I sensed this still, small voice whisper to my heart: *Davey, this is exactly what you're supposed to do. You'll never be fulfilled otherwise.*

I knew in the deepest part of me the voice was right. I answered the call to full-time ministry that day. And the moment my heart was set to ministry, I never looked back. It has been the most fulfilling thing I could ever imagine doing with my life. A friend of mine says a true calling from God is a burden plus an opportunity. That an opportunity without a burden is just a job that will leave you feeling frustrated and unsatisfied. My heart had this new burden gripping it—a holy unrest that I didn't even fully understand but that I unmistakably felt.

Immediately after that day, doors for ministry began to open up. It's crazy how this happens—the minute you commit yourself to being obedient to God's calling on your life, you will feel His Spirit move in ways you never experienced before, presenting opportunities that seem supernatural—ones you couldn't have planned more perfectly if you had tried. Just three days later, I signed to receive a full-ride baseball scholarship at a small Christian school in South Carolina called Southern Wesleyan University to study ministry and communications. By the beginning of my college freshman year, my life had been turned upside down, and I was now on what seemed like a dead sprint toward something much bigger than myself.

The crazy thing is that I began my college career studying to be a pastor but didn't attend church regularly—I considered church to be dull and therefore optional. When I was a kid, church attendance was anything but optional. I had so much church attendance under my belt that my gold star chart was overflowing. If the sanctuary doors were open and the lights were on, our family was the first there and the last to leave. I joke all the time that I had a drug problem. I was *drug* to church every time the doors were open. Now, I'm extremely grateful my parents had me in church consistently. Seeds were being planted in my heart even when I didn't realize it, almost as if Jesus was capturing my heart through osmosis. But at the time, church was something I did, certainly not something I was passionate about.

Even as a freshman in college I couldn't get excited about church. I rarely, if ever, had seen anyone walk an aisle to respond to an altar call and give their life to Jesus, so the whole thing felt sort of pointless to me. The only environments where I had experienced Jesus's electric, exciting, life-shaking, and eternity-altering presence were conferences and youth camps.

Then one day, fall semester of my freshman year, the resident director of my dorm invited us to attend this new, fast-growing church that all the college kids were going to—NewSpring Church.

"You gotta check this place out," he told us. "They play rock music like Switchfoot!" At the time one of my favorite bands was Switchfoot, so it piqued my interest.

The next Sunday, my friend Kenneth and I got in a car and drove forty-five minutes to attend. On the way there, I swore up and down I'd never again drive forty-five minutes to attend a church service. No church was worth that kind of drive. Besides, I was skeptical of any church that was growing this fast—thinking something must be shady behind the scenes for a church to be rapidly exploding. And then we stepped into NewSpring Church.

The music was powerful, intense, and it actually felt like we were at a legitimate rock concert. The environment was electric. The worship was energizing. Remember that feeling I talked about experiencing when God called me to be a pastor? It was like that—every cell in my body was responding to the Spirit moving through that place. Still, I was skeptical. I braced myself for another boring message, filled with Bible stories I had heard a thousand times before.

Then the pastor stepped up and delivered an almost hour-long message that had us, in one moment, rolling with laughter; the next, feeling extremely challenged; and the next, crying. At the end of the message, I looked down at my watch and couldn't believe it was already over!

Then something amazing happened. The pastor invited people who wanted to give their life to Jesus, to receive forgiveness for all their wrongdoings and to begin a new life with Christ, to stand up. *Yeah right*, I thought to myself. *There's no way anyone stands up in front of all these people.* But to my utter shock, I watched dozens across the auditorium stand to their feet while the rest of the congregation cheered. I sat in awe for a few seconds, eventually coming to my senses enough to raise my hands in front of me and join the applause.

I walked out of that experience with my perspective completely changed. For the first time I had seen what church *could* be like. We decided we'd go back every week, despite the drive. And we did. Over the next couple of years, I began taking some of the guys on the baseball team with me, most of whom were not believers and were attending this Christian college purely because of the baseball program. To our amazement, that semester we saw fifteen of the guys on our roster give their lives to Jesus. The following semester forty more athletes at our school did the same thing as we began busing student athletes back and forth, week after week. Over those couple of years God broke my heart for people who are far from Him, who don't have the hope of a relationship with Jesus, and He opened my eyes to the potential impact one local church can have. He began calling me deeper into this idea of being a part of something much bigger than myself.

Little did I know there was an eighteen-year-old girl in Elkhart, Indiana, named Amanda Byars who was feeling the same sense of calling.

Also growing up as a pastor's kid, Amanda had been around ministry environments her whole life. She knew God had placed this significant call on her life to be a part of something much bigger than herself. In fact, right after we met and began dating, we read a book together called *The Barbarian Way* by Erwin McManus.

The book features a biblical character named John the Baptist—Jesus's cousin—who started a fast-growing, electrifying ministry in the wilderness right before Jesus came on the scene. John had a significant call on his life from the time he was born. In fact, his mom and dad, Zechariah and Elizabeth, thought they would never have kids. When an angel visited Zechariah and told him they'd conceive and give birth to a baby boy, Zechariah laughed.

I love Zechariah's response to the angel's prophecy. "How could this be?" he scoffed. "I'm old, and my wife is even older!" (There were no blue pills on the market at this time).

The angel told Zechariah his son would be the forerunner to the Savior of God's people. From the day he was born, he would have a special call on his life to prepare people's hearts for revival. But because Zechariah didn't believe, he was rendered mute—unable to speak—until the day John was born. And so it happened just as the angel predicted.

John was born, Zechariah's first word in nine months was naming his boy out loud, and during John's childhood his parents fostered the special call on his life.

One day John left home and decided to live in the wilderness. He purchased some new hipster camel hair threads and went on some weird Paleo diet of locusts and wild honey. He was certainly an eccentric dude.

For a few years he led a thriving ministry pointing people to the coming Messiah. When Jesus finally came on the scene, John was the one who baptized Him! In John's mind he had to think he was on the fast track to sitting at Jesus's right hand when He set up His ministry—one that was bound to be even grander than John's. Jesus even referred to John as the greatest man who ever lived (Matthew 11:11)! Life was good.

But a strange turn of events changed everything in John's life. He was arrested for calling out King Herod's sin and banished to prison. One night Herod threw a party, had a beer or ten, and beckoned his twelve-year-old daughter to do a provocative dance for all his guests. He was so pleased with her routine he promised to give her anything she asked for. At the behest of her mother, the girl asked for John's head . . . on a platter (Mark 6:17-29).

Just before John was beheaded he sent some of his disciples to Jesus to ask Him one question: Are You really the Messiah? John was sure that if Jesus was who He said He was, things would have turned out differently for John—he wouldn't be looking down the edge of an executioner's axe blade.

Jesus said something profound in response to John's inquiry. He referenced passages from prophets listing all the things the Messiah would do once He appeared on earth (Isaiah 29:18–19; 35:5–6; 42:6–7; 61:1–3; Daniel 12:2), ironically describing all the things John and his disciples had already witnessed Jesus do (Matthew 11:1–6). The interesting thing, though, is that Jesus left off one item from His list of miracles: "setting the prisoners free" (Isaiah 61:1).

Essentially Jesus left John pondering some questions: If nothing turns out the way you think it should—if the story doesn't go the way you would write it—will you still put your trust in Me? Will you trust there's something bigger than you going on here? Will you still believe I am who I say I am, even if I don't bring you what you think I should bring? Will you still follow My barbarian call on your life?

As Amanda and I read this book together, God began doing something remarkable in her heart to call her to a life of ministry as well. She wrote this in her journal at eighteen years old:

Father, this book that I am reading, The Barbarian Way, *is excellent! I love it! It inspires me and yet it makes me nervous because I know you have called us to live barbaric lives. I want that so badly for myself and yet it's easy to hesitate because it's not easy. It's hard. But when we are in danger, when I am in distress, when I am taking huge risks, when I am over my head, is when I am fully ALIVE! I love that. It's amazing how the hardest road is the most fulfilling ...*

Lord, I'm a barbarian.

And so I'm not praying small prayers anymore. I know you are far too powerful to hold back. So . . . Lord I am pleading, asking, begging, and wanting to be used by you. Not just used by you ... but used by you in a BIG way. I want to impact, to make a difference and to make a change, but more than just the average. I want to take on the Barbarian challenge and embrace the "more" that is out there for me.

I know that it will not be the most easy or simple thing. But I am positive and completely confident that no matter any challenge, I can soar through because You are behind me ... Because "The one who is in you is GREATER than the one who is in the world." And I know that no matter how hard Satan tries to attack me and get me down, he will never succeed because my foundation and my roots are far too secure to be moved by some bumps and bruises. I love you Father, so much. Thank you for drawing me in through a barbarian call.

"Davey, can I come in?" I hadn't even heard the knock at the door. The doctor's voice jolted me back to my senses.

The lights were back on in the hallway, and an aroma of freshly brewed coffee rushed into the room as the doctor opened the door.

What time is it? Was I sleeping? Is it morning already?
I had sat there all night, mostly in a half-sleep state. I wasn't sure if I had dreamed it or just pondered it, but it felt as though my whole life had flashed before my mind's eye, and I was back to asking questions. *Why would God allow this to happen when all we wanted to do was serve Him with our lives? There had to be another explanation, something I wasn't seeing. Surely God was setting us up for an incredible miracle. Surely He was coming to rescue us in the nick of time . . .*
The doctor walked toward me and pulled up a chair. This was it. Maybe the numbers were looking good! Maybe the swelling had gone down! Maybe our miracle was right around the corner!

"Mr. Blackburn, we ran the brain scan analysis. When trauma of this nature occurs in the brain, it begins to swell. The skull can sustain only a certain amount of swelling. If the brain continues to swell past that point, it has nowhere to go other than down and herniate into the brain stem, which will cause her . . ." My eyes glossed over. His voice began to trail off. Where was he going with this? What was he trying to tell me?

"Doctor, I'm not sure what all this means. What are you saying?" My voice was shaking as I forced the question out.

"What I'm trying to tell you is the brain scan came back negative." The doctor dropped his head and let out a sigh before continuing. "There is no brain activity. Medically speaking, Amanda has deceased. What's keeping her other organs functioning right now—her lungs, her heart, her kidneys—are the machines."

"She's . . . she's gone?" My heart started racing. The room began to spin.

"I'm sorry, Mr. Blackburn. We did everything we could. I'm so very sorry." He put his hand on my leg, looked at me with tears in his eyes, and rose to exit the room. "I'm going to leave you to say goodbye." He made his way to the door and closed the curtain behind him before leaving. The sea of faces peering in from the other side of the window disappeared behind it.

I turned to look at Amanda in disbelief. This wasn't supposed to happen! It wasn't supposed to end this way! Jesus was supposed to do a miracle! She was supposed to recover! Now I was left alone with my best friend, the only air in her lungs being pumped into her artificially.

How do you say goodbye to your spouse, your lover, your ministry companion, your best friend? How do you step into that moment without it completely swallowing you up? I stood over her, peering down at her face, silently begging her to come back to me ... and then it broke loose ... uncontrollable sobs erupted. I bent over, my forehead touching hers, the smell of dried blood and formaldehyde masking the sweet scent that normally caked her skin.

No! This can't be it! This can't be how it ends! I couldn't muster any audible words, but my thoughts screamed inside of me as my tears soaked her hair. *I'm so sorry baby! I'm so sorry!! I should have been there! It should have been me!!* I couldn't catch my breath. Sobs pulled out what little life I had in me as I nearly collapsed over her body. *Please, Lord! Raise her from the dead! Bring her back to me! I can't do this without her! I don't think I can live without her!*

I lay there for what seemed like hours. My body was now in a near fetal position next to her, both of my hands clutching one of hers. The sobs eventually subsided and I raised my head to look at her. Slowly crawling out of the bed, I wiped the tears from my cheeks, set her hand back next to her side. I leaned over and kissed her forehead ... one last time.

"I love you, baby. I love you so much. I always will." I turned toward the closed curtain and started for the door. She was gone and I could do nothing to change that. Every bit of adrenaline, every bit of hope that had built up in the last twenty-four hours had been deflated. I was completely numb and confused.

How could God have let something like this happen to someone who spent her life serving Him? I can understand others going through this—bad people, wicked people—but Amanda? She had a calling on her life! She loved Jesus! Her life meant so much to so many people! She breathed life into everyone she interacted with! *How could He let this happen?*

These questions and more swirled in my head as I exited her hospital room into the embrace of family members waiting outside. What do you do when you feel you're promised something, called to something, but the outcome leaves you empty, disappointed, hurt, confused? What do you do when the calling turns out differently than expected—when God's promises don't line up with your present reality? And what do *I* do with God now that it seems His calling actually led us *into* this tragedy? If He were God, couldn't He have prevented this? And if He were good why *wouldn't* He have?

4

HOLDING ON TO HOME

"Davey! This is it! This is our house!"

Amanda came skipping around the hallway of this empty, newly renovated split-level on Sunnyfield Court. Her eyes sparkled like a child opening up her first American Girl doll on Christmas morning. It was November 2011, and we were making our rounds with a Realtor, trying to find a place to plant our roots in this new city. This was the first stop on what I sensed would be a long day of hunting in a city we knew little about.

I looked into her beautiful, azure eyes and paused for a moment before I spoke. I couldn't believe we were actually *here*. We had actually made it to Indy. I grinned and thought about how faithful God had been to us over the past couple of years, even though most things hadn't gone as we'd planned.

Amanda and I had touched down only a week before in Indianapolis. We arrived after a year of wrestling with a holy discontent about our comfortable lives and jobs in Greenville, South Carolina. What made the unrest even more complicated was the feeling that God was calling us to start a church in a major metropolitan city. You ever felt a stirring of this nature? Some gnawing notion that there has to be more for you in life— an unsettling that keeps you up at night and wakes you up early in the morning? We certainly felt it and for months couldn't shake it.

A year before we moved to Indy, I had been working at NewSpring Church—the church I commuted to and bused classmates to during college—for almost four years. It was my first job after graduation, and, at that time, my dream job. When I first started, the church was reaching seven to eight thousand people during their weekend services under the leadership and dynamic teaching of Pastor Perry Noble. It was exploding with growth. My job was to help launch their first satellite campus in Greenville, thirty minutes from their main campus in Anderson. Greenville promised to be a trendy and up-and-coming city to live in and an even more fantastic place to start a new campus. From day one it was downright exhilarating! Amanda and I both thrived in this ministry context.

Over the next two-and-a-half years of marriage and ministry, Amanda and I walked through all the firsts together—first apartment, first house, first vacation as a married couple, first jobs, first ministry. We couldn't believe this dream life and dream job God had given us. Each week we witnessed dozens of people (both adults and students) come to know Jesus as their personal Savior. The challenges of the growing ministry energized us. We were learning how to love people, minister to them, and help them discover their own purpose in Christ. Most importantly, God was confirming in us every step of the way that we were indeed called to spend our lives building His church.

Sure, there were ups and downs, as all newly married couples experience. We were learning to communicate with each other and learning to be considerate of each other's needs, but overall we were living the dream. We just *knew* we would be at NewSpring for the rest of our lives. Why would we ever leave?

Then, in November 2010, something happened. The church started going through another major growth season—starting three or four more campuses—and because of that, some major restructuring of the staff was in order. This meant my role as a teaching pastor in our student ministry would shift. The plan was to align the two student ministries by broadcasting one message from Anderson across all of the campuses, so I would no longer be able to use my unique passion for preaching and team-building the way I had been. I began wrestling with God about how Amanda and I would fit in with this new vision and direction NewSpring was headed. We both felt completely torn.

As new campuses were launching, I began to feel pressure from our leadership to move to another new city and start one of the new campuses. But this was the last thing I wanted to do. Amanda and I wrestled because we had begun settling roots and developing meaningful friendships in Greenville, and now we were feeling pulled toward a new transition. It felt like the winds of change might sweep us up like a storm blowing over a small tree, roots and all. After living in seven different cities since birth, I was sick to my stomach at the thought of moving and starting over *again*!

Then, in January 2011, Pastor Perry was leading an all-staff meeting and began casting vision about the new campuses.

"Perhaps we'll start five more campuses this year!" he said. Everyone in the room erupted with cheers. "Perhaps those campus pastors are in this room right now." I felt a figurative elbow to my side from my boss who sat across the room. He cleared his throat and looked at me.

My head sank. I couldn't get my heart around the idea of being a campus pastor. I knew leading the operations of a campus would keep me only mildly fulfilled, but I felt I would eventually grow bored with the role. I knew I'd be handed a template to execute on my campus, with little room to experiment and take risks. The pioneer and entrepreneur in me was screaming for a challenge.

"Perhaps we'll start a church-planting network this next year,"
Perry said. And all of a sudden, something happened. My heart
leapt. You know when you're at a rock concert and you hear this
dissonant tone—a minor chord—that your ears intuitively know
is off-key, and the band lingers on that tone until you feel like
you're going to go crazy, and then they finally resolve it with a
major chord? It's like *healing* to your eardrums. That's what
happened to my heart that morning. Something about church
planting resonated with my soul.

I had talked about starting a church in college but killed
the dream when NewSpring asked me to come on staff. Almost
immediately after my heart leaped at the prospect of starting a
church, I felt a wave of guilt come over me—almost as if I were
betraying this church I loved so much by even the thought of
leaving. So I suppressed the idea. I killed it—or tried to at least—
and resolved to just keep working through this transition at
NewSpring.

A couple of months later I was having lunch with a church
planter in Asheville, North Carolina. He asked me what was
going on in my life, and I began loosely explaining to him the
transition Amanda and I were undergoing. Before I could finish,
he interrupted and said, "Davey, I think you're called to start a
church." His directness seemed abrasive and startled me a little.

"Uh. I don't think so. God hasn't told me that." I've always
been very skeptical of people, especially pastors, who try to tell
you what they think God is calling you to do. "If He wants me to
plant a church, I'm pretty sure He'll make that abundantly clear
to me."

He sat back in the booth, put his hands up in front of him
somewhat defensively, and retorted, "I just think God has His
hand on some people's lives in such a way that He tells them, 'Do
what your hand finds to do, for I am with you.'"

That sounded like the dumbest thing I'd ever heard. When does God tell people to do what they *want* to do?! After all, didn't God pluck me from what I was wanting to do with my life my senior year of high school and redirect my life to ministry? This guy was crazy and clearly didn't know how God operates!

I left that lunch frustrated. The next morning I opened my Bible and picked up where I had been reading from the day before. I got to 1 Samuel 10:7, where a guy named Saul was being chosen as the king of the Israelite people. The man who led his coronation, Samuel, looked at him and said, "Now when these signs meet you, *do what your hand finds to do, for God is with you*" (ESV, emphasis mine). I couldn't believe it! This was the exact thing the pastor told me the day before! Sitting there in my living room, my face grew flush and my knees went weak. I slowly got up from the couch and walked into the bedroom to show Amanda.

"Honey, what's wrong? You look like you just saw a ghost."

"Um. Something really weird just happened." I told her about my conversation the day before with this church planter and then showed her what I had just read in Samuel. Her eyes widened.

"What do you think that means? Are we supposed to start a church?" Now *she* looked like she had just seen a ghost.

"I don't know, but I think we're supposed to start praying about it for sure."

So for the next several months we did. We spent countless sleepless nights and early mornings on our faces, begging God to show us what we were supposed to do. I wish I could say things clarified for us as we prayed, but they didn't. In fact, oftentimes things got more confusing.

Our relationship became strained as I had trouble figuring out what direction our lives were supposed to take, and Amanda grew frustrated that I seemed distant and uncommunicative.

I didn't know at the time that she was struggling with the prospect of moving and starting a church. She recorded her concerns in her journal, telling God how she was feeling and asking Him to guide us and lead us, without burdening me with her concerns.

She loved the idea of a comfortable house, a convenient lifestyle, starting a family, and settling down to raise our kids. Outwardly she seemed supportive and encouraging, but inwardly she was wrestling with the idea of attempting something that brought with it so many unknowns. How would we make money? Where would we live? Were we going to have to go backward in terms of our lifestyle? Would we be able to do something this difficult? What if we failed?

One Sunday in May of that year, a church plant team in Greenville asked me to fill in for their pastor who was on vacation. Amanda attended both services that I preached, and she wrote this in her journal the next day:

Jesus, you just blew my mind yesterday. Davey spoke at a start-up church here in Greenville yesterday. They started about 9 months ago and are [running] about 250.

As I was getting ready to go, I thought, well this will be good to see what it would be like if we started a church. Not really thinking much of it. But as soon as I came in and was greeted and someone showed me to my seat—my heart was just touched.

Then we started singing "I called and you answered and you came to my rescue and I wanna be where you are. In our life, be lifted up, in our world, be lifted up, in our love be lifted up."

Jesus, I just wanted to cry. I feel like you broke down my walls and broke my heart for the possibility of us starting a church.

I've never felt that way before. Honestly, I've never loved the idea because I KNOW how much work it would take, how uncomfortable it would be, and how risky it would be. But then Davey got up to speak about boldness. The one thing that really stuck with me was "safe doesn't see movements of God." Gut. Check. Father. I want so badly to be a part of a massive movement of you. But I also know that one of my biggest weaknesses is comfort.

But there was just something about yesterday that I've never felt before. Instead of dreading the idea and dreading the unknown, I got to see a glimpse of what it could look like and I honestly got SO excited.

Which is crazy because just two days ago I told Davey "If you feel like God is moving us, I think I would be ok with that." I don't want to try and assume what your plans are, Jesus, and I don't want to manipulate anything.

I beg that you would guide Davey and his heart to your will . . . not to his agenda, desires, and escape. But if anything does come out of this, Father—I just want to praise you and thank you for the fact that you care so much about me and my heart that you would enable me and get me to the point where I would be ok with leaving or moving.

It brings tears to my eyes to think about that song.

"I called and you answered" because Davey and I have been calling out to you for months for your direction and I feel like you are answering us, Jesus. I have never felt you so real and so sovereign before and I can't thank you enough for it.

Again, Jesus—I don't want to guess what you are doing . . . and if it ends up that we stay put for a long time—well then I'm gonna need your help.

You are good, Father. Your will is perfect and I just want to be IN it, no matter where it is. I love you and praise you so much for being all-knowing, completely sovereign and perfect.

Something changed that day. I didn't even know we hadn't been on the same page prior to that conversation, but now I could sense a unity that had not been there. We both just wanted to be in the center of God's will, together.

About a month later I was sitting on my back deck reading again in 1 Samuel, this time in chapter 31. Saul and his son Jonathan were killed in battle. An Amalekite from the Israelite camp came to David—the man scheduled to succeed Saul as king—reported to him what happened, and gave him Saul's crown. In that moment that same still, small voice impressed on my heart, *Davey, if I want you to start a church, I'll bring it to you. You won't be able to stop it.*

That was it. I was furious. I was fed up with all this ambiguity. That morning on my back deck I started yelling at God—out loud! "God I'm tired of this! Would You just tell us what we're supposed to do already! I've had it! You have to do something *today*! Something extreme! You have to release me from my burden for Greenville if You want us to move."

That same morning my boss, Howard, the campus pastor of the Greenville campus, called our whole staff into the conference room. I was seated at his immediate left.

"Guys, my role is changing here at NewSpring," he began. "I'm leaving the Greenville campus to take another role in our organization."

Shock filled the room, and then almost simultaneously my staff's eyes darted at me as if they expected Howard next to pass over the leadership to me. There was just one problem: this was the first I had heard about this.

"You guys are going to be in good hands because David Nasim is taking over here at this campus." Howard gestured to a different David sitting across the table.

There you go, Davey. You're released. It was the voice. *Your burden is no longer for this campus. It's for what I'm calling you to next.*

I couldn't believe it. I walked out of that meeting, stepped outside, and called my friend and fellow student pastor, Brad Cooper. "Coop, you have to talk me off a ledge. I think God's calling Amanda and me to start a church."

Brad listened, but instead of answering my question, or helping me find more clarity, he added even more complexity. "Davey, I want you to consider taking a position over here at Central Student Ministry of NewSpring supporting all the other campuses, but I need to know something in two weeks. Why don't you ask God if He'll give you extreme clarity about all this over the next two weeks."

Two weeks? Two weeks seemed like a ridiculously fast amount of time considering we had been begging God for *months* for clarity and hadn't received it. But I told Coop that Amanda and I would be praying and that we would let him know what we decided.

The very next day Amanda got a phone call from her sister in Elkhart, Indiana, saying she was going into labor—two weeks early.

Amanda came to me as soon as she found out. "We *have* to go see her, Davey. I can't miss the birth of my first niece!"

I consented, thinking it might be a good time for us to get away. A different pace and different place often provides a different perspective. Besides, if there was one city Amanda and I had talked about moving to, it was Indianapolis, my birthplace, the city where we used to meet up during our long-distance dating relationship, and where we eventually got engaged. I thought it would be good to drive through Indy and see if we got any special feeling that we were supposed to move there.

The day before we left for Indianapolis, I sat with a childhood friend and his wife, Guy and Holly Howard. Guy had played baseball with me from the time we were seven years old all the way through college. He and Holly were preparing to depart for long-term mission work in Cambodia the next week. He caught me up on their process and then looked at me and said, "How can we be praying for you guys?"

I looked back at him wondering if I should share what was going on. I took a deep breath and then said, "I think God's calling Amanda and me to start a church."

Guy leaned forward and looked at me inquisitively. "Really? Where do you feel like you're being called?"

"I know this doesn't make sense, considering you and I grew up in Birmingham, Alabama, but I think He's calling us to Indianapolis." What happened next would be a moment I'll remember forever. Guy shifted in his seat, obviously uncomfortable with what I had just said. He glanced at Holly, and she stared back at him.

"Guy, you *have* to tell him," she said.

"Tell me what?" This was really weird.

"Davey, this is bizarre. This has never happened to me before."

He paused as if he couldn't believe what he was about to say. "I had a dream a few nights ago that Holly and I were coming back from the mission field to visit you at your church . . . in Indianapolis."

"What? Come on, man. Quit pulling my chain," I said, half expecting to see Guy's telltale smirk come over his face. But it didn't. In fact, I'd never seen a more serious expression on his face in the entire time I'd known him.

"No, Davey. It was so vivid I woke Holly up and said, 'What the heck are Davey and Amanda doing in Indianapolis?'"

Immediately the air was sucked out of the room and I was speechless. I had always been very skeptical of God speaking to people in dreams, but now here I was, sitting face-to-face with what seemed like a legitimate and timely message from the Lord.

We wrapped up dinner, awkwardness still lingering in the air.

Part of me thought what Guy had claimed to experience was utterly ridiculous. At the same time something about it all resonated deeply in my soul.

Two nights later Amanda and I found ourselves in Elkhart at dinner with one of her childhood friends and her husband. We had driven through Indianapolis, hoping to get some kind of special feeling that we were meant to be there, but nothing happened. Now at dinner, we were asking this couple who had just moved to Indy from Chicago if they'd been able to find a great church to plug in to. Amanda's friend cut into the conversation and looked us both directly in the eyes.

"We've been talking about this. We think you two should move to Indy and start a church. We'd be your first members!"

I couldn't believe it. I fumbled through some kind of response about how we loved where God had us right now. Amanda and I got back in the car and looked at each other with utter disbelief.

And then she started crying.

We both knew what this meant. We had asked, God had answered, and we both just wanted to be where He was calling us to be.

When we returned home from Elkhart, I set up a phone call with one of my mentors, Pastor Kevin Myers. That day on the phone, I shared with him everything that had transpired, and he lovingly supported me and helped me see that this is how God typically calls people to do the seemingly impossible. Amanda was waiting nervously for me to get off the phone and come back inside to find out what Kevin had told me. She and I both knew that God often speaks to us through godly council to either confirm or challenge whatever He's doing in our life.

Now, as I walked back into our living room, I could tell she knew the look on my face said it all: We were going to move to Indianapolis to start a church and we didn't have a clue what the first step was. But at least we were going to do it together.

I took Amanda by the hand, and we knelt down by the couch in our living room. I scanned the room and saw all the leather furniture, the cozy vintage frames that lined our walls, and the rustic trunks stacked as side tables. Then I looked at her and said, "Babe, are you going to be okay if we don't have any of this stuff? If we have to cash it all in to follow God's calling?"

She burst into tears and nodded.

I pulled her close to me and held her. What little bit of strength I had that was holding my own emotion at bay crumbled, and together we knelt there on our living room floor, weeping and holding each other. God was calling us. And we had to go. And neither one of us knew what was waiting for us in Indy.

Now, just six months later, I stood in another living room, holding my Amanda's hands. This time her face was full of excitement and relief from finally having made it to Indy and finding a place in which she could begin to rebuild our home.

"I know this is the one!" she repeated to me.

"Okay, okay. Listen, babe. This is the first house we've looked at. We can't just jump at the first one. Let's take a look at a few more, and then if we still like this one, we'll come back to it." I knew she was anxious to get into a place of our own again. I knew that for her, it meant comfort and stability and having a space to fill with furniture, pictures, and all of her little personal touches. But we had no idea where in the city we were going to start the church. We had no idea where the good schools were or where it was safe to raise a family. I wanted to be wise about our next move.

But of course, after looking at about twenty more houses, we found ourselves right back in the living room of the house on Sunnyfield Court, and Amanda looked at me and smiled.

"I told you this was going to be our house," she teased me. I just gave her that you're-always-right grin.

We had already decided on an amount we felt comfortable spending on a house, given the nature of our church-planting situation and not being sure where income was going to come from for the next few years. That amount was quite a lowball offer for this house, but we went to our Realtor and asked him to make the offer anyway.

He looked at us with an encouraging grin. "Why not try?! It's been on the market for a little while."

Unfortunately the Realtor on the other end of the equation laughed us off the table. She didn't even bother to make a counteroffer, saying they had turned down three offers much higher than this one. She told us we'd do better to come back with a higher figure if we wanted to even begin the negotiation process.

Amanda and I were crushed, but we felt the Lord had given us this number and it was the max we were willing to spend. We prayed about it together that night and decided that if God didn't

want us to be in this house, He'd slam the door shut. But if He
wanted us there, He'd open it back up. It was in His hands, and
we weren't going to manipulate the process. Amanda's grandmother had always told her faith was living without scheming.

The next day we went into our Realtor's office and told
him, "Put down the same exact offer as before." This time not so
encouragingly, he stared at us in surprise.

"Are you sure? You could very easily lose the ability to even
negotiate for this house if you do that."

"We're sure."

And we were. We knew if God wanted us to be in this house,
nothing could stop it from happening.

Surprisingly, and quite miraculously, the seller *accepted* the
offer and Amanda and I became the new owners of this quaint
little split-level on Sunnyfield Court. This is what we would call
home for the next four years.

This was the house where we started our church with four
people and one kid. We did childcare in our master bedroom—
the only room with a TV. The kids watched VeggieTales while the
adults met in the living room. I can't tell you how many nights
Amanda and I climbed into bed to discover Goldfish crackers
buried in our sheets.

This was the house where we brought our son, Weston, home
from the hospital. Amanda transformed the office upstairs into
a cute vintage baseball-themed nursery for him. This was the
house where we cried together when a big donor came through
in the nick of time to pull us through another tough financial
season at the church. This was where we cried together and
prayed together and grew together. This was home.

And this was also the house where tragedy struck that
morning of November 10. This was the house where I found
Amanda on our living room floor with three gunshot wounds.

This was the house that was used for ministry, where we made some of our greatest memories, and where everything changed in a heartbeat.

Now there was no going back to this house.

I left the hospital in the afternoon of November 11 without Amanda, exhausted and in complete shock. In a whirlwind twenty-four hours, my best friend and wife had been pronounced legally dead, we had met with the organ donation representatives, and I'd watched all hope of her recovering from this incident immediately dissipate.

Nothing can prepare you for such waves of emotion. Only forty-eight hours earlier I had kissed her goodbye and left for work to begin a normal week. Now I was sitting in the passenger seat of Amanda's car, my mom driving. Amanda's gray flip-flops still sat on the floorboard. I pulled off my hat and looked at the blood stained on the underside of the brim. My eyes were cloudy and stinging from so many tears shed. The sun was shining through the car windows and, now with no hat to block it, invaded my already irritated corneas.

As we drove past the exit to our Sunnyfield Court house I realized I now had no home, no place for Weston and me to lay our heads. My home had become a crime scene. It's been said that home is where the heart is, but where is home when your heart has been stolen from you? Where is home when your heart has been crushed? Where is home when your life has been upended in a moment? Where is *my* home when Amanda *was* my home?

We pulled in to my grandparents' house, which would prove to be the first of four different houses I'd call home over the next four months. I was now a drifter, a transient. I had learned to deal with the fact that Amanda and I would probably have many different *houses* in our lifetime doing ministry, but the one thing that gave my heart peace is that I'd always have one *home*: Amanda. Now she was gone.

I sat on my grandparents' couch for the next several hours staring off at nothing in shock and dismay. Every once in a while I would be jolted by harsh, uncontrollable sobs.

A few hours passed and my assistant, Megan, stopped by the house with a suitcase full of clothes and toiletry items for Weston and me, along with a few toys from Weston's toy box. My parents had sent people into the Sunnyfield Court house to gather up some personal items that we'd need for the next who-knows-how-long. I looked at the suitcase and realized I didn't know when I *wouldn't* be living out of one of these.

"We found a bunch of Amanda's journals, Davey," Megan told me. "We thought you'd like to read some of them when you're ready." Her voice cracked a little as she held back tears, trying to be strong for me.

I picked up one of the journals and let it fall open to a random page. The soft strokes of Amanda's handwriting brought more tears to my eyes. This entry happened to be from the day after we moved to Indianapolis, November 11, 2011, exactly four years previous.

Well . . . we made it!

We are officially in Indianapolis!

I can't even believe it.

Jesus you are faithful in your promises. Thank you for getting us here. Thank you that we are actually here. It was so awesome as we drove in last night we saw the cityscape and it was such an inspiring view. I don't think I will ever forget that. I just felt a peace coming here yesterday and I cried while I listened to the lyrics of this song. "I will take up my cross and follow Lord where you lead me." I remember when Davey and I knew we were called to go to Indy (and hadn't told anyone yet). We were at Fuse and they played that song and I just cried. Two different kinds of tears but all with the same meaning. We're here ... and it's time to get busy. Jesus, direct us every step. I pray we would never look back. I pray that we would never lose heart. When it gets difficult and discouraging I pray that you will remind me "I will take up my cross and follow Lord where you lead me ... I will take up my cross and follow wherever you lead."

Her words cascaded over my shredded heart. She felt so close in that moment—almost like her words carried with them a part of her, like I was having a conversation with my best friend again.

In that moment, sitting on my grandparents' couch, lamenting the loss of home, a thought struck me: *Maybe we're not supposed to feel at home in this world.* Maybe this Sunnyfield Court house on that cul-de-sac, a symbol of our very own bodies, a tent that was built for a special calling and purpose but that was now ransacked by evil, sin, hatred, and darkness, was not meant to last forever. It was never meant to last forever.

Maybe we were never built to find our fulfillment and sense of belonging fully and finally here on earth, "where moth and rust destroy and where thieves break in and steal" (Matthew 6:19 ESV). Instead, even in that moment, I could feel my heart longing for an otherworldly place—one that would last forever, one that could not be shaken or torn down, one that could not be stolen from me. This is the only place that captures the full essence of my heart's longing: heaven.

Didn't Jesus say that He left earth after rising from the dead to "go to prepare a place" for us (John 14:2 ESV)? I thought about how in Jesus's ministry He moved around from place to place, house to house, city to city to bring the good news of the kingdom of God to people from all walks of life. He had "no place to lay his head" (Luke 9:58 NIV). I wonder if following Jesus ushers us into this same lifestyle and calling, until we finally arrive at the place He's been preparing for us.

I imagined Amanda stepping onto streets of gold of her new home—her permanent home—the only true home her heart was created for. I imagined her taking little Everette Grace by the hand, saying,

Well, Evie ... we made it!

We are officially in heaven!

I can't even believe it.

Jesus you are faithful in your promises. Thank you for getting us here.

Thank you that we are actually here. It was so awesome as we drove in last night we saw the cityscape and it was such an inspiring view. I don't think I will ever forget that. I just felt a peace coming here ...

Home is where the heart is. But more poignantly, home is where the soul is. And my soul belongs to heaven. My lasting home is in heaven.

And now more than ever my soul *longs* for heaven. Now more than ever, I realize that in my time here on earth I'm an alien, a wanderer, a transient, homeless. I'm just passing through.

Now more than ever, I realize how trivial things of this world and this life can be. Now more than ever, I realize my time here is brief, a vapor, here today and gone tomorrow. Now more than ever, I realize I find the most fulfillment when I spend my life, my time, my resources, my possessions as a tool for ministry, as a medium to convince others to find their home in heaven too.

Now more than ever, the depths of my heart are holding on to home, my true home. I long for heaven.

Unfortunately even as this thought concluded, I found myself sitting on my grandparents' couch—still on earth, in a temporary home, now wondering how I was ever going to survive without Amanda.

5

WHAT IF?

THE NEXT FEW DAYS I WALKED AROUND IN A FOG. MY GRANDPAR-
ents' house became a base camp for friends and families who
came into town for the funeral. Groups of people brought food
over, and as each arrived, they wanted to talk to me, offer their
condolences, and give me their dealing-with-loss theology in
a tweetable phrase. Grief books came pouring into the mail.
Letters, cards, gift cards, diapers and wipes for Weston, figurines,
snow globes, frames, and wind chimes.

If it could be shipped, we received it.

I didn't want to hear another trite Hallmark phrase, whether
it was theologically sound or not.

"Heaven just gained another angel."

"God must have needed her more than we did."

"You won't always feel this way. Time heals."

"I'm just grateful you're young and you have time to find love
again."

"She's in a better place."

Each one of these phrases I could have easily taken into a
theological debate arena and ripped to shreds, but I just sat there,
gritting my teeth, nodding politely with each passing statement,
knowing people just wanted to help. But sometimes there is
really nothing you can do to help except just show up. Just sit
with someone in their grief. Just hold their hand.

All I wanted was someone to hug me, to tell me they loved me, to remind me that they were here for me. Then one morning my mom did just that, and I got irritated with her because it felt like she was hovering. I guess all I really wanted was *Amanda* to hug me, tell me she loved me, and that she was here for me—and for Weston. But she wasn't, and she wouldn't be. I'd never feel the warmth of her hug again. It was gone. She was gone.

And on some level it felt like it was my fault.

What many people didn't realize is that while I was wrestling with sorrow, sadness, loss, and shock, I was also wrestling with a level of guilt I'd never felt before. You see, when I left that Tuesday morning for the gym, I didn't lock the front door.

We hardly ever locked our doors when we left the house. We were tucked back on a cul-de-sac in a neighborhood that had been historically safe. These men who broke into my house, who at this point were still on the loose, had unhindered access to my home, my stuff, and my family. Here I was, the man of the house, supposed to be the protector, the defender, the fighter for my family, and I wasn't there in the most pivotal moment of my family's life. I couldn't take it. I couldn't shake this guilt!

God, why couldn't I have been there?! What if I hadn't gone to the gym that morning? What if I hadn't been in such a hurry to leave? What if I had come home earlier? What if I had locked the door?!

Three weeks before all of this happened, I took two weeks off work. We were coming off a very busy summer and fall at the church and I wanted to spend two weeks with Amanda, resting and preparing for what was next. Amanda and I spent the first of those weeks on a staycation doing house projects.

We had talked about putting the house up for sale in the spring and possibly finding a larger house to prepare for the arrival of Evie and quite possibly more kids. Amanda's heart had just recently been stirred by the idea of fostering kids and providing a stable home for those who didn't have one. We'd had several discussions about the prospect, so moving to a bigger home was fresh in our minds.

One day during that week I was at a local hardware store, picking up supplies, and came across some door hardware. We had only one functional key for the front door and had been handing it back and forth. Most of the time, she was the one at home with Weston while I was at work, so we kept that key on her key ring. The deadbolt on the front door—which could be opened only by that one key—was fairly old and rickety, so I called Amanda to get her thoughts about buying new hardware for our exterior doors.

"Oh, honey. Don't do that! Those are so expensive." She pushed back on me. She was always thinking practically and frugally. "If we sell the house in the spring, the new homeowners will change the locks anyways. Let them deal with that."

I saw her point, so I relented, picked up the paint supplies we needed, and left. Of course, now, I was thinking what a small expense that would have been to avoid all that had happened. *Why didn't I just get the new locks? Why didn't I at least make extra copies of the key so I could have taken one with me that morning and locked the door?*

Amanda's keys were on her bedside table the morning I left. I was never very good at being quiet in the mornings when I got up before her, and if I woke her by searching for her keys, I knew she'd be upset. So I left without locking the door.

I left without locking the door. What if I hadn't? This would all be different! She would still be here!

One of the things people so rarely acknowledge about guilt is how paralyzing it is. It steals all of your energy and motivation. It makes it impossible to walk out the next steps of any process, especially the grief process. Life requires a certain tenacity—a dog in the fight—to survive, but guilt tends to rip that fighting spirit right out from under you. Grief in and of itself is suffocating—but guilt on top of grief? It steals your ability to do just about anything.

I sat there feeling as though I had a constant throbbing headache of the soul. Beat after beat, it felt like knives were stabbing my heart over and over. But add to that a layer of guilt—the burden of knowing that I could have prevented Amanda's death had I just made that one change . . . had that one little detail altered. It was excruciating.

On top of everything, the media was blowing up my email and voicemail inboxes. People wanted to know what had happened, and although many were supportive and wanted to help, the loudest in the bunch were those who were pandering to the lowest common denominators. Some had jumped to the worst-case scenarios and were spreading hate and lies as they concocted and circulated conspiracy theories of my involvement in my wife's murder.

NewSpring Church sent a crew to Indy to help me and my family navigate the media firestorm we were in. We sat together as a family, huddled in a bunker, and tried to wrap our minds around what had just happened to us, what we had just lost. All the while the media remained a dull noise in the background.

All the to-dos of that week loomed over our heads—a casket and a gravesite needed to be picked out, the funeral needed to be planned, arrangements needed to be made—and we just couldn't gain clarity of thought to do any of it. Here we were, a family of pastors who normally stepped into this kind of service for others, but we were now paralyzed, unable to minister to ourselves.

No one should have to pick out a casket and a gravesite for a twenty-eight-year-old woman. No one should be planning a funeral for a young mother! Especially one who had a clean bill of health and was expecting to welcome her second child into this world. I sat there with my family and couldn't help but feel helpless and somewhat responsible.

I looked at her dad, Phil, across the room. His furrowed brow reminded me of Amanda when she would focus. Weston has the same look when he's intent on something.

Amanda and her dad shared a special bond. Ever since Amanda and I met, their relationship began to evolve into an even deeper connection. As a pastor he understood that with me, Amanda's life would be consumed by ministry. During her senior year of high school, they would often go on runs together and talk about the heartaches of helping people. He is an incredible counselor to people, and Amanda's dream was to counsel people as well.

Although both loved people earnestly, the catchphrase they often shared was "people suck." Anytime her dad would come home clearly drained from a hard day of leading people, Amanda would just look at him, grin, and say, "Dad, people suck." She was able to pull out the lighthearted side of him like no one else, and yet she was able to coerce the depth of his wisdom as well.

After Amanda and I married and entered ministry, she and I would stay with her mom and dad for long weekends just to have them counsel us. We'd sit in front of a wood-burning fire and drink coffee all morning, laughing, crying, and swapping war stories of the ministry grind.

Personally, I've always had an incredible relationship with Phil as well. I was so comfortable talking to him and Amanda's mom about personal things. They even did our premarital counseling.

I used to ask him how I could love and lead Amanda better. Some of my favorite conversations with him were surrounding his daughter, how to guard and protect her heart and be a better husband to her. He always reminded me so much of Amanda. There were times when she would laugh, and her face would practically morph into her dad's face right in front of me. It made it really difficult to kiss her in those moments—which I'm sure her dad secretly relished.

I remember the first time I met Phil. I was so intimidated by stories Gavin had told me about how strict he was. It was the morning after Amanda and I were set up on our blind date. I attended First Baptist Church in Elkhart where Phil was the music pastor, and after the service he found me in the atrium to introduce himself. I hoped beyond all hope he didn't notice my hands were shaking and my armpits were sweaty.

I found out later that Gavin had majorly exaggerated what I should expect. Truth was, he was one of the nicest guys I had ever met. His reputation for being tough came from his grave concern for his daughters' purity, well-being, and hearts. He was going to make sure that whoever they were interested in not only took good care of them but loved Jesus and honored them as daughters of God.

After church that day—the first day I met him—we all went out to eat hot wings. Little did I know this was a tradition and a litmus test in the Byars family. If someone was going to date

Phil's girls, he made sure they could stomach hot wings, like some kind of rite of passage into manhood.

I sat next to Amanda at Wings Etc., picked up the menu, and said, "Hmmm, what's good here?" Without hesitation she reached across me and pointed to the hottest wings on the menu. She was going to make sure I didn't order something weak like teriyaki or honey barbecue!

Suddenly, Gavin's voice brought me back to reality, sitting in my grandparents' living room.

"There's bound to be a lot of people at her service with all the media attention out there. What venue should we use?"

"That's a good point, Gavin." Phil turned his attention to me.

"Davey, do you have any friends in town who pastor a church with a large auditorium?"

I looked at him and couldn't help but be overcome with guilt. This man had trusted me with the protection of his daughter. My thoughts began to wander to the day I asked him for his daughter's hand in marriage.

Phil and I were at their house that day, and for some reason Amber was with us, so the three of us piled into his jeep and drove down the Byars' long driveway to Arni's Restaurant. Amber thought it was amusing that she was going to sit in on the infamous asking-permission-to-marry conversation. Gavin had proposed to her a couple of weeks before, and she was glowing with delight over her left ring finger, now clad with a beautiful new rock.

There is nothing like driving down a rural road with country music playing on the radio. It can bring a sense of nostalgia to even the most hipster city dweller—there's something so simple and carefree about those southern guitar licks. As we made the turn onto County Road 200, a new song by the band Heartland called "I Loved Her First" started playing. It was a song about a father giving his daughter away in marriage. I could have sworn in that moment that Amber and Phil had concocted some kind of conspiracy against me, knowing this would tug at my heart-strings and make me even more nervous to follow through with the impending conversation.

I remember it seemed just about every country song released that summer was about a father giving away his daughter! Each time I would hear one, I'd almost impulsively drive up to Phil's house in tears and beg forgiveness for taking his daughter away from him. These songs touched me *that much*!

We pulled into Arni's, ordered three Cokes and a pizza to split, and I knew I couldn't delay the conversation any further. I launched in. "Mr. Byars, I want to ask for your daughter's hand in marriage."

He smirked, looked over at Amber wryly, and replied, "I'm sorry son, but Gavin already beat you to it."

Amber and he erupted in laughter, and after a couple seconds I followed with my own nervous chuckle. I was grateful for a little humor to break the ice.

For the next several minutes I did my best to explain to him how I would love and cherish Amanda as long as I lived. I described to him my plan for providing for her. I did my best to assure him that I would follow Jesus's direction for our lives the best I could. As I finished my well-prepared speech, he looked at me and told me he was thrilled to give me his blessing. But something in his eyes caught my attention. I could see a little twinge, almost as if his heart was saying to me:

Remember, son, I loved her first.

In that moment I couldn't help but think about how much Amanda admired her dad. I'm convinced this is why she was so confident in who she was in Christ. He showed her early on in her life that her value didn't lie in the grades she brought home, how she performed in the sports arena, or what a boy said about her. He instilled in her that her value was inherent, that she was a daughter of King Jesus, and that sons and daughters of the King never have to settle for second best. It was Phil who taught Amanda how to handle God's Word, how to seek wisdom whatever the cost, and how to love people well.

I felt a significant weight of responsibility that day at Arni's, which made the guilt all the more compounded sitting there in my grandparents' living room looking across at Phil. I felt like I had failed him, like I had failed her.

Phil must have recognized what was going on in my countenance. As conversation about the funeral plans began to wrap up that evening, he looked at me and said, "Davey, can we talk? Can I take you to breakfast tomorrow?"

The next morning, sitting in a booth at one of Phil's favorite breakfast joints, my pulse raced with anxiousness about admitting my guilt to him. "What's going on in your heart right now, son?" He looked at me, his eyes heavy with hurt and fatigue.

I hesitated a moment, not sure how this conversation was going to pan out, and then I unloaded.

"I'm having a lot of trouble right now. I feel like I failed you, Dad. I feel like I failed Amanda. I feel like I should have been there to protect her. I keep thinking about all the things I could have done differently, and maybe this could have been prevented."

I told him about the weight I felt that day leaving Arni's eight years before. I told him I felt the role of protector shift from him to me as he walked her down the aisle to me at our wedding. I told him about another moment I had with God one early January morning in 2009.

"I was reading my Bible and sipping a cup of coffee while Amanda was still asleep. I read Ephesians 5:25–28: 'Husbands, love your wives, just as Christ loved the church and gave himself up for her to make her holy, cleansing her by the washing with water through the word, and to present her to himself as a radiant church, without stain or wrinkle or any other blemish, but holy and blameless. In this same way, husbands ought to love their wives as their own bodies' (NIV).

"I remember the force of these words hitting me like a tsunami, Phil. I've heard this verse preached time and again, but for some reason the responsibility of being a husband sat on my shoulders much heavier that morning. I felt the Lord speak to my heart and remind me Amanda wasn't mine. That she had been stewarded to me by our heavenly Father for a season, that I was to love her, pursue her, cherish her, and . . ."—I paused for a moment as the thought sank in—". . . protect her."

Phil stared at me while tears began to well up in my eyes.

I continued. "So I put down my coffee and Bible, got up from my chair in the living room, walked into our bedroom, and lay down next to Amanda. I cuddled up to her with tears streaming down my face and told Jesus I would do my best to steward the responsibility He'd blessed me with. I thanked Him for the gift of friendship, companionship, love, intimacy, and marriage. And now, Dad, I've failed."

Phil put down his coffee and tilted his head. "You feel like you failed in the responsibility to *protect* her?"

I looked down at the plate of breakfast in front of me, not feeling much like eating any of it, and nodded.

"Davey, I need you to look at me. You couldn't have prevented this. It wouldn't have mattered what you did."

"But, Dad, I didn't lock the front door. *What if I had?!*"

"Davey, the investigators told us that the men they suspect had already broken into two locked doors that morning! The officer on assignment said he thinks they saw you leave for the gym as they were leaving the other house on your street. They were coming into your house no matter what."

This helped a little, but I still couldn't shake the thought that I could have altered this whole thing.

"Davey, you feel like *you* could have prevented this. Don't you think God could have prevented it?"

I looked up through the tears that were welling up in my eyes. Of course I did, but it hurt to even consider that God could have but didn't.

"Yeah, I certainly believe He *could* have."

"You're right. He very easily could have. But He didn't. For some reason He allowed this to happen. And honestly, Davey, we're not going to know why on this side of eternity. If there is one thing I've learned in this life it's that God's thoughts are higher than mine, His ways are beyond mine, and His plan sometimes can't be understood in the moment. But He does work all things into His beautiful master plan."

The waiter approached the table to top off our coffees and hand Phil the check. He waved me off as I stuck out my hand to try and intercept it. Some things would never change about our relationship.

"Davey, I got a phone call this morning from Dave Hunt."

Dave was the funeral director who was taking care of the arrangements that week for Amanda. He and his wife had attended a church in Crawfordsville, where Phil had been employed for a few years, and they were taking the loss of Amanda as if she were one of their own daughters. "He told me he left the hospital after we got the test results back for Amanda. He was praying about how to handle everything and talking to his wife, Karen, about what casket could be used for Amanda." I listened intently.

"Anyway, Karen had almost forgotten to tell Dave that they had just received a mistake order last week for a casket. She held on to it until they could decide how to ship it back. Davey, it's made out of reclaimed barn wood."

I almost fell out of the booth. I couldn't believe it. Before Amanda was killed, she had gained a reputation in Indianapolis for her vintage furniture and home decor business, which she called The Weathered Willow. She would reclaim free or cheap pieces of furniture, restore them, and sell them for a profit. One of her favorite things to work with was reclaimed barn wood. I thought about the wall tapestry she had just made out of barn wood for Weston's nursery, on which was written a verse from 1 Samuel: "For the rest of his days he will be given over to the Lord."

Even Amanda understood through the anxieties of pregnancy, scares of miscarriage, and uncertainty of bringing a child into this world that Weston really belonged to the Lord.

Remember, son, I loved her first . . . just as I loved Weston first.

"There's more, Davey. Robin and Amber went to check out Traders Point Church's auditorium where we decided to do the celebration of life service. As the lady in charge of facilities walked them into the auditorium, she was explaining to them how they had just finished renovations. Davey, the whole front of the stage and the walls are covered in reclaimed barn wood."

I couldn't believe what I was hearing. It was almost as if all of this had been staged. Like there was this massive orchestration going on around me that had been set into motion months and years before this week. Phil leaned in closer as if he wasn't finished.

"Amber told me about what happened when you guys went to the hospital the other night to say your final goodbyes. She told me about the OR doctor."

I had almost missed the significance of this moment until Phil mentioned it on the coattails of these other details. A couple of nights before, while we were standing around Amanda's hospital bed saying our final goodbyes before they wheeled her into the operating room for organ donation, a young man walked into the room. Amber looked up from Amanda's bedside, saw this man, and her face lit up.

"Chris! What are you doing here?"

"Amber, I'm so very sorry ... about everything. This is all just unbelievable." Chris was in scrubs and held a clipboard by his side. His eyes were moist and red.

"Do you work here?" Amber looked at him confused.

"Actually, I'm the OR doctor assigned to Amanda. I'll be there by her side as we harvest her organs and take her off the ventilator."

Amber gasped and then almost immediately must have realized how confused Gavin and I looked. "Davey, Gavin. This is Chris. He went to college with Amanda, James, and me in Florida. We all used to eat lunch together every day."

Now as I sat there across from Phil in the diner, the realization of how profound that moment was hit me. Tears streamed down my face. The fact that God would make sure Amanda wasn't alone as her body took its final breath. That someone would be standing beside her who was not just a believer but also a friend. It felt so personal. This God who often feels distant, removed from our pain, otherworldly, put His thumbprint on our story in such an intimate way.

"Davey, God wasn't surprised by this. He's orchestrated things ahead of time to show us that He's *in* this! He's working a master plan that none of us understand, but He's in control! He's the *author* and *perfecter* of our faith."

Seeing I was still trying to wrap my mind around all that was being said here, Phil shifted in his booth and lowered his voice. "Davey, you're missing the most important part of that Ephesians passage. God gave her to you. He gave her to me. He gave her to us. She was a gift, and there was going to come a day you were going to give her back, whether that was when she was twenty-eight years old or eighty-eight years old.

"You see, He thought her up. He thought this family up. He thought the two of you up. He knew the number of hairs on her head. He knew her most intimate thoughts. He numbered her days. He brought her to you. He *stewarded* her to you . . . for a season. And He loves her more than you or I ever could."

Phil put down his fork and continued. "Here's the deal: We could all but kill ourselves replaying over and over how we could have prevented this. And that's exactly what most people do. They let guilt and grief paralyze them and they never emerge from it. Or we could do something different. We could trust that during the whole time there was—and is—a higher power in control, that God is weaving something beautiful out of this. Remember, son *He* loved her first."

I couldn't hold it in any longer. I blurted it out through the sobs.

"If God cared so much, why did He let this happen? Why didn't *He* protect her?!"

Phil looked back at me and said softly and deliberately, "I believe He did. Davey, what do you do when Weston falls down and skins his knee or when he gets hurt?"

"Um . . ." I sniffled a little as I wiped my face clean, not sure where he was going with this. "I pick him up," I said. "I hold him, let him cry, and then I kiss the bruise to 'make it all better.'"

"Of course you do. Every good parent does that. There's something about a parent's touch that makes it all better, even when you're in pain. It's a touch that only a parent has. Davey, God is a perfect heavenly Father. Don't you think in those final moments He scooped Amanda up, held her, let her cry, and then in a moment—I mean this with all sincerity—kissed it with a power that only the Master Healer has and made it all better? You see, I believe He protected her in ways neither you nor I could have."

Sitting there in booth number nine of this little breakfast diner, a tremendous rush of peace invaded my spirit. The fact that God would be so personal to orchestrate all of this just to speak into my situation, into my pain, the assurance that He is in control. I guess I hadn't thought about the fact that this didn't surprise Him. That He wasn't shocked. And that He'd been preparing all of us for the day. That when He brought her into my life He knew November 10, 2015, would come—the day His little girl would be brought back to Him. And what I was beginning to realize is my willingness to trust God's plan and give this situation over to Him became the very act of presenting Amanda to the Father, "holy and blameless" (Ephesians 5:27 NIV).

A profound thought filled my spirit that day. I could look at this as a coincidental string of events, or I could begin to see this for what it really was, a providential story that a loving heavenly Father was writing. And if I *truly* loved Amanda I could *completely* trust her to Jesus's perfect love and plan. His love and protection is infinitely better than mine could ever be.

As we left the diner that morning, the still, small voice echoed in my mind . . .

Remember, son, I loved her first.

PART 2

THE BATTLE HAS ONLY JUST BEGUN

6

STEAL THE SPEAR

"You're on in ten minutes." A voice came from the door. "They're doing the final mic and feed checks."

I was sitting in the greenroom at Traders Point Christian Church. Pastor Perry Noble had surrounded me with a team of people and pastors, spearheaded by Suzanne Swift, to help me know exactly how to handle everything that was going to happen in the next couple of weeks—including this interview I was about to do with *Good Morning America*.

A week had passed since the tragedy, Amanda's celebration service had been two days before, and still no arrests had been made. Instead, I found myself caught in a media firestorm, every local and national news outlet covering the story of this pastor's pregnant wife who had been tragically murdered in her home while her fifteen-month-old slept upstairs in his crib.

To them, this was headline, a sensational story—and everyone wanted the exclusive. To me this was a nightmare, a blur. I couldn't believe what was happening. I was sure any moment I was going to wake up at home, in our bed, next to Amanda, and discover it had all been the worst, most vivid dream of all time. I sat on a leather couch in the corner of the chilly room and began reflecting on Amanda's celebration service just a few days before. I couldn't believe there were almost two thousand people in attendance and another ten thousand who watched the live stream on the Web. Hundreds had responded to Pastor Perry's message to give their life to Jesus. Outside of celebrity funerals, who has that many people looking on during their funeral? It seemed everyone had been touched by Amanda's life and its senseless ending.

My family and I decided what Amanda would have wanted was a simple and powerful worship service. The teams that pulled it all together could not have done a better job. I was dumbfounded by the impact Amanda's death was having across our country.

I thought about the text I received from Chase the day after the service. I had coached baseball with him at a local middle school, and Amanda and I had grown fond of him and his fiancé, Rachel. They visited our church a couple of times, but having grown up in very skeptical homes, they hadn't actually received the idea that God wanted a real relationship with them and that He'd made that relationship available through Jesus's death on the cross.

"I want you to know I gave my life to Jesus last night at Amanda's service," Chase had texted me. "You guys have made such an impact on me."

I thought about the several families in our neighborhood who knew Amanda and who also attended the service. Amanda was always such a great neighbor, making it a point to build relationships with people in a very unassuming and casual manner. She was passionate about making a difference for Christ wherever we lived. When we moved into the neighborhood, she made cookies for each household on our cul-de-sac and invited them to church meetings.

Often people would walk their dogs and stop to talk to her while she was painting furniture in our driveway, her sleeves rolled up, trying to soak in every ounce of sun she could possibly manage. I thought about Ryan and Melissa who lived just down the street. Amanda had recently felt a specific burden of theirs and had tried to invite them to church. I found out later that both of them attended the celebration service and both decided to receive Jesus as their Lord and Savior that night.

"Would you like some coffee, Davey?" Suzanne's team member, Amy, broke into my thoughts and extended a white ceramic mug my way.

"Thank you. That would be wonderful."

I swiveled to take the brimming cup of black coffee from Amy and then turned back to the TV screen in front of me. Indiana is always chilly in the middle of November, and this hot liquid was a welcome jolt to my weary body and sore throat. I was beginning to feel the effects of a week with virtually no sleep, my body aching to escape into some sweet dream. My nerves moved a million vibrations per minute.

The night before, I reluctantly took two Tylenol PMs in an attempt to catch a few hours of rest. It was now 7:15 a.m., I was ten minutes away from going live with George Stephanopoulos on *Good Morning America*, and my mind trudged through the fog the medication had left behind.

This was the first of what would be many interviews over the next couple of weeks. Everyone was vying for time to know what I had to say about what had happened. I was beyond grateful to have Suzanne present and available to help me navigate through this process. I had no idea what I would be doing without her guidance.

Suzanne had spent nine years on staff at NewSpring, filling many different roles, and now she was serving as the public relations director for the church. She and I had worked together when I was on staff, and it was comforting to have someone I could trust to buffer me from this media frenzy as well as help me decide what requests I should actually accept.

Out of the corner of my eye I watched her enter the room, grab her iPhone off the table, and take the seat next to me.

"How do you feel?" she asked.

"I'm okay. I'm just a little overwhelmed with all of this." I hesitated, not wanting to display the full breadth of my uneasiness. "What do you think they're going to ask me?"

I was extremely comfortable talking in front of people, having been thrust on a theatrical stage by my mom since I was a kid. Now as a pastor I was well trained in maintaining composure on stage and speaking into a camera when necessary. But this seemed worlds different.

My calling and career path had also trained me to recognize big moments, and this was the biggest I'd ever experienced. Literally overnight I had gone from small church-plant pastor in an obscure neighborhood in Indianapolis to having my face, and the face of my murdered wife, plastered on every screen in the country. No matter where I went, I couldn't escape the reminder of what had transpired.

I wanted to escape all of it. I wanted to rewind to November 9, take Weston and Amanda to some hidden cabin in the Carolinas, and live out the rest of our days there, safe from anyone and anything that could disrupt the life and family we had dreamed for ourselves. But now something told me that obscurity was no longer going to be a possibility in this lifetime.

I also wasn't sure how I was going to respond on live TV. Truth was, my emotions were quite unpredictable the past week. One minute I was feeling a weird peace and calm I couldn't explain, and the next minute I was bursting into sudden and horrific weeping.

On top of that, I knew these moments in front of the national news were more monumental than anything I'd ever experienced. All I could think about was how there was more than just Amanda and me at stake. I knew people wanted to know if my faith had faltered, if everything I taught prior to this was real, tangible, and sustaining when a great crisis hit my own life.

How would I reconcile what I had preached about Jesus, His love, and God's forgiveness of sins with what had just been taken from me? It was like the whole world was waiting to see what I was going to do next.

Some people were even convinced that I had something to do with the murder. Just a few days before, some of the biggest names in the news media had all but openly accused me of being behind it all. Broadcasting trolls were scouring news articles to add their two cents; people were creating websites and Facebook pages to highlight their conspiracy theories. To them, I was just another drama-filled story.

To my heart, these accusations were like a violent twist to the dagger that had already been shoved through it just days earlier; it felt like having your leg cut off and then watching while the wound gets seared with a red-hot iron. I tried to reconcile how my heart could both break for a group of people who were clearly reacting from their own life hurts and be infuriated with them at the same time.

Suzanne looked back at me and could tell my mind was swirling.

"Just be yourself," she said. "Let what's in your heart come out. Remember, everyone out there wants to tell *their* version of the story. You're the only one who knows and can tell the *true* version of the story. You can tell a *better* story than the evil and hatred that has ripped your family apart. The world needs to see the light that was Amanda's life in the midst of such darkness and despair."

She was right. But it didn't make it any easier. I looked up at her, took a big breath, and exhaled loudly. Seeing I was still struggling, she turned and faced me.

"Okay, Preacher, you remember in the Bible, when David was on the run from King Saul because the king was trying to kill him?"

"Yeah?" I looked up at her, not sure what she was getting at.

The story of David had always been one of my childhood favorites—and not just because we share a name. This runt of a shepherd boy gets plucked up from the sheep fields and chosen to be the next king of God's people. His brothers scoff when he's chosen, half out of jealousy, half out of doubt that he could actually fit the role. He wasn't built to be a warrior or a politician. He was a musician, always carrying around his harp, and probably wearing skinny jeans, scarves, and deep V-neck T-shirts.

But despite his shortcomings, as a young man David stepped into his calling and slew the nine-foot-tall giant—no, not André, Goliath—with just a sling and a stone. People began to take notice of him, and the king, Saul, made him a commander in the Israelite army. Shortly after that, Saul began suffering from frequent anxiety attacks, so he called David into his palace regularly to play the harp for him as music therapy. Saul became a mentor to David—and his son, Jonathan, became David's best friend.

Soon, however, Saul grew jealous of David and his success. He heard songs ringing through the streets: "Saul has slain his thousands, and David his tens of thousands" (1 Samuel 18:7 NIV). One day while David was playing the harp for Saul, the king pulled out his spear and tried to pin David to the wall with it. David narrowly escaped and spent the next several years running for his life from Saul, who continued to hunt him with the intention of killing him.

"Imagine how painful that must have been for David," Suzanne said. "His mentor and father figure throws a *spear* at him and tries to take him out. In a moment, David loses everything he has and spends the next few years dodging Saul and his militia men."

As Suzanne described it, I put myself in David's shoes. I could now almost empathize with the hurt, loss, and betrayal he felt.

"And then one day David has a chance to take revenge when he stumbles on Saul's camp while Saul is asleep," Suzanne continued. "But, instead of throwing his own spear to kill Saul and put an end to the whole mess, he simply *steals* Saul's spear and walks away."

I looked at her confused. What did this have to do with me? What was the application?

"Davey, instead of throwing your own spears at those who have been throwing them at you, just *steal* the spear and tell a better story. God is a *much* better avenger than you. He'll take care of these accusations in His own time. These people are hurt people just like Saul was, and *hurt* people tend to *hurt* people. Remember, how Saul is eventually silenced in the story? He falls on his own spear and dies!" (First Samuel 31 tells of Saul falling on his own *sword*, while 2 Samuel 1 seems to indicate it was his *spear*. Some Bible scholars attribute the seeming contradiction to "sword" being a generic term for weapon.)

I chuckled at the thought. What a brush of irony and poetic justice and what a brilliant concept. When people throw spears at you, don't throw spears back. Just steal their spear, and eventually they'll fall on their own. They'll self-destruct. *All I have to do is walk this thing out faithfully and God will take care of avenging me . . . and Amanda.*

"Thank you, Suzanne. I needed that." I took a deep breath and exhaled. "Okay. I think I'm ready." We got up from the couch, made our way down the hallway, and walked into the room filled with lights, cameras, and microphones.

Okay, Jesus I whispered to myself before I stepped into my interview. *Help me to speak from my heart. I know You're in control of all of this. I know You'll give me the words to say. Help me to honor You and honor Amanda, and give me the agility to dodge and steal the spears.*

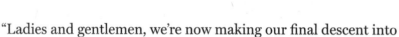

"Ladies and gentlemen, we're now making our final descent into Indianapolis. Please make sure your tray tables and seats are in the upright and locked position. Thank you for flying with us here at Delta Airlines. We'll be on the ground shortly."

My head was leaning against the plexiglass as I stared out the window of this Boeing 737. I stared at a sea of clouds that created a thick barrier between the plane and the ground. Pastor Perry had flown me down to South Carolina to get away for a few days. My week at NewSpring, ducking the media and seeing a couple of counselors and pastors, had been more necessary than I even realized at the time.

Jake Beaty, NewSpring's care pastor, hadn't left my side for the entire week, and for some reason I had quickly felt like I could open up to him about my confusion, heartache, anger, and shock. Talking through the trauma of what had taken place the last couple of weeks almost felt like I was talking to Jesus Himself about it all.

Yet as valuable as that had been for me, I still couldn't wrap my mind around what had happened. It didn't seem like reality. I just kept waiting to wake up from this horrible nightmare. I had trouble sleeping. My body felt sluggish and my eyes heavy, but most nights, sleep eluded me. I felt jumpy, nervous, anxious, looking over my shoulder all the time.

When sleep finally *would* come I would wake in a panic, thinking I had woken from a terrible nightmare, half expecting to find Amanda lying there by my side in our master bedroom at Sunnyfield Court. Each morning as I woke up in a strange, lonely bed, it reminded me of reality, and the knife in my stomach was plunged a little deeper.

"What are you thinking about?" came a voice next to me.

It was Derek, our church's worship pastor. He and his wife, Ashley, had spent the week accompanying me in South Carolina. Over the last almost three years, they had become Amanda's and my closest friends. We couldn't believe when Derek and Ashley actually accepted the job offer I made them in December 2012.

Derek had spent three years at Hillsong College in Sydney, Australia, as a student in their worship track. Two years into his studies, the oversight at Hillsong did something extremely rare and gave him worship and production leadership over an extension site. After graduating from college, Derek took a job at a church in Texas but quickly realized it was not a right fit for him, so he resigned and put résumés out to the top twenty-five fastest-growing churches in the country. Resonate was certainly *not* one of them, but fortunately for us, NewSpring was. We were forwarded his information and I quickly set up a phone call.

After a series of conversations, we invited them up to spend a weekend at our church. They visited in November 2012 between interviewing at several massive churches. We might have had fifteen people at our service that week. Amanda and I *loved* Derek and Ashley immediately—they were so easy to be around, and you could tell they carried Jesus's presence with them wherever they went—but we also thought there was no way they'd ever wind up with us.

When Derek called me two weeks later saying they felt called to help us build Resonate Church, we were floored. The four of us quickly grew close over the next few years, sharing in the most difficult seasons of church planting—where people left the church, always leaving a trail of hurtful words in their wake—and also the exciting seasons, where new people would come, and we'd walk with them as they gave their hearts to Jesus. We all four found so much joy in witnessing lives drastically change.

Amanda and Ashley enjoyed a close ministry friendship neither one of them had ever experienced with anyone else. And although Derek and I were as different as two people could be, we enjoyed spending time together and complemented each other in ministry well.

Now, here were Derek and Ashley, caught so unexpectedly in the middle of caring for me, standing beside me, carrying the weight of the church as I tried to get a handle on my circumstances, while sorting through their own shock and grief of losing their great friend.

"I'm not sure how I'm going to feel about our city," I answered in response to his question. "I'm afraid I'm going to hate it for what it did to Amanda." I was beginning to feel this new emotion stirring inside of me that I quite frankly had never dealt with in my lifetime, especially to this degree.

Two nights before, news broke that arrests had been made, and for the first time I saw the three men who were allegedly involved in Amanda's murder. Up to this point her killer had been a faceless person at large, so my emotions had been distracted by shock, loss, sadness, and disbelief.

But now there was a face to it. Not just one but three. And I had seen them and begun to feel emotions I'd never felt before—anger, hatred, rage, and despair. How do you process all the emotions brought on by those who've taken the most important thing in your life from you? Was I supposed to *forgive* them for what they did? Surely Jesus's teaching on forgiveness didn't apply to this extreme of a situation! How was I even going to forgive myself? How was I supposed to move on with my life without Amanda?

The night before we sat on that plane, I had hit an all-time low. In addition to dealing with the murder, I had been warned by investigators that unsubstantiated reports of sexual assault might leak from the press. I appreciated being preempted but didn't know how to even process this new information. My mind began to run away with what could have happened in those last forty-five minutes of Amanda's life. I felt this unexpected part of me rise to the surface, this part of myself I had never known, and that part of me wanted to *kill* these men and then take my own life. I just wanted to die. I felt like I had nothing left to live for. Everything I was living for had been taken from me.

Derek and Ashley sat with me that night as I was floundering in despair. On the last leg of our flight, upon touchdown, I secretly hoped the pilot would lose control and cause all of us to go up in flames. I always used to feel a little bit of anxiety right before wheels touched down, but not this time. I wasn't scared to die anymore. At this point, death actually seemed it would be a welcome relief.

"I think we just have to take this a step at a time." Derek was surprising me with how much wisdom and poise he was bringing to this situation. "Remember what we talked about last night? We can't change anything that has happened, but we do have a choice as to how we respond from here."

I wouldn't have wanted to hear this from anyone else, but I knew he was hurting too, and it seemed less like he was preaching at me and more like he was reminding himself.

I lifted my head off the window's surface and looked at him. "What do you think you'll do?" he asked me. "Where will you stay?"

"I don't know. The Andersons offered to let Weston and me stay there for a bit. That might be nice." Eric and Nikki Anderson were a couple who had joined our church two years before. They were one of the first established families with teenagers to get involved at Resonate. The thought of living with them brought a sense of comfort and stability to the whirlwind that was now my life.

"Do you ever think you'll go back to your house?"

I thought for a minute before responding. "I can't imagine doing so," I told him.

The thought of walking back into my living room made me sick to my stomach. All I could see, in my mind's eye, was Amanda lying there helplessly, unconscious and struggling for air.

"My cousin said her in-laws will be in Florida from January to April, and their house is available. But I don't want to stay anywhere by myself."

Just then an idea popped into my head and I blurted, "After I spend a couple of weeks with the Andersons, and when the house my cousin was telling me about comes available, what do you think about you and Ashley living with me? I think it'd be nice to just have people around and for Weston to have some kind of consistent womanly presence in the house. Ashley is so caring and motherly, I think it would be good for him."

"Actually she and I talked about it last night," Derek admitted. "Our lease on our apartment is up in January, so it would work out really well."

For just a moment, the anxiety that had been pressing in so firmly around me let up and I felt like I could breathe. I couldn't think of anyone else I'd want to have live with me, and I certainly couldn't see Weston and me living alone. The thought of being by ourselves terrified me.

"Davey, let me ask you something," Derek continued. "What do you think Amanda would want you to do next?"

I sat there for a moment. I couldn't say I hadn't spent some time considering it. After all, God had called us *both* to Indianapolis. So much of our story involved wrestling through each decision *together*. It was *our* story. Was I still called to this city without Amanda? And the thought still hovered over my heart: would I need to leave because the constant reminder of Amanda's murder would loom on every street I drove down?

Would I loathe these neighborhoods that had essentially produced Amanda's killers? Would I be able to step into the same city where she and I had spent the last four years sharing joys, heartaches, and memories? At that moment a memory I had almost forgotten hijacked my thoughts.

It was summer 2014, just before Weston was born. Amanda and I had been going through Dave Ramsey's Financial Peace plan and getting our household ready for the arrival of our first baby, which entailed making sure life insurance and a will were in place. I had been doing all the preparations for this and decided she and I needed to go for a walk to discuss who would get Weston if something happened to both of us.

As we turned down the wide street in the neighborhood across from ours, trees dipping over our heads from the weight of the full summer leaves, I asked her, "What would we do with Weston if something happened to both of us?"

"Oh man. That's a tough question," she responded, a studied look on her face.

We deliberated together for a bit. It was tough to decide which of her siblings we'd want to ask to carry that burden, but we finally decided on Gavin and Amber since James and Angela didn't have any kids yet. They had just recently discovered they were pregnant with their first, and Amanda and I thought it'd be a bit overwhelming if Weston were forced to join their family as well.

"Okay, let me ask you another question," I continued. "What would you do if something happened to me?" I asked her, knowing this was a tough but necessary question.

"Davey, can we not talk about this? This is too depressing to even think about!"

"No, it's important. Dave Ramsey says we need to have these conversations."

"*Ugh*. Okay," she grunted. "Well, I suppose Weston and I would move in with my parents back in Elkhart and figure things out." She paused for a moment and then led with her own question. "Your turn. What would you do if something happened to me?"

"I don't know ... I truly can't imagine that." I stared ahead at the street, lined with beautiful oak trees, now a sagging, crowded canopy dangling over the road. I thought about it for a second but was at a loss, so I looked back at her and asked, "What would you want me to do?"

She stopped midstep, looked up at my eyes, and began without hesitation. "Davey, we've given our lives to this church. We've cashed in everything, literally everything, to get it up and going. It's like our second baby and I can't imagine giving it up for adoption after going through all these labor pains." She stared even deeper into my eyes, and I could tell she wasn't taking this lightly. "I'd want for you to pour out the rest of your life building this church and reaching this city."

A sudden jolt of turbulence jarred me back to the conversation with Derek. I recoiled from the memory and snapped my head in his direction. "She would want me to stay here in Indy and figure out a way to keep building Resonate to reach this city." Tears began to fill my eyes as I suddenly realized the pain and difficulty this could entail, the prospect of stepping into all this brokenness. I had to turn back away from Derek, knowing I could burst into tears at any moment.

"I know she would, Davey. In fact, I need to show you something." He pulled out a plain black spiral notebook. "This is one of Amanda's journals you gave Ashley to read."

Earlier, Ashley, Megan, and I had spent a couple of nights in my grandparents' house reading through some of Amanda's journals. It was all we could do to try to retain some sense of her presence. I knew there were only a handful of people Amanda would have opened her entire life up to, and Megan and Ashley were two of them. So after reading most of the journals myself, I gave each of them a notebook to read through.

"She told me I had to show you this entry. Amanda loved this city, Davey. She loved our church, and she loved *your* calling."

My hands were shaking as I opened up to the dog-eared page halfway through the notebook and began reading:

Esther 4:14

And who knows but that you have come to royal position for such a time as this?

Man, I am such a lucky girl. We are sitting in a hotel room at the J.W. Marriott on the 29th floor, overlooking all of Indianapolis right now, sipping my Starbucks coffee, reading my Bible, and reflecting on just how blessed I am. Father I don't know how to thank you for how good you have been to me. I have the sweetest husband and most thoughtful man ever. We got sushi last night and he took us to a hotel that had chocolate covered strawberries and sparkling [grape juice] waiting for us with an incredible nighttime skyline view. And we're spending all day together downtown. He's just the best! Thank you for giving me an incredible man! Thank you so much!

Father it's inspiring to look over this huge city and to think it's ours. That the harvest is so ripe. That 82% of people here don't go to church. That's around 1.6 million people. Father I beg you for this city. I beg you to use us to turn it upside down. I beg you to use Resonate to change Indianapolis drastically. We're here and willing to do whatever it takes, Father. I know that with that will surely come a lot of heartache and trials and sacrifice, more than we have already experienced. But I know that there is a great cost to see a great movement. And we are here and ready to do whatever you tell us. Thank you, Thank you, Thank you for calling us here.

I love this city. I love being a part of something bigger than myself.

You're wonderful, Jesus. Your plan is perfect. Thank you for being all knowing. Thank you for the work you have already done. Make yourself known in this city, Jesus. May we glorify you. I love you.

Tears flooded my eyes as I finished the entry, and I turned to look out the window again, the notebook still on my lap. At that very moment, as if a stage curtain were being pulled back to signal the start of a production, the clouds opened up and the plane descended for landing. Stretched out in front of me, like a portrait in a museum, was the landscape of Indianapolis—this city we had dedicated our lives to, this city that had taken

Amanda's life, this city that held so many precious memories, and this city that Amanda loved.

In that moment my heart did something miraculous and strange. It grew. It expanded, almost as if I felt in all my faculties the full expanse of both my love and Amanda's love for this city. Somehow in this moment, the Lord gifted me enough grace not *only* not to grow bitter toward this city but to grow *compassionate* toward its brokenness, to hurt for it, to long to see it redeemed and restored . . . to love it.

Derek spoke next, softly but deliberately. "Davey, what you have to ask yourself is, Are you willing to step into brokenness for the benefit of others . . . for the benefit of our city? Who knows, maybe that verse from Esther at the beginning of Amanda's journal entry is true of you. Maybe you've come to position, have been given a platform, for such a time as this."

I looked out the window at the JW Marriott, Victory Field, Lucas Oil Stadium, and the grid of streets that comprised Indianapolis. Even as I stared at its orderly landscape, all I could think about was how chaotic and disjointed my life felt.

"I don't know, Derek. I just don't know."

7

FIGHTING FOR FORGIVENESS

Two weeks later—now six weeks after I said goodbye to Amanda—I sat on the side of the stage at a youth conference in downtown Indianapolis. One of my old youth pastors, Scott Simmons, was in charge of booking bands and speakers for the event, and when I heard Elevation Worship was going to be there, I reached out to see if I could attend one of the sessions. He was happy to reserve a place for me; Amber; her brother, James; and his wife, Angela.

There are few places that make me feel completely at home— places that seem to wick away the worries and stresses of life. One of those places has been sitting fireside on a crisp late-fall Indiana morning with Amanda and her family, cup of coffee in hand, and no agenda for the day. Amanda's parents, siblings, and their spouses had become more than just in-laws to me over the past few years. They were some of my best friends.

Another place is in an arena or auditorium full of people worshipping Jesus. It's an environment that has always transported me to a state in my soul where it doesn't matter what is going on in life. In these settings, heaven seems to open up for a brief glimpse, giving me eternal clarity and perspective, and assuring me nothing else mattered in this world as much as singing to Jesus.

And now, there I stood, singing through the intermittent moments when my emotions would grip me during an

125

instrumental build or a vocalist's run. In my peripheral vision, a sea of six thousand teenagers raised their hands and hearts in worship. Amber leaned over, elbowed me, and pointed out at the crowd. "Isn't it amazing to see young people worship?! It gives me goose bumps every time!"

For a brief moment, I let my attention wander away from the stage and land on this gathering of students spread out in front of me. Individual faces began to emerge from the sea of people, and I focused on the unique features of these students, some with their eyes closed and hands raised, some with big smiles across their faces as they watched the lights, some clutching their chests as if to say, "I wish I could physically pull out my heart and offer it up to God right now."

And then one face struck my attention. It was a young African American boy who looked to be about twelve or thirteen years old. He stood with an inquisitive look on his face, studying the band members and the other kids around him. You could almost see the battle raging inside of him, the longing to join in and participate but also his hesitancy because of what his disengaged friends standing beside him might think of him.

As I watched this boy, something strange happened in my heart. An image flashed across my memory of the mug shots of the three black men arrested for Amanda's murder. For a moment, I no longer saw this young man standing in front of me. I saw Larry Taylor—the man being charged with pulling the trigger and taking Amanda's life. I can't quite properly explain the swell of emotions that rose up in my heart in that moment.

On the one hand, there was a *hatred* for this boy because of his resemblance to the man who took Amanda from me. This was immediately followed by a stab of fear and guilt for even thinking such a prejudiced thought. Then, it was hatred for myself, or maybe just alarm, for what this whole situation might be doing to me—what it could turn me into. When had I become this person who could have such a vengeful thought about another human being? Why all of a sudden did these three men create new thoughts in me toward an entire ethnic group?

Just then, another thought came over me, a small whisper to my soul that cut right through my whirlwind of emotions: *Davey, what if Larry Taylor had experienced something like this conference when he was twelve years old? What if he had been given the opportunity to respond to Jesus's love and forgiveness? How different would your life be now?*

Then, one more thought that almost made me lose my breath: *How many more twelve-year-old Larry Taylors are walking the streets of your city?*

I couldn't believe it. Was it possible God was trying to plant in me the seed of a vision for a movement in our city? Was it possible that He could use my story, Amanda's story, to intercept young kids and teenagers before they resorted to a life of drugs, gangs, and violence? What if God was going to take this terrible event and do something bigger and more beautiful with it than Amanda or I could have ever imagined?

Leaving the conference that day, I wasn't sure what to do with what I thought God had said. Had I really heard what I thought I heard? Could any of the idea be possible? How would I be equipped? And if God was really calling me to this vision, what was I supposed to do next?

I once read staggering statistics linking male inmates with their being raised in fatherless homes. I also read that Indianapolis was beginning to see an uptick in violent crime due to gang migration from the Chicago area in order to traffic drugs to other larger cities in the Midwest: Cincinnati, Louisville, and Columbus. I was discovering that Indiana, "The Crossroads of America," and more specifically Indianapolis, was becoming Central Station for operations of violent crime, drugs, and gang-related activity.

A few days after the conference I had coffee with one of Amanda's old youth pastors. For their anonymity I'll call him Shaun and his wife Kristen. During coffee I was quickly reminded that when God calls us to something, He is the one who equips us. He always makes His way known. He never asks us to do something for which He doesn't give us clear directions, even though sometimes they may be given all at once and sometimes one step at a time.

Shaun had spent a few years attending seminary in California and was now back pastoring a church in Indianapolis. He asked me to coffee to find out how I was doing after everything that had happened. We ordered and sat down at Hubbard and Cravens on Forty-Ninth Street for what, unbeknownst to me, was going to be a vision-shifting and life-transformational conversation.

"How are you, *really*, Davey?" This was the first question Shaun asked me.

I guess being a pastor himself, he anticipated my tendency to put on a pretense and spit out some pithy theological phrase to avoid admitting how deeply I was really struggling. I was too broken and tired that day to fake it with him, and he asked, so I let down my defenses.

Tears immediately began welling up in my eyes, and I tried my best to explain to him the emotions I was struggling with— loneliness and the longing to just talk to Amanda being the weightiest. Then, I eventually got around to sharing with him some of the feelings of hatred and prejudice that had recently and unexpectedly surfaced in me.

I whispered to him in the coffee shop, embarrassed about the feelings that had come up so unexpectedly at the youth conference a few days before. I told him what I thought about when I saw that young African American boy from across the arena, and what I heard God say to me in response to those thoughts. I hung my head in shame and waited for him to tell me what I should do next.

He sat back and listened until I came to a stopping point when he then leaned forward and said, "Davey, I can't quite understand fully. I can't even pretend to imagine what you're going through. But I keep putting myself in your shoes when it comes to my wife."

Shaun's wife, Kristen, had been one of Amanda's high school small-group leaders, and both of them had always been extremely fond of Amanda.

"Kristen has been wrestling with a lot of fear lately. She's really jumpy and almost paranoid all the time, as I imagine a lot of women who have heard Amanda's story are. But what compounds it is that the getaway car the men used to escape in was found on our block."

Shaun and Kristen live in a rough neighborhood not too far from my old house. Their ministry philosophy regarding the inner city was what we call, in the church world, "incarnational," meaning rather than helping families in the inner city from far away in the suburbs, they decided to live in the *midst* of it and do life alongside of the people living there. I admired their tenacity to embrace discomfort and live with the people they were ministering to. After all, wasn't this how Jesus did ministry? Instead of requiring us to climb our way to Him with good behavior, He graciously left His comfortable position in heaven and came to us.

As I listened to Shaun, I couldn't believe the coincidental nature of what he was sharing with me.

"Davey, I step out my front door and I look at the house across the street from me, and I know for a fact that the teenagers that live there are caught up in drugs and gang-related activity. On a good day, these kids are good kids. On a bad day, they would put a bullet in anyone's head. Before Amanda was killed, this fact made me hurt for these kids. Now, I'm beginning to feel more than just hurt."

He leaned in really close, and lowered his voice like I had before. "I'm beginning to feel hatred too."

I looked at him through misty eyes. I felt such a sense of relief to hear another pastor admit to feeling what I had been feeling. I could hardly believe it. All my fears of him merely reprimanding me for what I was feeling melted away.

"Davey, what you're feeling ... what I'm feeling ... is normal. But you know as well as I do it doesn't make it right ... don't you?"

I nodded as I looked up from my coffee cup. "But how do I get rid of these feelings? Every African American man I see now makes me think of these guys!"

"Let me ask you something. How did you feel when people accused you of murdering Amanda?"

Man, what a loaded question that was. How could I even communicate the level of hurt I felt with accusations like that? I felt fortunate Shaun didn't give me much time to answer. He continued.

"Have you ever heard stories of husbands murdering their wives?"

I looked at him a little confused. "Um, yeah ..."

"Of *course* you have. That's because these stories are everywhere. That is why it was so easy for people who don't know you to almost immediately jump to conclusions that you were the one who did it. Anyone who knows you, and who knew Amanda, knows it would be impossible, that it's absurd to even assume, because that's not you."

I nodded.

"Just because *some* husbands have murdered their wives doesn't mean every husband is a murderer. And it certainly doesn't mean you murdered Amanda."

My mind started to compute what he was saying, but before I could interject, he asked me another question. "Have you ever heard stories of pastors using their platform for personal monetary gain?"

"Yeah." I nodded.

"But just because *some* pastors have done that doesn't mean *all* pastors do that, you know?"

I nodded again.

"So do you see why it would be so easy for some people who don't know you to accuse you of doing that same thing? I *know* you, so I know that wasn't your intention by going on national television. I know that you actually care for people, especially people who are hurting. But do you see how people can jump to those conclusions?"

"By making assumptions," I replied. "Generalizations." I saw where he was going now.

"You see, racism and bigotry occur when we take a few isolated instances and make them normative for an entire group of people. Not every husband kills his wife, though *some* have. Not every pastor is out for greedy gain, though *some* have been. And not every black man is a murderer and thief, though *some* are . . . and so are some white men, and so are some Hispanic men, and so are some *men,* regardless of color.

"You see, Davey, race isn't the driving force of hatred—*sin* is. The problem with our nation today is that instead of leaning in and seeking to understand the situation and feelings of another party, we throw stones and accuse."

It was all making sense. Finally, this was something that sounded true and that I could stand on. My emotions of hatred are normal because I'm human and I'm sinful. But if I let my emotions drive me, I'm a victim of shifty whims that are neither predictable nor helpful.

"So how do I get rid of these feelings?" I asked him.

"Davey, I want to talk about that vision God gave you at that conference. There's something to that. You see, our neighborhood revitalization association recently requested a former drug dealer from the community—yes, a black man—to attend one of our meetings and offer insight as to how they can prevent teenagers from making destructive decisions. We really wanted to understand the other side.

"The only way you can get rid of racism and hatred is seeking to understand the other side.

"You know what he told us? He said the biggest thing driving young black men to gangs and drugs and crime was, 'We didn't have any options.' He told us, 'There was nothing going on in or around the neighborhood that offered us an alternative. We didn't have family relationships, we didn't have responsibility that interested us, and we felt like we were fighting for survival, so we turned to drugs, gangs, and violence.'"

Shaun leaned forward and looked me in the eye. "Davey, that's why I've had a dream to build some kind of community center for the kids in this area. A place where they can come and belong and channel their creative energies into healthy outlets. And most importantly where they can hear about the love of Jesus! That's what turns hatred around!"

Immediately I thought about how Amanda and I used to talk about the same thing. In fact, she and I used to run from our house to downtown on this seven-mile trail that cuts right through the Riverside community—the White River Parkway Trail. I told Shaun about it.

"Oh yeah, I know that route very well!" He said, his eyes brightening as he leaned in a little closer. I continued.

"At one point the trail opens up to a huge park with dilapidated fields and a beautiful view of the cityscape behind it. The first time I saw it I told Amanda, 'Babe, this would be an incredible place to build a community center for inner-city youth one day.' From that day, every time Amanda and I would run by it we would pray that God would allow us to build a community center on this location!"

Shaun took this all in and drew another sip of his coffee. "Can you show me where this is on a map?"

I pulled out my iPhone and opened up Maps, pinching the screen to the exact location of the park at Cold Spring and Thirtieth Street.

"Wow, yeah," he said. "This area is just south of us and is actually *the* hot button spot for our city when it comes to drug trafficking and violence.

"You know what you need to do? You really need to get in touch with Pastor Martin Smith." (I've changed his name for privacy reasons.) "He's a black pastor with a very historic congregation in that community. You may have heard of him. He's received a lot of media attention recently for speaking out against the crime in his community. He would be a *great* resource to get something started up there."

I made a mental note to touch base with Martin Smith sometime in the near future, but frankly I was still too torn up emotionally to even begin thinking about trying to *do* anything at this point. Not to mention, my mind felt so clouded in shock that I couldn't fathom trying to move the ball forward on anything. Frankly, I still just wanted to run away from everything.

Shaun and I wrapped up our conversation, he prayed for me, and I left the coffee shop.

Later that afternoon, I sat down for coffee with a member of our congregation named Mike, a business lawyer who helps entrepreneurs get the legal aspects of their businesses established.

After about an hour of chatting, we got up from the table and began to walk toward our cars. "Davey, one more thing. I'm so sorry to bother you with this right now, but a client of mine has been wanting me to get in touch with you since Amanda passed. Maybe you've heard of him. He's received a lot of media attention recently for speaking out against the crime in his community. His name is Pastor Martin Smith."

I couldn't believe it. Twice in one day this Pastor Smith's name had been mentioned to me. I've learned that when things like this happen it's usually the Lord trying to get your attention. So I decided to listen.

"Give me his number. I'll contact him as soon as possible."

8

BUILT FOR THE BURDEN

THE VERY NEXT WEEK I WENT TO COFFEE WITH PASTOR SMITH. Frankly, I wasn't sure where this coffee was going to lead, but I sensed the Lord wanted this connection to be made, so I opened up with him about everything. I shared all that had transpired to lead us to this moment and explained to him this dream I had of establishing a community center for underprivileged youth.

"Davey." He shook his head, almost in disbelief that this conversation was happening. "You have no idea how long I've been praying something like this would happen for this community. It's definitely needed." He spent the next two hours schooling me on the complexity of the culture of the Riverside area—the racial tensions, the economic deterioration, the lack of spiritual vitality, and the undergirding traditionalism of the church community. Then he shifted the conversation.

"I need to ask you a question, Davey." He paused for a moment to emphasize the next part, "How do you feel about these guys that killed your wife?"

I opened my mouth to speak.

"Wait, before you answer, you have to know something. When I heard about this, I was devastated. I was on an airplane, sitting on the runway about to leave for vacation, and I felt like my heart was ripped out of my chest for you. Before they arrested the men who did this, I was hoping beyond all hope that they would be white, so the stereotype wouldn't be reinforced. Then they arrested them and I saw their pictures in the news, and that they were black, and I thought, *Oh no, dear God, no.* I know I'm not the only one in the black community who felt this way."

Wow. This question felt even more loaded now than it had the week prior when I was talking to Shaun. I didn't know how to unpack everything that had been going on in my heart concerning the three men who killed Amanda—especially to a black pastor. How could I explain the racism that had surfaced in my heart? How could I tell him about the anger, the hatred? I didn't know how to explain it all to him, but over the next half hour I tried.

"I'm trying to forgive these guys," I began. *Trying* was certainly the operative word. I knew the Lord had yet to do a tremendous work in my heart before I could ever *feel* like forgiving. But I also knew I had a role to play in the whole deal.

"Why?" Martin interjected, not so much out of curiosity but almost as if he was prying a little more into my motives. "Why would you try to forgive them? I mean, I saw you come out on national television and tell the country that you've chosen to forgive them, which was quite a statement to make. There are a lot of people who probably think you're crazy!"

I chuckled at the thought. I guess it does look kind of absurd to tell a national news correspondent, a week after your wife has been brutally murdered, that you're extending forgiveness to her killer.

"Because I know it's the right thing to do, Martin. I mean, I've preached dozens of sermons on how it's the right thing to do. I've preached about how holding on to bitterness and unforgiveness is a cancer that only destroys you and the people you love the most. You think you're getting revenge or retribution on the perpetrator by harboring resentment, but the reality is, it doesn't do *any* harm to them. It's like swallowing rat poison and expecting it to hurt the other person. Unforgiveness only destroys you!"

"But you can't possibly *feel* like forgiving!" Martin retorted. "I mean, I'll be honest. I felt hatred in *my* heart when I heard about Amanda."

"Yeah. I definitely don't feel like it. I'm not sure if I ever will."

What Martin didn't understand was that, as confused as I was about everything else going on, for some reason *this* was the one thing I felt confident was the right thing to do. "But I wonder if in order to *truly* forgive someone you *must* also feel the full weight of anger and hatred. I wonder if *not* feeling those emotions actually cheapens the act of forgiveness."

Martin looked at me and tilted his head like he needed to ponder what I was saying.

"Martin," I went on, "let me tell you my story about how I met Jesus." Something in me was determined to help him understand how I was processing this.

"I was seven years old growing up in Birmingham, Alabama. My dad was a pastor, so I grew up going to church regularly. One evening I attended an Easter play at Gardendale Baptist Church with a friend and his family. It was one of those productions where they lead you around in groups to different rooms and in each room there was a new scene of the story."

"Oh, you mean like one of those Judgment Houses?" Martin recalled.

Judgment Houses were a popular church alternative to Halloween when I was growing up. A production would be put on in a church or a school about someone dying, facing the final judgment of their life. They'd take you into a room where the heat was turned up to ninety degrees, create some fiery effects, and cast members dressed up in scary demon costumes would "torture" other cast members in the room. Of course, the room represented hell.

After this, cast members would take you to a peaceful, white room where a man dressed up as Jesus and others dressed in robes as angels would hug and talk to you. Then they would take you into another room and explain how you could get into heaven and escape hell.

Maybe some of these productions were done tastefully, but for the most part, I remember it quite literally scaring the hell out of me and all of my friends. Of course, after walking through the rooms, we all wanted to go to heaven, so we'd say the prayer they told us to say and we'd pick up our Get out of Hell Free card on the way out.

"Yeah, this play was the same type but much different in nature," I explained. "In this production they just walked you through different rooms with scenes that portrayed the life of Jesus. I remember it being done really well. Jesus was depicted in a way I'd never seen Him before. They showed Him caring for hurting people, loving people who had made mistakes and were ostracized from society because of it. He healed people who were broken and sick. It was the first time I remember being *drawn* to this Jesus guy!

"And then they led us into a room where they acted out the religious leaders of the day being furious at Jesus for the following He had amassed and the things He was claiming, like being the Son of God! They put Him on trial illegally, mocked Him, beat Him, flogged Him, and then voted to kill Him. I'll never forget the next thing the cast members did.

"They led us into the sanctuary where they had constructed this scene of Jesus on the cross. I had never seen Jesus's death depicted in such vivid detail. Martin, it was like a live version of the *Passion of the Christ* movie! For a moment I forgot I was watching a reenactment."

Martin raised his eyebrows, clearly intrigued with where I was going with this. I continued, "Finally the pastor came out and shared with us how we're all sinful and broken. How my mistakes, my shortcomings, my sin has separated me from a relationship with God and that because of my sin, I deserved death and to be separated from God for all of eternity. He said that my sin deserved capital punishment... no matter how small or trite I think my sin is.

"I mean, come on, I was seven! *How many bad things could I have done!?* But something about what he said really resonated with me. Then he told us how God loves us so much, and wants that relationship to be restored so badly that He sent His only Son, Jesus, to die for us, to take our place, and to take on Himself the penalty for our sin.

"Then he said something that I'll never forget. He said, 'Your sin and my sin murdered Jesus.' Here I was, having for the first time seen how amazing Jesus was and then seeing the brutality in which they treated Him!"

When I said this, Martin's brow furrowed, and he leaned forward slightly in his seat.

"*Then* the lights shifted and focused everything back on Jesus hanging on the cross, and He cried out something I'll never forget. He cried out, 'Father, *forgive* them for they don't know what they are doing!' The scene froze again and the pastor continued. 'That forgiveness is offered to you today. All you have to do is receive it.'

"Martin, before I realized what was going on, my heart was pounding out of my chest and my face was red hot! Tears started streaming down my cheeks, and I was so embarrassed by what my friend and his family were going to think about me I walked down to the end of the pew, knelt down, and begged God for forgiveness. I just kept repeating, 'I'm sorry, Jesus! I didn't know my sin did that to You!'

"That day I made the decision to give Jesus my life, receive the offer for the forgiveness of my sins, and be transformed into a new person with new perspectives and a new way of life."

"Wow," Martin slowly shook his head. "You're so right. My sin *murdered* Jesus, and yet He extended forgiveness to me."

"Exactly. So, of course to someone who's never received Jesus's forgiveness, it looks *crazy* to see me extend forgiveness. That's because it's impossible to extend forgiveness if I haven't *experienced* forgiveness for my sins! The truth is, I'm a conduit for God's forgiveness. But at the same time, when I realize what I've been forgiven from, it's a spiritual impossibility for me to *experience* forgiveness and then hold on to it for myself—I'm compelled to *extend* it too!"

"Man, that's good," Martin exclaimed. "And what's amazing is that this means you're going to be fighting hatred with love. I mean you can't fight fire with fire. It only exacerbates it. If you try to fight hatred with hatred it only makes it worse! You have to fight hatred with *love* and *forgiveness!*" Martin took a breath. His next question would rattle me a bit.

"Davey, I just had a thought: Do you feel like these men are your enemy?"

"Um. Well. Maybe. I don't know. I guess," I stammered.

"I don't. Well at least not your true enemy. I believe your true enemy is God's enemy, Satan, and everything he represents: hatred, evil, violence, malice, rage, envy, strife . . . you get the picture. Every time you spread the love of Jesus and tell someone about how they can experience His love and forgiveness, I just imagine you're giving the Enemy a swift kick in the nuts! *That's revenge!!*"

"Ba-ha-ha!" I almost exploded with shock at what had just come out of his mouth. "That's hilarious! I love that thought! A swift kick in the nuts. Hmmm. So I don't need to try to scheme revenge against these men. I need to participate in *spiritual* revenge on the real enemy?"

"Exactly." Pastor M. smiled and nodded.

I was so glad Martin and I had gotten connected. I felt that in this two-hour conversation, years of perspective had just been layered onto my soul. I felt a little lighter just being around him. Nothing could prepare me, however, for what he was about to say next.

"One more question," he continued, a little more slowly. "How do you feel about these guys' families?"

"Excuse me?" I didn't understand what he was asking. It seemed like an odd question. Why would he bring up their families? Frankly, I hadn't even considered them and told him just that.

He shifted forward in his seat, lowered his voice, and said, "Well, they think you're infuriated with them."

What?! What does he mean "they think?!" How would he know this?

"About two weeks after Amanda was killed, during the time all the arrests were being made, I got a phone call from a pastor friend of mine who was freaking out because the cops were searching his home. He and his wife had been foster parents to Larry Taylor for the past six years."

The statement felt like a giant fist in my stomach. It nearly knocked all the breath out of me, and I burst into tears. How many people have their wife murdered and shortly afterward discover they are now relationally two arm's lengths away from the killer?

Martin let my sobs quell and then continued softly. "Davey. Let me tell you Larry's story." I leaned back in my seat.

"His dad has been in prison most of his life, and his mom, strung out on drugs, didn't want to deal with him anymore. So when Larry was twelve years old she dropped him off at her sister's doorstep. She left him, Davey. Rejected him. Abandoned him.

"This started a cycle of hurt and anger in his heart. My friend told me that over the next six years, they tried to help him get off the drugs that had already created a stronghold on his mind and body. If they kept him on house arrest, he would detox and start to seem normal. Then they'd start trying to mainstream him into school and the community, and so on.

"Each time they did, though, he would leave the house for school and wouldn't come home for days, only to wind up back on their doorstep a few days later, once again strung out on drugs. Then the cycle would start all over again."

I couldn't believe it. Just a few days before, I had met with Coach Phil McIntyre, the baseball coach at North Central High School, the school where I coached and had spent a few years substitute teaching when we first moved to Indy. Coach McIntyre had told me that two of the guys arrested for Amanda's murder had gone to school at North Central. I remember the whole rest of the day all I could wonder was: *Had I subbed for one of their classes? Had I ever unknowingly interacted with the guys who would kill my wife?*

Now, this black pastor I had just met, but whom Jesus obviously and providentially directed me to, was telling me he knew the killer's parents?!

I couldn't deny it. This wasn't normal. Now these guys weren't just faceless, nameless criminals. They were men ... men who used to be boys, each of them with a devastating story. I had never once thought about their stories, their hurt, and their pasts, until their stories senselessly and brutally plunged into mine.

In that moment, as I sat across from Pastor Martin Smith in that coffee shop, all I could do was stare ahead, through reddened, tear-filled eyes and into dead space in disbelief. *What are You up to, Jesus? What the heck are You up to?*

"Davey, you need to understand. I believe what God wants to do here is nothing short of historic. I believe the opportunity your story has to break racial tensions and sinful strongholds that has held our city in bondage for decades is unprecedented."

As these words fell from Martin's mouth, I thought to myself, *No! I can't handle this weight! I can't handle this story! I can't handle this responsibility! It's too crushing! It's too much! I'm not strong enough! I'd rather have Amanda back!*

Right there, in the middle of that coffee shop, uncontrollable sobs shook my body, and I buried my eyes in my hands. I tried to choke them back, feeling the obvious stares from everyone around me. I tried to stop the sobs, but they just kept rushing out of me.

I'll never forget what happened next. Martin leaned forward, placed his hand on my shoulder, and began repeating over and over, "Davey, you were built for this. You were built for this. I saw it in you from a distance and I see it in you now up close. You were built for this. You have been placed in this position for a time such as this. *You were built for this!*"

A sense of empowerment flooded my body. Maybe we are all somehow built for the plight we're facing. Maybe in every task God gives us in life, He's also given us the tools to face the task, the grace to face the day and finish the work. I would soon, however, discover I needed more than just a few tools for what I'd be facing. I would need an arsenal.

9

GUTTED BY GRIEF

The lights from the Christmas tree shimmered in my peripheral vision as I sat on the leather couch staring, eyes fixed, as
if examining something delicate in front of me, yet processing
absolutely nothing occurring around me. I sat pensive and in
a trance while my mom carried a neatly wrapped Christmas
package over to Weston.

It was the night before Thanksgiving, and the entire family
had assembled in Elkhart to celebrate together. I suppose none
of us would have actually termed what we were doing as "celebrating." In fact, it was impossible to imagine doing anything
traditional for Thanksgiving at this point, let alone celebrating.
This was a holiday that by its very nature had always called for us
to hit the pause button, gather our families together, reflect, and
be thankful for the things and people we had been given—and
now all we could think about was the *one* person who had been
taken from us just two weeks before.

A void lay at the center of our hearts and in the painfully
obvious empty seat in the middle of the room.

My parents; my brother, Jonathan; and his wife, Tessa, had
all traveled back to Indiana to spend Thanksgiving with Weston,
myself, and Amanda's extended family rather than continuing
with the original plan of a Blackburn-family-only Thanksgiving.
Amanda and I had always alternated holidays with families—
my family for Thanksgiving one year and then Christmas the

next. The lot for Thanksgiving fell on my family this year, and Mom had booked a cabin in Tennessee for the six of us, plus Weston, to hunker down for the holiday week and celebrate both Thanksgiving and an early Christmas together.

Amanda had been uncharacteristically enthusiastic about spending Thanksgiving with my family this year. She absolutely loved my mom, dad, brother, and sister-in-law. Despite her deep love for them, though, I could always see a tinge of sadness in her eyes when we were with my family, since she was missing out on her own family's festivities.

This year, however, she had mentioned multiple times how excited she was to spend Thanksgiving with the Blackburns.

Weston was at such a fun age, and she couldn't wait to see what kind of new Thanksgiving and Christmas activities Nonna (what Weston called my mom) had planned for him. It was two years earlier, on another Thanksgiving stay at a cabin in Tennessee, that Amanda and I discovered some incredible news about how our life would drastically change.

"Hey, I brought a pregnancy test to take while we're there this weekend." Amanda was in the passenger seat of our rental car, looking cozy in her Gap vest and scarf while a winter storm was brewing outside the window. Her soft blond highlights accentuated her smile as she grinned at me. Something about her face glowed more the past couple of weeks, and secretly I had begun to wonder if she might in fact be carrying a baby in her belly.

I nearly swerved off the road with excitement. "Really?! Do you think you might be . . . I mean how do you feel? Are you feeling like you're . . . like you're pregnant??" The thought of us having a baby elated me. There was something about our love creating *something* out of *nothing* that seemed so miraculous and life changing. It made me love Amanda all the more. The thought of this little human possessing character traits of both of us almost caused me to explode with joy!

Would it be a girl? Would it be a boy? What would we name him . . . or her? Would he be a great athlete or a bookworm? Would she want to dance or be a tomboy? Which one of us would he most resemble—extroverted and wide open like his daddy or quiet, balanced, reserved, and intentional like his mommy? It was so exciting to think about the possibility of Amanda being pregnant, and I could hardly retain the patience to find out.

"Let's take it now! I'll pull into the 7-Eleven at the next exit! Come on!"

"Davey, no! That's disgusting! I'm not taking a pregnancy test at a gas station! *Ew!*"

Amanda was always so clean and tidy, and I loved her for it. In fact, in the first rental car we had been issued on this trip, the interior had the slight scent of residual cigarette smoke, and the smell almost made Amanda sick. I knew she wouldn't be happy when we got in the car, but her near rebellion against riding for the next seven hours with that residual cigarette smoke odor had me wondering if her olfactory sense was heightened beyond the norm.

Couple that with the fact that she'd been napping much more than usual recently, and I was almost sure something was up. At this point, I was more than ready to find out if we were going to have a baby and had no qualms about my wife taking a pregnancy test in a backcountry gas station bathroom, despite how dirty it might be!

"I'm not going to take it until Thanksgiving morning," she continued. "I think it might be a really fun way to start off Thanksgiving, being thankful for a new life God gave us." I couldn't argue with her when she gave me that sweet smile. I could tell she was as excited about this as I was—even more than I ever thought she could be.

For five years of marriage we had held the idea of having kids at bay for the sake of building our friendship, making memories together, and, more recently, getting the new church plant off the ground. Many couples go on a five-year or ten-year plan, but we decided we were just going to stay prayerful and trust God's timing for that particular season— whenever that might be.

Each quarter she and I would take a small romantic getaway to rest, recoup, reconnect, and have serious conversations about what we projected the next ninety days to look like for our life and ministry. We would always bring up the timeline of starting a family, and until this previous quarter we would always unswervingly and without hesitation look at each other and say, "Nah. Not yet." We loved our pace of life and weren't sure how we could add another element into that rhythm, especially one as big as a human being we'd be responsible for.

Amanda was always keen on balance in life, and it was difficult enough maintaining a healthy balance while in the throes of starting a church. Adding kids to our life up to that point seemed nearly impossible.

But something had shifted a few weeks before this. Amanda and I went on a trip to Chicago with Derek and Ashley to attend a church leadership conference and spend a couple of days in the city. One night in our Michigan Avenue hotel room I brought it up to her. "What would you say if I told you I think I want to start trying to have a baby?" I braced myself for the expected reaction, and when it didn't come I was shocked.

"That's funny, Davey. I've been thinking about it for a month now. It would be a pretty ideal time if we got pregnant soon because that would put a baby arriving in July. That's not too busy of a season for us as a church. It would be perfect!"

"Amanda Grace—" (I always called her by both names. In fact, I said the two together so often, many of our friends actually assumed she had one of those Deep South double names.) "What are you saying?"

"I'm saying, I think I'm ready to start trying." She smiled at me, and I couldn't help but grin back at her. For some strange reason, the idea of adding a baby to the equation now peeled back a whole new dimension of love I felt for her, even in that moment.

Just as quickly as the romantic moment was developing in front of me, I had to open my mouth and ruin it. "Well, whether we get pregnant right away or not, it sure is going to be fun to start practicing!!"

She rolled her eyes and blushed as I wrapped my arms around the small of her back and pulled her close to me.

Now, three weeks later, we drove our rented Kia Sorento to our destination cabin, wondering if we had actually made the pregnancy official. If so, it certainly didn't take long, and while I was thrilled about the possibility of being pregnant I was also secretly lamenting the fact that we didn't get the opportunity to "practice" more.

"So Thanksgiving morning it is," I agreed. "Tomorrow might be the longest day of my life!" I tilted my head back against my headrest and stared at the road in front of me, watching the sun dip below the horizon. I had this feeling we were on the cusp of something really beautiful and amazing—a brand new adventure.

Two days later, I didn't even need an alarm to get me out of bed. "Hey! It's Thanksgiving morning! Get your tail up, get in the bathroom, and take that pregnancy test!" I shook Amanda awake as soon as I could. She let out a sarcastic groan and smiled at me and, peeling the comforter back, made her way to the bathroom.

"Aren't you going to come with me?" Amanda asked me. I smiled thinking about how shameless she was. Peeing on a stick in front of me seemed completely normal to her. I loved that our friendship was that open.

In that moment, I couldn't help but be reminded of our wedding night—arriving at the Conrad Chicago Hotel. We had driven two hours from Elkhart to Chicago, it was past midnight, and the Starbucks coffee we had grabbed on the way was calling on both of our bladders by the time we stepped into the room. Completely disregarding the swanky setting, the bubbly champagne, and chocolate-covered strawberries on the bed, not to mention the romantic music coming from the speaker on the nightstand, Amanda bolted directly to the toilet to pee . . . and left the bathroom door open while she did!

"Seriously?!" I hollered after her. "The first time I'm going to see you naked and this is how you're going to do it?!"

She laughed and reached for the door to shut it.

"Davey!" Amanda's voice jarred me back to the present. "Did you hear me? How long does the box say we need to wait before the results show up?"

"Oh! Sorry . . . Umm, lemme see." I grabbed the little Walgreens box and held it up to the light. "Says three to four minutes."

Those three minutes seemed like the longest of my life. Amanda and I sat on the cold tile of the bathroom floor in that rental cabin in Tennessee holding our breath as we counted.

"Okay. Three minutes is up," Amanda said, pulling the stick from behind her back and holding it up. We both gasped.

"It's positive," she blurted in disbelief. "Oh my gosh, Davey! It's positive! We're pregnant!"

The two dashes forming a plus sign were unmistakable! I couldn't believe it! Tears welled up in my eyes as Amanda threw herself into my arms. We were pregnant! A little life we had created was forming inside of my beautiful wife! It was by far one of the happiest days of my life, Thanksgiving 2013.

I blinked to squeeze a tear out of my eye. As I did, the twinkling holiday lights surrounding me blurred, and instead of wiping away the residual moisture to clear my vision, I continued in my daze. I couldn't even muster the motivation to wipe a tear from my cheek.

Energy seemed to completely elude me. It was now two years later, Thanksgiving 2015, and I was at James and Angela's house instead of being back at the cabin where we announced to my family our pregnancy with Weston and where we intended on announcing our pregnancy with Evie. Our plans had changed, as our entire lives had now been completely upended. Weston sat on the floor in front of me as my mom brought him a package to unwrap. My dad sat on a chair adjacent to me while Jonathan and Tessa sat coiled on the couch across from me. There was an empty seat next to me, glaring at me, a constant reminder there would be an empty seat next to me this entire holiday season and for the rest of my life.

Weston seemed the most normal of any of us. At almost sixteen months he had no idea how much his life had just been drastically altered. He waddled to my mom enthusiastically, reached to take the gift, and ripped through the paper wrapping to reveal a plastic basketball goal and set.

"Amanda picked this out for him." My mom looked up at me, her eyes moist and a quiver in her lip. "She was so excited about getting him one of these and had been talking about it for a while."

Of course she had. She always joked about brainwashing Weston into liking basketball more than baseball since basketball was her favorite sport and baseball was mine. We had just spent an afternoon in Chicago, dreaming about our kids playing sports, spending Saturday mornings at the ballpark, and being courtside for each of their games.

Now we would never share those experiences. Now those dreams were dead.

Sinking to the floor, I covered my face with my hands, and my whole body shook with tears. I had been trying my best to hold the torrent of emotions back long enough to spend these few moments opening presents with Weston, attempting to make this somewhat normal for him, but watching him open up a present his mommy had picked out for him not two months before was too much for me to contain.

She should be here! She should be watching him open this! She should be opening up her own gifts right now!! She should be showing him how to shoot a basketball and cheering for him when he makes his first basket. Why, God?! Why?!

My insides were screaming and fighting to burst out of my body. Everything in me ached—the pain too unbearable to contain. It was as if someone were holding my head under water, the pressure building, my bones crying out for oxygen, but just before exploding, just before the relief of slipping into death, I'd be allowed to resurface long enough to take a deep breath, only to be thrust under again. It was pure torture. Over and over again, grief held a vise grip on my heart.

For the next few days around the family, I couldn't sense or discern anything going on around me. Thanksgiving just seemed to *happen*. The family gathered, ate, watched football, and talked, but there wasn't much laughter. It seemed quiet, like we all expected Amanda's familiar laugh to slice through the heaviness in the room. I kept glancing over at the kitchen, expecting to see her beaming face and gleaming crystal blue eyes as she joined the gals in food prep, their conversation of Black Friday shopping schemes filling the room.

Instead it felt like the holiday was more happening *to* us than anything else. Almost as if "normal" were going on all around us while we were being held in this surreal numbness. Bloodshot eyes filled the Byars' living room, no one feeling like they had any more tears to cry, and yet the smallest memory, or trinket, or picture that reminded us of Amanda would trigger the onset of more sobs from someone as they dismissed themself from the room.

Black Friday tradition with the Byars had always gone like this: The boys would do their thing in the morning, go out for a big breakfast, and maybe go to the gun range while the girls watched the kids. In the afternoon, the girls would go shopping while the boys supervised the kids' naps and watched football. The girls would always come home in time for all of us to do dinner together.

As for me, I would watch football with the guys but secretly anticipate the girls returning. My absolute favorite thing would be when Amanda walked in the house after shopping with all the girls. I'd meet her halfway in the hallway, give her a big hug, and she'd whisper in my ear, "Hey, you. I missed you." Even after seven years of marriage, this would cause butterflies to dance in my stomach.

This year, however, none of the guys even wanted to look at a gun. The girls still went shopping, and the boys congregated at Gavin's house for football. Around 6:30 that evening, Audrey, my oldest niece, four years old, bounded through the living room as she saw headlights come around the bend and pull into the driveway.

"Mommy's home!" she yelled.

Instinctively I jumped out of my seat and started for the hallway to meet Amanda. All of a sudden, as if a bus hit me, I remembered she wasn't returning with them. She didn't go shopping. Glancing around to make sure no one was watching, I leaned against the wall, my back hitting it with a thud, and I slid down into a fetal position. Another wave of grief, another torrent of tears.

I had just finished reading C. S. Lewis's *A Grief Observed* that morning. Lewis lost his wife to cancer, and this book comprised his journal entries during that time, published by a family member after his death. Lewis was the only writer I'd read up to that point who had truly been able to articulate everything I was feeling. He mentioned feeling after his wife's death as though he had a limb amputated from his body. Similar to the way amputees often experience what's called "phantom limb phenomenon," I seemed to be reaching to scratch an itch on a leg that was no longer present, and the itch wouldn't go away.

As I sat on the floor of Gavin's hallway, I thought about a couple of other times this phenomenon had happened. Just a few weeks before, after Amanda was killed, Gavin and some others were accompanying me to the City-County Building while I reported to discuss updates on the case with investigators.

As we were leaving, Gavin received a phone call from a few of my staff members who were scouting out cemeteries and burial plots for Amanda's body. I overheard Gavin talking to them about the three options they had visited. Without thinking about what I was doing, I looked at Gavin and asked, "What did Am—" I stopped. *Was I seriously about to ask, "What did Amanda think about it?"* It was habit for me to ask Amanda's opinion on most things, especially big decisions I didn't feel I had the ability to make alone. Out of instinct, I had just turned to ask for Amanda's opinion yet again.

I thought about how, when I had landed on one of my flights to Greenville, South Carolina, earlier that week, I'd reached for my phone to text Amanda that I had landed safely and midtext came to my senses and realized what I was doing. The itch. It was there. But my limb wasn't.

I didn't know what else to do but continue to type the text to her. I needed to tell her how much I missed her and how excruciatingly painful it was to think that I'd never see her again on this side of eternity. I knew it was crazy, but it seemed the only way to get some semblance of relief from the itch.

I hit Send on my phone:

Hey babe. I know this seems crazy but I'm missing you way more than you can know. You remember how I used to call you when I was driving in the car and you knew I was driving in the car because the call was so random. I miss that. I miss that about you, that you knew me better than I knew me. I really can't believe you're gone. None of this makes sense to me. The past two days have been really emotional. I'm sorry I'm blabbering but I just feel like I have so much to tell you and I wish I could tell you all of it. I love you so much. One day I know you'll meet me halfway in the halls of heaven, and I'll give you the biggest hug

I've ever given you and you'll whisper in my ear, "Hey you, I missed you" just like you used to.

10

RUNNING TOWARD THE ROAR

SEVERAL DAYS LATER I WAS BACK IN INDY AND TYPED OUT ANOTHER text—this time to Pastor Levi Lusko.

Back at the end of October, Amanda and I took a train to Chicago for a romantic getaway. I had recently learned of Pastor Levi and heard his story of losing his five-year-old daughter, Lenya, to a freak asthma attack. Amanda and I sat in tears on that train ride listening over podcast to him preach a sermon on what God was teaching him about life, death, pain, healing, and grief.

We both marveled at his strength as he declared that through it all, God was still God and God was still good. I remember thinking, *I can't imagine going through that level of pain and having that kind of faith and resolve.* All the while, I secretly feared our own season of pain was just around the corner.

My fingers fumbled as I shakily crafted the text to Pastor Levi. It was Thursday, December 10, and he had reached out to me via text nine days before to offer his condolences and make his help available. I was in the middle of reading his book *Through the Eyes of a Lion*, written in the wake of losing Lenya.

Levi. Thank you for writing Through the Eyes of a Lion. I'm having a particularly rough 2 days. I'm not sure how I can go on feeling this way every day. The reality and finality of never seeing Amanda again on this side of eternity is setting in deeply with me. On top of that, yesterday I followed a couple rabbit trails of conspiracy theorists, haters, trolls, and nay-sayers picking apart everything I say. It made me want to crawl into a hole and never say anything ever again. Your book is really helping me gain some perspective on things.

I had just spent the last two nights sick to my stomach, restless, feverish as I took trip after trip to the bathroom. I had never experienced a bug or food poisoning that lasted this long, so something told me it wasn't virus related but rather a physical reaction to grief, emotion, and stress.

The gnawing in my stomach would subside during the day while I was distracted with my parenting duties, only to come back with a vengeance during the night, leaving me lying in bed, staring at the ceiling, trying to fall asleep. Everything about the night seemed dark, like this cloud enveloping me, sucking the life out of me, leaving me paranoid and jumpy at every sound from the blackness. It seemed as though I'd never be able to shake the knot that had welled up in my soul.

Weston and I were staying at the Andersons' house until I could figure out what we were to do next.

Now I lay on their couch, curled up under a blanket as chills and spells of cold sweats laid siege to my body. My head swam every time I tried to sit up, and all I wanted to do was sleep until I couldn't feel anything anymore.

No matter where I was, everything seemed to remind me of Amanda. Just six weeks before, the Andersons had hosted a Halloween costume party for all the volunteers in our church. Amanda, Weston, and I went as the superhero family from the Pixar movie *The Incredibles*. As Amanda and I were getting ready that night, pulling on our spandex costumes, I admired the little baby bump beginning to form on her stomach—soon to be the fourth member of our family.

From across our bedroom, I said to her, "We're going to have to tell everyone tonight, babe. There's no way you're going to be able to hide that bump much longer!" Normally, I prided myself on having tact, but I was just too excited about our second baby.

"I know! It's getting bad!"

She looked so adorable in her boots, mask, and tights, even with her baby bump. I could hardly take my eyes off her the whole night.

It was there, in the Andersons' living room during a rousing game of Fishbowl, that we announced to many of our closest friends we were having Baby Number Two. Everyone was so ecstatic. Hugs were exchanged, high fives were handed out. It was a joyous night. Now I lay on the couch, in that same living room, one wrong move from being forced to sprint to the bathroom again—still trying to wrap my mind around the gutting that had occurred to my beautiful family.

Nothing prepares you for when the torrent of grief hits; it comes out of nowhere. In settings where you think you may be an emotional wreck, you do okay. Then grief often overtakes you when you least expect it.

I found myself, many times, longing for the initial state of shock once more. That seemed to be God's grace in my life, holding the weight of loss off my shoulders. I'm convinced I would have died from a broken heart, crumbled under grief's grip, had God not buffered it in waves. Even still, grief's waves and breakers always took me off guard.

The week before, I had gone to see the new James Bond movie, trying to distract myself from everything and just to spend some time with the guys. I walked out of the movie theater, heart pounding, unable to catch my breath from a near anxiety attack when one of the opening scenes showed a woman being shot in the head and executed by a man.

Earlier that same week, I got into my car, and the Bluetooth connection between my phone and car stereo reset itself without my prompting, which means it defaulted to playing the first song alphabetically in my library. That song just happened to be a song that was played during our wedding, just before Amanda walked down the aisle. The opening cord progression threw me into a nearly uncontrollable fury.

As soon as I recognized the song, I pounded the dial of the stereo to turn it completely off and drove in silence the rest of the way, fuming between involuntary whimpers.

That whole week I had been waking up in cold sweats from multiple distinct nightmares, each equally terrifying and equally vivid. One was of Amanda wanting to divorce me as she fell asleep. I knew, in my dream, that if she dozed off, the divorce was final. As she began to close her eyes, I begged and pleaded her not to go and to give us another chance. Still, she closed her eyes and faded away.

I jolted awake in a cold sweat—betrayal, abandonment, and anger toward my murdered wife immediately swelling inside me. *Why was I feeling those emotions?!* I glanced at my phone to check the time. It was 6:37 a.m.

In another dream, my father-in-law; my best friend, Kenneth; and I were CIA agents staking out an abandoned warehouse. As we made our way through the building, this feeling of a cloak of darkness began to surround us. Kenneth walked into a room and the two of us followed not far behind. As I entered and turned around to shut the door, I saw Kenneth bolt toward me with a look of terror on his face. He let out the most bloodcurdling cry I'd ever experienced.

"We're dead!" he screamed. Just then, there was a terrible explosion—a bomb went off, killing all of us as I woke up in another cold sweat. Again, 6:37 a.m.

I began to receive text messages from random people, folks I didn't hear from often, telling me they felt prompted to pray for me at 6:37 every morning. These texts came from at least three different people, none of whom knew each other or were connected in any way. I didn't know what this could mean. There was definitely something beyond the natural taking place here.

The night and the morning both terrified me. The night because the darkness somehow seemed to give my thoughts permission to wander to dark places, not to mention every bone in my body resisted falling asleep for fear of having another nightmare.

But the morning was no better. I'd wake up from a nightmare in a panic. Relieved to realize it was a dream, I would think maybe *everything* had been a dream, and I would reach beside me to pull Amanda close—but she wouldn't be there. It was like losing her all over again, and again, and again, and again.

There I was now, lying nearly lifeless on the Andersons' couch at 3:30 in the afternoon, sick as a dog, trying to figure out how I was going to make the dinner plans with the Agricolas—a family from our church—I had scheduled for that evening.

Just then Levi responded to my text:

Davey. It's an honor to help any way I can. I wrote the book I wished I had been able to read when Lenya went home. I know what you mean with it "setting in . . ." It feels sickening and overwhelming, far too much to bear. Like you have been just gutted. Because you have. In those most difficult moments for me, it would help to remember not to unnecessarily experience days of separation I might never have to actually go through. It makes no sense to think of what it will feel like in 10 years or 14 months for that matter because Jesus could return in the night or I could go to heaven driving to work tomorrow morning . . . so all we have to get through is TODAY. And we get to do that one minute at a time. I'm sorry for the morons who hopefully will never have to know the horror of what you are walking through but feel the freedom to pile on with their words . . . don't hate them just completely ignore them and run your race. Jesus has trusted you with this trial and will give you the grace to steward it with grace and power. Keep Running Toward the Roar!

Keep running toward the roar. I wasn't really sure what that meant, but I guessed it was something in the book I hadn't read yet. It sure sounded empowering. I grabbed the book, which happened to be lying beside me on the couch, and rifled through the pages to find a chapter with a title that resembled the phrase *running toward the roar.* Sure enough, it was in chapter 11.

What I read next would become one of the single most healing and empowering things I had ever experienced in my life and would completely change the trajectory of how I walked through my pain. Levi wrote,

I am fascinated by the way lions hunt. I've read that it's the lionesses that actually do the "lion's share" of the work. The males are obviously incredibly intimidating, with their manes and their ferocious roars, but it's the chicks you really have to watch out for.

The fact that lionesses do not have a big, recognizable mane actually helps them sneak up on whatever they are hunting. They lie in wait, hidden in the tall grass, motionless like statues. I listened to a sermon by Pastor Brian Houston in which he said the males do play an important, albeit small, role. While the females stalk their prey from behind, the king of the jungle will come from the front and let loose one of those roars that gives him his spot at the top of the food chain. This sound is so powerful it can be heard for up to five miles away. Hearing that terrifying noise causes the gazelle or antelope to run as far as they can away from whatever made that sound.

What they don't know is that as scary as it sounded, the one who did the roaring is more bark than bite. So away they go—directly into the path of the real threat: the waiting lioness. In other words, the prey's instincts are wrong. Going with their gut causes them to make the last mistake of their short, little lives. It's counterintuitive, but the right choice would be to override their emotions and run toward the roar.[2]

As I read Levi's words, I couldn't help but think about how in 1 Peter 5:8, the Bible uses the analogy of Satan as a lion—how he prowls around us like a *roaring* lion, seeking whom he could devour. I wondered if maybe the way *out* of my pain was actually *into* my pain, through my pain, right into the roar of my greatest enemy.

As a Christian, I knew I wasn't in danger of actually being devoured by Satan, even if my circumstances made me feel like I was. I am a believer, and therefore he has no claim over my life. I am a new creation, no longer a slave to the curse of sin and death. So the Enemy couldn't ultimately destroy me. However, what the Enemy could do was scare me into being devoured by pain and fear.

In fact, his intention is to steal, kill, and destroy. He wants to steal my joy, kill my hope, and destroy the purposes God has for my life.

In that moment, I realized that because my pain was so terrifyingly messy and unpredictable, I had been running away from it. I'd been trying to box up the pain and suppress it—and it wasn't working. In fact, it was booby-trapping me. Perhaps this was the explanation for the physical sickness I'd been dealing with.

By running *away* from the pain I was running straight *into* an ambush. I was afraid of stepping into the pain, letting my heart feel the full weight of it, working through it, and trusting the Lord's promise to strengthen and help me. It made me feel too exposed and vulnerable. I realized if I continued in this I might never actually come to a place of true healing. If I didn't do something about this, months, years, even decades down the road, the pain would ambush me and take me out with even greater ferocity.

I decided right there, on that black leather couch in the Andersons' living room, that instead of running away from the pain I was going to start running toward it. I decided to embrace it, to deal with it head-on: one day, one minute at a time. Even if it felt like it was going to kill me, I had to take my first step: I had to join the Agricola family for dinner that night.

Jeff and Angela Agricola were the family Amanda nannied for when we first moved to Indy. I'll never forget Amanda spending countless hours praying God would direct her to a job where she could interact with people who didn't know Jesus, so her job could also be her ministry—since that was her heart. The Lord led her to Angela Agricola and her two little boys, Brady and Cooper.

Amanda was a natural with the Agricola boys. It was always her dream to mother two boys, so she took on Brady and Cooper as her own. I helped her babysit on occasion and often swung by the Agricolas' during a lunch break. While watching Amanda in her nanny role, I'd daydream about having our own kids. Seeing her with the Agricola boys gave me great confidence in the mom she would be to our own children one day.

A few months into working for Angela, Amanda had grown to love Angela and their friendship was beginning to blossom.

In September 2012, our church was having our first Sunday service and Amanda really wanted to invite Angela to attend. But they'd had a few conversations about faith, and knowing where Angela stood spiritually made Amanda leery about how she might respond to an invite.

As a scientist, Angela was a self-proclaimed atheist, holding to the belief that science and rational thought disproved the existence of God. Amanda, however, was convinced God had put Angela in her life for a reason and was determined to love her new friend into God's family.

One afternoon as they were chatting, Amanda slid an invite flyer to Angela and asked her to come to our launch service. Probably more from a place of friendliness and support than of genuine interest, Angela agreed to attend. At the end of the service, when I gave the invitation to receive the gift of Christ's sacrifice, Amanda and I were both shocked and delighted as Angela raised her hand to receive Christ! Amanda and I spent the next couple of years frequently grabbing coffee with Angela, walking her through her newfound faith.

Now, a month after Amanda's death, the Agricolas had invited me, Weston, Derek, and Ashley over to have dinner. Angela was really struggling with the loss of Amanda. After all, Amanda had been the one to tangibly show Angela who Jesus truly was, first by her kindness and servant's attitude in interacting with the boys, and eventually through her words.

We arrived at Jeff and Angela's house, and it didn't take long before I was sitting on the floor of the playroom, watching Ashley and Angela play with Weston, Brady, and Cooper. All I could think about was Amanda and how she used to dream of playdates with the Agricola boys. My stomach tumbled over and over the entire evening. I knew I was supposed to be there, but everything inside of me wanted to get up and walk out, to run away from it all. It was just too much to handle!

After dinner, I left with Weston to get him home for bedtime. I drove home and thought about how I had barely interacted with anyone the entire night. I mostly sat and looked on as Derek and Ashley carried on a conversation with Jeff and Angela. I should have felt strange or guilty or embarrassed about that— that would have been my "normal" response. But nothing about the grief process is normal.

Instead, on the way back to the Andersons' house that night, I drove in silence. Weston was tuckered out from playing with the Agricola boys and was barely able to keep his eyes open. I couldn't get comfortable in my seat. My stomach pains felt like they were leaking over my entire body now—achy, sore, and nauseating.

It almost felt as if my love for Amanda had nowhere to go now, no outlet, so pinned up inside of me it was festering, rotting, and turning into a horrific cancerous knot of sadness, grief, and terror.

I couldn't hold it in any longer. I had to do something about this. I was completely exhausted from harboring all this emotion. I pulled over to the shoulder, grabbed my phone, and cued up the stereo to the song from our wedding I had turned off before.

Run toward the roar, Davey, Run toward the roar.

I was determined to force myself to listen to it this time. I didn't know what was going to happen when I did, but I was tired of being on the defensive. It was time to attack this pain head-on.

As the song began, something in me snapped. There on the side of Highway 31, sounds that I could not even recognize as human spewed from a depth of my soul. This was the kind of sound that gives the term *ugly cry* new definition.

Almost involuntarily my body released the tension that had been brewing for all this time. And once it started, it wouldn't stop. I cried and I cried and I cried. And even when it would have made sense to stop, I just let myself keep crying.

In that moment I realized something powerful and cathartic. I hadn't let myself do this yet. Had I cried? Oh, absolutely! But I hadn't let myself sob uncontrollably. I hadn't been alone long enough to do so. And as I sat in my car on the side of the road, I let wave after wave of grief overtake me. My eyes felt like they were bleeding tears; the veins in my neck felt like at any minute they were going to explode under the tension of my sobs. Weston didn't budge. His eyes were closed now, and his little chest rose and fell rhythmically. As he drifted into peaceful sleep in the backseat, I cradled myself in the front and wept violently and inconsolably.

I played the song again and again—not sure how many times exactly—but pass after pass through the chorus and bridge, I wept. And then, all of a sudden, it was over. It was done. Just as abruptly as it had begun, it ended. I had no more tears. I couldn't cry anymore.

Then something strange occurred: I didn't feel like I *needed* to cry anymore. It was almost as if when I finally confronted the pain, met it head-on, and wrestled it to the ground, it overtook me for a moment but then vanished. *Poof!* It was the strangest thing I had ever experienced.

What was even more shocking was my stomach didn't hurt anymore. My body didn't ache either. The knot that had formed in my gut had been carefully untied and massaged to normalcy. I felt this strange sense of peace, a peace that surpassed my ability to understand or quantify. The waves of grief hit with ferocity but almost immediately were followed by what felt like waves of *grace*.

I put the car back in gear, a little stunned, and drove home.

Back at the Andersons' house I sat on the couch, suddenly feeling more empowered than I'd ever felt in my life, like some kind of superhuman strength had overtaken me. I grabbed a notebook and began writing as I thought about the things that had been terrifying me:

- *Run toward the roar*
- *Start preaching again at Resonate*
- *Get up at 5:00 a.m. every morning and read the Bible*
- *Read through all of Amanda's journals*
- *Go back into the Sunnyfield Court house*

As I wrote, I felt the horror of these things course through my veins. I had no idea how I was going to tackle each of these, but I was determined to approach things on offense now. No more running away from the roar.

11

TRAGEDY TO TRIUMPH

Two weeks later I sat by the fire at Amanda's parents' house. It was Christmas, and Weston and I were staying with Phil and Robin for the week. There was no Christmas tree up as Robin had decided to skip decorating for the holidays this year. Understandably, she couldn't bring herself to get into the festive mood.

Despite the lack of seasonal decor, her house still felt like home—cozy, warm, and with hints of Amanda sprinkled everywhere. It's amazing how much a daughter resembles her mother when it comes to keeping a home, and at this point Weston and I craved that familiarity.

"I think we need to go back into the house as a family," I hesitantly suggested as the three of us sipped our morning coffee. I began to explain to them my new outlook on dealing with grief and running toward the roar. "I just think we should face our greatest fears head-on."

To my surprise, Robin and Phil both immediately agreed. They thought it would help them gain some type of closure. The last time Robin had seen Amanda alive and in person was in September, when she and the girls took all the kids to the apple orchard for the day. Phil's last interaction with her was over FaceTime while he and James were on a wilderness trip in Colorado. They each thought it would be a healing experience to spend some time as a family sorting through Amanda's things and packing up the house.

We agreed on a weekend in February, they excused themselves to get ready for work, and I refilled my coffee cup. I sat back down, closer to the fire, and picked up a book on the coffee table that had caught my attention earlier that morning, *Fresh Faith* by Jim Cymbala and Dean Merrill.

I'd read it when I was in college, but something drew me to open it up again that morning. As I began thumbing through the pages, I noticed a reference the authors made to King David. Intrigued, I looked closer.

If you know the story of David you can understand why I'm drawn to it. The mess and the beauty of his story give me hope that God can use my mess as well. As I leaned in a little further to what the authors wrote, however, I realized this was a part of David's story I had never actually seen before (a rarity for a pastor!). It was the story about David's wife and kids being captured.

David was still on the run from King Saul and his men when he decided to take refuge among the Philistine army, which seemed a little crazy because the Philistines were his *enemies*! David was, of course, the unassuming shepherd boy who had killed the Philistine champion, Goliath. So how amazing is it that they would even let him into their camp?

Somehow David convinced them he deserted the Israelite army and that he wanted to fight for their side. Over time he built such a trust with Achish, the commander to whom he's assigned, that he was allowed to come and go as he pleased—as long as he reported back what he'd been doing every day.

David and his men went out each day and raided the camps of other enemy nations—the Geshurites, the Girzites, the Amalekites, and the Cellulites (no, not really). Then, in order to retain the trust of Achish and the Philistine commanders, David came home and reported that he'd been sacking the Israelite camps. This persisted day after day.

One day the Philistines called their entire military force to go to battle against the Israelites. David and his men joined the conscription, but as they lined up for battle, the other Philistine commanders told Achish they couldn't trust David. They were afraid that, in the middle of battle, David and his men would double-cross them. So they sent them away. David and his men began the slow, dejected march back to their campground in Ziklag.

As they approached the crest of the hill that overlooked Ziklag, they noticed smoke coming up from their camp. They rushed into the camp but it was too late. Their city had been burned and each of their wives and children carried away by the Amalekite army. David had messed with the enemy too much and retaliation was due, and this time it was his wife and children who would pay.

I put the book down, peered over at the fire, and began to whisper, "Lord, are You trying to show me something here? This is crazy! David had his wife stolen from him by the enemy?!" I felt the prompting to keep reading to see how David responded to his tragedy that felt eerily similar to mine. I mean, my wife and daughter had *also* been stolen by a great enemy. This is one of my favorite parts about Scripture: if we look closely, we can find ourselves in it. So I continued reading.

I have to admit, I fully expected David to go into William Wallace mode at this point. I thought he would probably explode into a fury of vengeance and cut the throats of every Amalekite responsible (which, if you keep reading, he eventually did do). But what struck me as miraculous was what he did *first*.

In 1 Samuel, David and his men "wept until they had no more strength to weep" (30:4 ESV). This sounded all too familiar, especially given my roadside experience not a week earlier. But then what happened next made me all the more intrigued. David motioned to the priest and said, "Bring me the ephod."

What is an ephod? I wondered. *Surely this is some ancient weapon or instrument of torture David was intending on using against the Amalekites.* So I looked it up. I was surprised and a little confused to discover that instead of a weapon, an ephod was a linen cloth the priest would put on before they stepped into the tabernacle to make sacrifices to God on the people's behalf. The Bible also refers to it as a "garment of praise."

Wait, what? Why would David ask for a garment of praise? Why would he ask to put on an ephod when he had just lost his wife and kids?! The last thing I wanted to do was *praise God for my circumstance!* This didn't make any sense to me.

Then, I suddenly remembered another instance in Scripture where David wore a linen ephod. In 2 Samuel 6, following one of his greatest victories in battle, David paraded into the city, triumphant, a conqueror—and he *danced* in a linen ephod. The people made up chants about his triumphs and the women swooned over him as he showed off his moves.

The only two times David is portrayed wearing a linen ephod in the Scriptures are in his greatest *triumph* and his greatest *tragedy*. In both seemingly opposite situations, he put on a garment of praise. Even though he *felt* like focusing on the pain, he *chose* instead to look at his tragic circumstance through the perspective of praise for what God was going to do.

I was now both intrigued and miffed, so I kept reading the story.

David asked for the ephod and then prayed and asked God if he should take revenge on his wife's captors. God told David he should and that the victory would be his if he would do the hard part of stepping into the pain and the battle, if he'd *run toward the roar.* So David did as he was instructed, and as he and his men entered the Amalekite camp, they discovered all their wives and kids survived, and—even better—the Amalekites were too drunk to fight.

So David and his mighty men made a quick rout of the Amalekite army, killing nearly everyone in their camp and rescuing their wives and children.

I put the book down on the coffee table, trying to piece together what this meant for me. It seemed as though God had specifically led me to read this. I mean, this would be fantastic inspiration if I had the opportunity to rescue Amanda and Evie. It would make sense if God was trying to speak to me about storming into my house and pulling Amanda from the clutches of death, but I didn't have that opportunity!

I'm happy for David, God, but what does this have to do with me?!

No sooner did I have this thought than His still, small voice whispered to my soul. *Davey, I didn't show you this to teach you about rescue. I showed you this to teach you about restoration.*

I nearly gasped as these words pressed into my heart.

Davey, I'm a God who restores out of the ruin, and when I restore, I restore completely. David's life was not only restored, but in the process, I threw in a bonus—he completely destroyed the enemy. Davey, I want to use you to teach people about restoration, and in that process, you'll be a part of My plan to destroy the real enemy, Satan. As you run toward the roar, I'll begin to restore. Instead of focusing on your pain, focus on praise. I want to give you a purpose in the midst of your pain, and as you step into that purpose, your pain will be healed and you'll help to heal others as well.

I glanced at what remained of the fire, now only smoldering cinders, swelling with warm glows that began to grow blurry as tears welled up in my eyes. Could these dreams of growing old with Amanda, now dead at the hands of criminals, be somehow restored—resurrected into a greater dream? I knew something profound had been spoken to my heart, and almost immediately it had become a fire in my bones, something I couldn't hold in. I knew I had just been given the first sermon for my return to preaching at my beloved church.

A little more than a month later, I sat next to a different fireplace. This time at a new house where Derek, Ashley, Weston, and I were living. My cousin's in-laws offered us to live in their house while they were snow birding in Florida.

It was 5:07 a.m., and the coffee was percolating in the background. The black of night was still very present in the Indiana February sky. Refusing to be woken up in a cold sweat at 6:37 anymore, I had spent the last month setting my alarm for 5:00 a.m. My nightmares were beginning to subside and 6:37 didn't freak me out the way it had before.

For the first two weeks of this new early regimen, I'd hold my breath for nearly the entire thirty-seventh minute of the sixth hour while watching the clock. I still had people texting me at that time, and there still seemed something sinister about that minute, but the last couple of days I had actually unknowingly rolled right through the minute, too engrossed in what I was reading.

I began opening up my Bible and reading from about 5:30 to 6:30 every morning, and each time I did, the darkness and distress that previously seemed to overshadow the morning retreated. My anxiety gradually subsided and my outlook on the day seemed brighter.

Falling asleep each night was still a bit difficult. Some days were so packed with activity between Weston and the church that once I went to bed and the distractions slowed down, it gave room for my mind to speed up. Sleep still eluded me many nights, but now the mornings began to feel different—brighter. I actually looked forward to the mornings again.

God's promise that "His mercies . . . are new every morning" (Lamentations 3:22–23 ESV) was becoming more and more of a reality to me with each passing day. I felt a nearness to God I had never felt in my life. The Bible says of itself that it's a "lamp to my feet and a light to my path" (Psalm 119:105 ESV). I felt the light of God's Word quite literally driving out darkness each and every morning and warming my soul.

I was also feeling a nearness to Amanda. After reading my Bible, I'd pick up Amanda's prayer journals. Each entry took my breath away. I couldn't believe how connected Amanda was to Jesus. I knew she was serious about her relationship with the Lord and that she displayed a trust in Him I had always envied, but I was amazed to read how she processed everything we had walked through the last five years and was transparent with God about it all.

As a kid she journaled sporadically but became more consistent as a senior in high school. But for some reason when God began calling us to Indianapolis to start a church, the frequency of her journaling greatly increased. I was amazed to see this girl confess to God her fears, insecurities, doubts, and frustrations. I was also amazed at the depth of wisdom that flowed from her pen.

Each entry seemed to begin with some observation of what she read in the Bible that morning. Then she would vent her frustrations about whatever she was going through. You could nearly taste her emotions as you read them. However, almost without exception, there would be this turn in the middle of the entry where she'd write something like, *God that's how I feel, but this is what I know your Word says is true. Show me where I'm wrong in this. Show me where my heart needs to change. Help me to surrender my emotions to your Truth.*

I had spent the last month devouring her journals. Once I assembled all of them and put them in chronological order, I started with the first and couldn't put them down. I was now getting near the end of them and couldn't believe the life her prayers were speaking into me. Each time I read an entry where she prayed for me, or for Weston, I'd lose it. My heart would seize up with this mixture of joy, sorrow, and pain. Joy for how much it made me adore her all the more, and sorrow for the reminder of what was no longer in my life.

I truly couldn't believe how much she prayed for me! I couldn't believe how much she prayed for me about things she never even told me about. I could tell in her entries she knew addressing me with some of these things probably would *not* have gone over well, so instead of trying to be the Holy Spirit in my life, she would pray that the *real* Holy Spirit would inspire me to change.

When I looked back on the timing of these prayers, I could follow my own timeline of conviction and growth. It was truly remarkable. Talk about the power of a praying wife. Ironically, I was beginning to feel like her prayers had even more power in my life now than before she went to be with Jesus.

A couple of times, I posted entries that were meaningful to me on social media. I couldn't believe the response they received. People were clamoring to hear what Amanda had to say in these journals. Obviously I used discretion, only posting words I knew Amanda would have publicly shared in a counseling session or a Q and A at church. Regardless, it felt right and good that Amanda's words were being used to minister to so many people, even as she was in heaven. That's who she was when she was here, and it only made sense for her legacy to continue after she was gone.

Never in a million years could Amanda have known how her *personal* devotional time was going to affect so many people. I think about this often, now, as a pastor, when I'm encouraging those I serve to spend time with God in the Word. I think about the magnitude and the possibility of this. This is not just about "getting some time to yourself" each day. You have no idea how your personal quiet time, how your small prayers, could be shaping and shifting the world around you. It's actually quite a miracle.

On one occasion, after reading one of Amanda's journals, Megan approached me and mentioned the idea of publishing some of them.

"When I read how she communicated with Jesus, it makes me want to have that kind of relationship with Him," she said to me. I completely agreed. I was also inspired and challenged by the depth of her friendship with Jesus. He was truly her first love!

Considering the possibility that Amanda's quiet time could potentially speak into the hearts of tens if not hundreds of thousands of people choked me up even more. As Megan and I discussed further, I began thinking about how this is actually true of all of us. By that I mean that the only thing of value we have to offer people publicly comes from our personal devotional life. What we do behind closed doors directly affects other people. You can't give away what you don't possess. Amanda definitely possessed a nearness to Jesus that was *so* evident in what she gave away on a daily basis.

Anyway, on this particular morning I was fiercely missing Amanda and begging God to show me something in her journals that would be especially healing for me—some prayer that would inject a sense of empowerment in my spirit.

Amanda's family and I were going back into the Sunnyfield Court house later that morning and planned to spend the weekend packing everything up. I was terrified for what emotional highs and lows the weekend held for us. I just needed to hear from God, to hear from Amanda, that everything was going to be okay.

I picked up a red composition notebook—her last volume of entries—unfolded the dog-eared page, and began reading:

I just read a devotional about not giving up and this woman talked about how she could barely get herself out of bed in the morning to face another day. She talked about how she had walked through a divorce, her mom dying of cancer, and her daughter being diagnosed with a terminal disease. Father, my heart breaks to hear that. I can't imagine the feelings and thoughts that go through her head every morning as she tries to face another day. It just puts my world into total perspective. Lord, you have protected me from so many heart-breaking things. You have covered me and my family, and I'm so thankful for your grace and protection.

I know it may not be like this forever, and you may have things ahead of us that are unbearable. I just want to take the time to thank you for blessing our lives like you have. Thank you for the health of my family. Thank you for [the] support and love of my family. Thank you for an amazing husband and the bond we share—our crazy, hilarious Weston and our baby on the way. Please continue to watch over us and protect us from illness and injuries. Help us to take advantage of our health and serve you whole-heartedly because you've allowed us to. And when the valleys do come, please keep our family strong. Keep our eyes on you. I love you, Lord.

Are you kidding me? I was completely amazed. Exactly when I needed it. Exactly when *we* needed it, her prayers were there, covering us, going before us, making a way. I closed the journal, whispered a deep, heartfelt *thank you* to Jesus, and walked upstairs to get dressed for the day.

Two hours later, my dad and I pulled into the driveway of the Sunnyfield Court house. It was the first time I'd been in the driveway since the morning of November 10, pacing on the phone while Amanda struggled for life inside.

"You sure you don't want me to go in with you?" my dad asked. He is one of the kindest, most compassionate, and most self-sacrificing men I've ever met. He had driven seven hours, through the night, just to stand beside me on this day. He knew it was going to be extremely difficult for me to walk into the house, and he wanted to make sure I knew he was available if I needed a crutch to lean on.

"No, Dad. I need to do this by myself. Can you do me one favor, though?"

He nodded.

"Can you intercept Amanda's family before they come in? I want to have my time in there before anyone else comes in."

"Of course, son." My dad turned in his seat and looked me square in the eye. "I love you and I'm proud of you," he whispered.

I choked back tears, reached for the latch on the door, and climbed out of the vehicle. Each foot felt like it weighed a hundred pounds as I planted it on the ground. I consciously willed myself forward with each step I took toward the front door. The last time I had opened this door, I walked into my greatest nightmare. Only three months later, I could feel the same quickening of my heartbeat and the hair beginning to stand up on the back of my neck. I reached the top step of the porch and stood for a second staring at the front door.

Run toward the roar, Davey. Run toward the roar. Take this house back from the Enemy. You and Amanda devoted this house to Jesus several years ago. You devoted every activity of the house to ministry. Now, take back what the Enemy did here and devote it again to ministry. Restore this house. Restore her story. Restore your story.

I reached for my headphones and plugged the jack into the bottom of my phone. I remembered walking in three months before, seeing Amanda lying on the floor, and chucking my headphones out of my ears to get to her side as fast as I could. Now my hands nearly convulsed as I placed each bud in my ear and scrolled through the library on my iTunes worship playlist that began with "Nothing Is Wasted." I tapped Play on my phone, reached for the door handle, turned it, and walked over the threshold, linen ephod in hand.

PART 3

WHAT THE ENEMY MEANT FOR EVIL

12

A NEW SEASON OF
CONTENTMENT

THE MAN SITTING ACROSS FROM ME GAZED AT THE LOOK ON MY FACE, his soft, dark eyes and raised brows a stark contrast to his white beard and deep, soothing voice. He leaned toward his desk and lowered his voice, his tone deepening to a rich, grandfatherly delivery.

"Davey, do you think Amanda would have still said yes to Jesus about moving to Indianapolis if she knew she was going to lose her life four years into it?"

I was sitting in the office and headquarters of Dr. John Walker's Christian leader resource and renewal center in Tampa, Florida, called Blessing Ranch. It was March and the weather in Florida was perfect—seventy degrees and not too humid— the kind of weather you would order if you could ask God for a perfect day, and a welcome retreat from a harsh and enduring Indiana winter.

Dr. Walker specializes in counseling pastors and church leaders through difficult situations. I was connected to him through two almost simultaneous sources. One was my long-time friend and mentor, Pastor Perry Noble. Pastor Perry had been outspoken about his struggle with depression and anxiety and was touting Dr. John Walker as the "savior of his life and ministry"—next to Jesus, of course.

The second person who had referred me to Dr. Walker was Pastor Tim Harlow. I was connected to Tim through my friend Bob Goff. Bob reached out to me shortly after Amanda passed and asked if I wanted to have dinner with him. I told Bob I'd move heaven and earth to connect with him, so Gavin, James, and I drove to Chicago one night to meet Bob during one of his speaking engagements.

The pastor of the church where Bob spoke was Tim Harlow, an extremely kind man who had spent over twenty years building Parkview Christian Church in the suburbs of Chicago.

After Tim and I were introduced, he asked me, "Have you seen a counselor yet?" Since I had always been the one counseling people, it seemed a little odd to me at first to make the switch to being on the receiving end. It wasn't that I had any shame about seeing a counselor. As I have always told my congregation, it's not bad people who need counseling; *all* people need counseling. And now I believed that statement more than ever. I just needed to find someone I could trust explicitly with such a delicate season.

I shook my head a little sheepishly.

"You *have* to go see my counselor," Tim insisted. "His name is John Walker. He quite literally saved my life and ministry."

From that moment, I was sold on Dr. Walker since two people I highly respected were, completely separately of each other, telling me the same thing. Tim was even gracious enough to cover my costs to see John for an entire week.

Now that I sat in Dr. Walker's office, in a plush leather chair, I tried to get a read on him. He reminded me of a softer, gentler version of the Dos Equis man, and after hearing a few stories of his life adventures, I certainly thought he could pass as "the most interesting man in the world."

"It's okay, I'll let you think about it for a minute." John motioned his hand to me, inviting me to ponder his query.

The question hit me like an earthquake. I had never considered this before, and even just the *thought* leveled me—the thought that God would allow someone to have the foresight to know she was walking into her own death. Could anyone possibly have the kind of emotional strength to deal with the knowledge of her impending death and walk forward anyway?

Father, not my will, but yours be done.

I couldn't answer him right away. I couldn't think of many people who would jump at the chance to die for Jesus. After all, how many people does Jesus *ask* to do that? Certainly not many! He normally asks us to *live* for Him. But die?

I sat there and ruminated for what felt like hours, although I'm sure it was no more than a couple of minutes. As I reflected, a few memories gradually began surfacing in my mind. I suddenly remembered reading a journal entry Amanda wrote after our last Sunday service at NewSpring before moving to Indy to plant Resonate. I reached into my book bag, pulled out the notebook, flipped to find the correct page, handed it to Dr. Walker, and nearly whispered, "I want to show you a couple of things if you're okay with that."

The entry read:

Jesus, thank you for that message yesterday. It was awesome and such a good perspective for me to be reminded of. Job 42:12: "The Lord blessed the latter part of Job's life more than the first." Davey said the other day, God must have big things in store for us because we are leaving what we think is the greatest church in the world and the greatest city in the world. And it's encouraging to me when you give and you take away and yet I can say, "Blessed be your name" because you are working everything out for a perfect purpose. Jesus I needed that perspective yesterday. Give me strength to not hold on to the material things. I'm starting day #1 today for packing. Help me Jesus to just trust you through these next two weeks. Please encourage my spirit and sustain me. Help me to remember what you have in store. I love you. Give me faith to trust what you say.

He handed the notebook back to me and raised his eyebrows. "Wow. She was quite a woman, wasn't she?"

I dropped my eyes and stared at the top of his desk. "Yeah. That's not even the start of it."

I reached for another notebook from my pack, took a moment to locate the entry I was thinking about, and handed it to him. It was the entry Megan had earlier pointed out to me that Amanda wrote the morning after we moved to Indy: November 12, 2011. She concluded it with *"I will take up my cross and follow wherever you lead."*

"Amazing." Dr. Walker shook his head and looked up at me after reading the entry.

"There's more. The weekend before she was killed I took my leadership team and their spouses on a planning retreat to Cincinnati. We wanted to get off-site to forecast for 2016, which seems incredibly ironic to me now because none of us could have seen what was actually coming, let alone prepare for it. One night I had the team gather in a little room on the top floor of the hotel. It was the old fitness room so there were mirrors all around and terrible lighting, but it was the only private room we could find. I asked our worship leader if he'd lead us in singing, and then we spent some time in prayer together."

I pulled open my phone and retrieved a picture of the scene, showing it to Dr. Walker. He looked at the photo and exhaled as he studied it, his shoulders visibly slumping. The whole team was in a circle that filled the room. I was kneeling in the center of everyone with my hands resting on my knees. Amanda, facing the camera and a bit blurry, stood in the circle.

"Dr. Walker, I felt this overwhelming presence of God in the room that night, unlike any presence I've ever felt before. I couldn't even stand up it felt so thick. I opened the floor for anyone to pray. There was silence for a couple of minutes, and then Amanda led with the most genuine prayer I've ever heard. She said through her tears, 'Jesus, I'm sorry for the times I make my life about my agenda. I want my agenda for my life to be *Your* agenda for my life. Tonight, I surrender to Your agenda for my life.'"

A lump began to form in my throat as I recounted that night and the sincerity of her prayer. I remember her prayer leading the way for each and every team member to pray their own prayer of surrender.

"We knew God was about to do something great through our surrender," I continued. "We just couldn't possibly know He was leading us into *this*."

"Man, Davey. That is both heartbreaking and beautiful." Dr. Walker wiped a tear away from his eye.

"One last thing," I added. "The morning before Amanda was killed, I walked into our bedroom at about 7:30 a.m. I had just finished some time reading the Bible and praying and I knew that she was up, doing the same. When I walked in the bedroom, however, I didn't see her in her normal reading spot, propped up on the edge of the bed. I peered around the corner to check the bathroom. She wasn't there either. Then I looked back toward her side of the bed, and there she was, on both knees, bowing beside the bed, in a posture of surrender."

I glanced down at the floor, wrestling with what I was about to say, eyes darting for something, anything to hold my gaze. It seemed so difficult to actually articulate what I was about to say next—which was that, yes, Amanda would have joyfully walked into her own death out of obedience to Jesus. Everything I knew about Amanda's character affirmed she would have done exactly that.

I finally mustered the courage to speak again.

"So . . . yes. I believe she would have said yes, even if she had known how all of this was going to take place. Because, for Amanda, no matter how much it hurt, she always chose the route of obedience over comfort."

"I agree, Davey. I'm confident she would have said yes."

The resolve in Dr. Walker's voice gave me a sense of comfort. "I asked you this for a reason," he told me. "If you can wrap your heart around what I want to teach you next, it will change your entire perspective moving forward. It won't change your circumstance, but it will change your perspective. You see, Davey, we often want God to work in *poof.*" He moved his hands like a magician, and I furrowed my brow, a little confused.

"We want God's work in our lives—healing, connection, relationships, career—to occur in what I call *poof.* Instantaneous. Without struggle. He snaps His fingers and we're fixed. But that's not how God works. He works in *process,* not *poof.* He has a long, arduous process laid out next for you, and it won't change your circumstances. But if you lean into His process, He'll change your perspective. And a right perspective will carry you through any circumstance. And I mean *any* circumstance. Including this one."

He paused for a moment to let that sink in and then continued. "You want to know what perspective I believe God wants you to learn next?"

I nodded and inched toward the edge of my chair, curious to hear what he had to say.

"When I heard you were coming to see me, I did as much research on you and Amanda as I possibly could. She was a special girl, Davey. From the outside looking in, she was one of the godliest women I have never had the privilege of knowing." I dropped my eyes and nodded in agreement, pained by the reminder that something this horrific happened to someone so beautiful, someone I loved so much, to the person in the world who *least* deserved to suffer the way she had.

"In fact, Davey, she was such an amazing woman, I found myself questioning, 'God, how could You have let this happen to such an incredible wife, mother, and follower of You?'"

Dr. Walker continued. "Then I was reminded of a trip I took to Rome a few years back. One day while visiting, we went on a tour of the ancient Coliseum. What a magnificent structure! At one point, the guide ushered us down to the dungeons where they housed the early Christians moments before they would meet their demise in front of thousands of jeering Roman citizens.

"Nero was the emperor at the time, and he hated everything about the movement of Christianity. You know in Hebrews 11 where it talks about people getting sawed in half, flogged, and decapitated? Many of these monstrosities were committed under Nero's reign."

I nodded solemnly as he continued.

"What's fascinating is Nero didn't ask these early Christians to recant Christ. Ancient Rome was a polytheistic society, meaning most Romans worshipped *multiple* gods. Nero merely asked these Christians to worship him *first*, before they worshipped anyone else—including Jesus. These early martyrs could have easily conceded to Nero's wishes, all the while secretly holding on to their love for Jesus in order to be spared their life.

"But they *didn't*. They chose Jesus over everything else. Over comfort, over health, over convenience, over safety, and, yes, even over life on earth."

I looked across the desk at Dr. Walker and squinted a little, physically trying to make sense of what he was telling me. I knew he saw the confusion and hurt in my eyes, but he continued.

"What struck me though, Davey, is that while we were down there, the tour guide began reading some written accounts of ancient historians, recalling how these early Christians did not cower in fear or recant their beliefs as many expected them to do. They walked into their deaths in a completely different manner . . . triumphantly. They didn't see themselves as victims of their situation. Instead they seemed to walk in victory!"

"Dr. Walker," I interjected. "I don't understand how they were able to do that! How did they have that kind of strength?!"

"You know why I believe they were able to do it?" Dr. Walker asked. "Many of these people actually *saw* Jesus after He was raised from the dead. It wasn't just hearsay to them. They *witnessed* Jesus gain victory over death and get up from the grave three days after He was killed. I think they knew that, since Jesus walked through suffering and was raised to new life, by His spirit and by His power, they too could walk through death with confidence.

"I think they also knew that on some level in order to share in Christ's resurrection, they were going to have to share in His suffering. Isn't this what the disciple Peter says in one of his books of the Bible? I mean remember, Peter was the guy who was crucified upside *down* because he didn't believe he was worthy to be executed in the same manner as Jesus."

John took a sip from his water glass and leaned in a little farther. "You see, Davey, I believe, in some ways, Amanda was a martyr. Sure, she probably wasn't killed as a direct result of her beliefs. However, she did give her life to a great calling and lost her life because of it.

LEFT: Amanda with
the sword during
our "First Look" on
our wedding day

BELOW: Our double
wedding (left to
right, Gavin, Amber,
Amanda, Me)

RIGHT: Finishing the San
Diego Marathon side-by-side
(Me, Amanda, and Amber)

BELOW: Proposing to Amanda at
White River State Park in Indy

TOP: Amber and Amanda with their dad at James and Angela's wedding

BOTTOM: Dressing up as the Incredibles for our last Halloween together

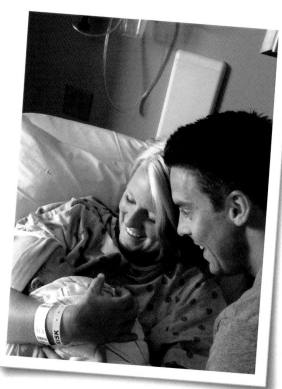

LEFT: Moments after Amanda gave birth to Weston

BELOW: "The Upper Room" of the hotel in Cincinnati days before Amanda's death

Running the Indy
Mini Marathon in
May of 2016 in honor
of Amanda (left to
right, Chad Gilbert,
Me, Allison Gilbert,
Ashley Barrett, Tayler
Anderson, and Amber)

Weston delivering
flowers to Amanda
and Evie's graveside

RIGHT: At one of many of Amanda's weekend vintage shows

BELOW: Discovering we were pregnant with Weston on Thanksgiving 2013

Amanda and
Angela Agricola

Bringing Weston home
from the hospital
to our Sunnyfield
Court house

TOP: Weston as a baby

BOTTOM: Amanda's family (left to right, Amber with Audrey and Raegan, Gavin, Dad, Angela, James, Mom, Me and Weston, and Amanda)

TOP: Amber holding Amanda's hand while she lay unconscious in the hospital on November 10th, 2015

BOTTOM: My family (left to right, Jono, Tessa, Dad, Mom, Me, Weston, and Amanda)

TOP: Some of the Israel team (left to right, Craig and Samantha Walker, Katie Bailey, Brad Cooper, Jason Moorhead, Perry Noble, Allison Kring, Me, Hyking Paul, Kelsey Massey, and Lauren Bryant)

BOTTOM: Kenneth Wagner and me at the 2016 World Series in Cleveland, OH

TOP: Our wedding day, August 1st, 2008

BOTTOM: Weston's first birthday, the only birthday
Amanda got to celebrate with him

ABOVE: Spending time with Levi Lusko after he reached out early in my grief journey

LEFT: The day Amanda and I first met outside of Steak and Shake

ABOVE: Amanda as everyone remembers her—full of joy and laughing

RIGHT: Kristi and I when we first started dating, attempting (unsuccessfully) to keep our relationship discreet

TOP: The first time Kristi and I made a public appearance as an official couple was at our annual Halloween party

BOTTOM: November of 2017, right after Kristi and I got engaged

TOP: December 17, 2017, our wedding day

BOTTOM: Just after we each saw each other for the first time on our wedding day

ABOVE: Cohen
was born in
November of 2019

RIGHT: From broken
to blended

"In fact, that picture you showed me of your team in the hotel fitness room reminds me of the Last Supper, where Jesus took His disciples to an *upper room* to share their last meal before He was crucified. He tells them His body is about to be broken and His blood poured out at the cross, and then He puts a towel around His waist and washes each of their feet, as a household servant would. It's a powerful image, Davey. In that passage, you can see His heart to lead the way in service and surrender in front of His best friends. When I look at this picture I can almost *see* Jesus's heart coming through Amanda. She was also leading the way in surrender in front of her closest friends."

I pulled up the picture again and zoomed in on the touchscreen. I could see Amanda's blurry, pixelated, furrowed brow. She would always wear that look when she was either deeply concentrating or sorting through conflicting feelings in her heart.

"You see, Davey, if your goal in this world is to make life easy and comfortable for yourself, joy and happiness will always elude you. This world is not comfortable or easy. Those who believe it *is* are only fooling themselves. It's a difficult world. We will all endure pain, heartache, suffering, and sadness. Some to a certain degree, and others to a greater degree. But we all experience it.

"Many people try to adhere to the belief that if you are following Jesus everything is going to be roses, daisies, sunshine, and rainbows, that you'll always be healthy and wealthy, that Jesus was a feather-haired hippy who just passed out suckers and hugs to everyone. The two problems with that philosophy are history and the Bible. Both tell us that those who followed Jesus the *closest* actually went through the *most* suffering.

"But life isn't difficult just for the Jesus follower. It's difficult for *everyone*. The Jesus follower is able to walk through difficulty differently. He has an anchor of hope to keep him grounded during the difficult times. So, instead of trying to make life easy, our goal should be this: *live well in a difficult world.*

"Davey, hear this: If you chase after happiness, it will flee from you. Chase holiness—become more like Jesus—and true happiness will cling to you . . . not a circumstantial happiness, but a joy that sees you through any circumstance."

I was amazed by Dr. Walker's words and wisdom. I took a moment to jot down some notes, my brain swirling with everything he had just said. Then I asked him another question.

"So, how do I chase holiness in this situation?"

Dr. Walker sat back in his chair, "Well, now. That is the question we're here to resolve, isn't it? And we'll tackle it just as soon as we get a cup of coffee. Cream? Sugar?"

I politely declined, and Dr. Walker left the room, leaving me mulling over my notes from the past hour of conversation, the question of how to experience joy in the midst of all of this still plaguing me.

A few minutes later Dr. Walker returned to the office and took a seat in the lounge chair across from me. By now I had moved to a couch on the other side of the room. A coffee table with a floral arrangement in the center separated the two of us.

"So you want to know how to pursue holiness, not happiness, in the midst of your situation?" Dr. Walker made a clicking noise inside his mouth and crinkled his eyebrows as if considering how he was going to craft his next words. After a few seconds he spoke again slowly and resolutely. "Suffer well."

For a minute, silence hung between the two of us. I thought maybe I knew what he meant. But I wasn't sure. What did it mean to suffer well? How exactly could I go about doing that? As if he were reading my mind, Dr. Walker continued.

"What I mean is you share in Jesus's suffering. When you come to a crossroads where you have to choose between comfort and following Jesus, you choose Jesus. Amanda did, and in doing so she was more like Jesus than *ever*, right before she met Him face-to-face. She followed well, suffered well, and then stepped into heaven. And the beautiful thing is, at the very moment she died, all of her suffering was immediately eliminated . . . undone."

I took a deep breath at the reminder of the last moment of Amanda's life. Dr. Walker continued.

"J. R. R. Tolkien once implied in his writing that when you cross over into heaven, everything sad that was done on earth becomes untrue! Like it never happened. Everything that was done to her in those final moments was immediately *undone*. She walked through the doorstep of eternity in victory, not as a victim . . . why? Because she had trusted Jesus for her salvation."

Dr. Walker folded his hands and began again. "Davey, earth is a place where what's been done can't be undone. So what you have to figure out now, since you can't change what's been done, is what to *do*. But as you figure that out, remember that heaven is a place where what's been done has *already* been undone, all because of what Jesus *already did* on the cross for us."

I sat back in my chair to let this thought marinate for a moment. His perspective on pain and suffering was simply amazing. "Dr. Walker, this is incredible. I've never heard perspective like this on tragedy from anyone."

"Well, it's impossible to retain this perspective as long as you think the here and now is all there is to life. Most people live intoxicated by this world . . . stuff, career, relationships, thrills.

They are lulled to believe that this is the best there is to life, when in fact God has so much more for each of us."

Suddenly I was reminded of an interaction I recently had with Weston and chuckled. "Ha! It's kind of like Weston and the zoo!" I blurted out. Dr. Walker gave me an inquisitive look, and I grinned, realizing he couldn't read my thoughts.

I launched into an explanation. "Just last week I planned to take Weston to the zoo in Indy. While I was getting ready to go, I sat him down to watch *Daniel Tiger*—you know, the *Mr. Rogers' Neighborhood* remake? I thought it fitting for him to watch since he was about to see a *real* tiger for the first time. Well, when it was time to load him and all our stuff in the car to leave, I turned *Daniel Tiger* off. He absolutely lost his mind and threw the biggest fit I've ever seen in my life!

"I tried my hardest to explain to him that we were going to see a *real* tiger, in person, but how do you rationalize with an eighteen-month-old who has never seen a real tiger before? He totally didn't get it!

"The whole way to the zoo he cried and cried and cried, like he was being tortured! He didn't realize that the animals I wanted to show him, the destination I had in mind for him, was so much greater than the cartoon animals he had been experiencing on screen all morning."

"Whoa! You should preach that, Davey! That's so good! That's exactly why we get bogged down in the midst of suffering. We scream when the TV is turned off on us, not realizing God is driving us to an even better destination!" Dr. Walker gave me an enormous grin, teeth gleaming through his beard.

"Davey, you remember that journal entry you showed me at the beginning of this conversation? Amanda talked about Job. Talk about a guy who suffered well. He was blessed with more wealth, power, and influence than anyone in the land *and* had a fantastic family. Then, all of it was taken from him in a matter of one day.

"He was left with a nagging wife and three friends who tried to tell him the reason this was happening to him was because he had sinned against God. His wife berated him, telling him he should curse God and die. But Job didn't. Like Amanda pointed out in the journal, God blessed Job's life greater in the second half than He did in the first half. Even in suffering, God has great blessing in store for us, as we walk faithfully with Him."

"Wait, didn't Job get mad at God?" I interrupted suddenly. "Didn't he doubt God? I mean it's pretty unrealistic to think someone could go through what Job did . . . um, what *I have* . . . and not doubt God!?"

"Well, yes. Job *questioned* God. But that's different than *doubting* God. Think about it. If he had doubted the existence of God in his suffering, why would he have talked to God so much? Much of the end of the book is dialogue between Job and God. Job is asking questions—but God isn't intimidated by Job's questions, just like He's not intimidated by our questions.

"In fact, I believe when we ask sincere questions of God, when we engage Him in our suffering, we may not get the *results* we're looking for, but we always gain something far greater—deeper *relationship* with Him. What do you think Weston will value more in the long run? A trip to the zoo or quality time with his daddy? We may not find all our answers in that relationship— at least not on this side of eternity—but we'll find something better . . . *healing.*"

As Dr. Walker said this, it triggered my memory of something I had recently read. *Something about what we gain. What we gain.* I tried to place the memory in my brain. Where had I seen that? *Hmmm. Oh! "The gain of loss!"* I had to tell him.

"Dr. Walker, a month ago I was given a book called *The Path of Loneliness*. It was written by Elisabeth Elliot. You know her story, right?"

"Absolutely I do! What an incredible and very fitting story to explore in your situation."

Elisabeth Elliot was the wife of Jim Elliot, the great missionary and martyr. The two of them were missionaries to South America and devoted their lives to spreading the good news of Jesus to impoverished and unreached people in Ecuador. They abandoned comfort and safety to connect people to Christ.

I had read a book by Elisabeth Elliot when I was eighteen years old called *Passion and Purity*. This book was very instrumental in my life in helping me settle with being single. I believe God used this book to prepare my heart to meet Amanda. A compilation of Elisabeth's prayer journals during the time she and Jim were dating, *Passion and Purity* is a raw account of her wrestling with whether God was calling her to marry Jim. She begged for contentment in her season of singleness and continually and actively wrote prayers surrendering to God's plan even if it meant doing ministry as a single woman the rest of her life.

As they sought Jesus's plan together, Jim and Elisabeth both felt God was calling them to get married and devote their lives to mission work. For the next two years, they would be considered a power couple, accomplishing much more for God's kingdom than they ever could apart, but something tragic happened that caused their good fortune to reverse. They would soon accomplish exceedingly more for the kingdom *apart* than they ever could have *together*.

Jim and four other missionaries had spent months airdropping supplies over an unreached and notoriously hostile South American tribe, known as the Huaorani. After some time they felt the Huaorani were returning friendly signals. Passionate about seeing this tribe come to faith in Jesus, Jim and his associates landed the plane on the shore of this tribe's territory. They were met by the arrival of a group of about ten Huaorani warriors. The natives attacked and killed each of the men. Elisabeth and the rest of the wives sat by, helplessly listening to the entire attack on shortwave radio.

Some time later, Elisabeth amazingly went into the same territory herself and shared the gospel, forgiveness, and the hope of heaven with the very tribe that had executed her husband.

Thirteen years later, Elisabeth was remarried to Addison Leitch, a professor of theology at Gordon-Conwell Theological Seminary. Elisabeth had found a new romance, and her capacity to love was being restored. However, just four years later, Addison died of cancer. She wrote *The Path of Loneliness* as a reflection on what God had taught her through the tragic loss of her two husbands.

"Dr. Walker, Elisabeth said in *The Path of Loneliness* that what she gained in relationship with the *Giver* far outweighed the loss of the *gift*."

"Wow! *What she gained in relationship with the Giver far outweighed the loss of the gift.*" Dr. Walker repeated as he jotted some notes in his notebook. He looked up at me at the last stroke of his pen. "And that's what I feel this next season is for you, Davey. It's about learning to be content again. We'll call it 'A New Season of Contentment.'" Dr. Walker loves giving helpful titles to things he teaches his patients.

"God used singleness to teach you contentment with Him and Him alone when you were eighteen. In this next season of singleness, as painful as it has been and is going to be, God wants to teach you how to be content with just Him once again."

I shook my head and glanced at my wedding band still on my left ring finger. "I don't know if I can, Dr. Walker. It's too painful."

"I know, Davey. Listen to me, Amanda led the way in surrender . . . and she's *still* leading the way. Now you have a choice to make. What's done can't be undone. You can't change this situation. So you have to ask yourself, Are you willing to surrender to God's plan in this? Are you willing to surrender to the *process* of discovering His purpose in your pain?"

I turned my head to stare out the window at the sunshine and palm trees, swaying in the warm Florida breeze. Something about being in the sun the whole week made me feel a little softer than I had been before, a little more ready, like I was melting. I could almost feel my heart warming up, thawing out the calloused and frozen fear that had been sitting there since November 10.

I wasn't quite sure what it would entail for me to surrender, and, frankly, in that moment I didn't understand exactly what Dr. Walker meant when he spoke of *purpose in my pain*. Not yet anyway. But God would soon place some key events in my life that would help provide more explanation.

13

THUMBPRINTS

A GUST OF WIND SWEPT UP THE GLOOMY STREET, BLOWING CANDY wrappers and empty beer cans out of the thistles and onto the sidewalks. I looked up and down Rader Street, one of many north-south streets that help to compose the grid of inner-city Indianapolis. Rows of neglected and rusted cars sat parked in both directions, hugging the curb and accessorizing the dilapidated neighborhood. It was early April, and the warmth my heart had begun to feel in Florida during my time with Dr. Walker was being cooled to an icy, dreary melancholy.

Normally in Indy, spring remained hidden behind the gray filter of late winter until early May. This year was no exception. I glanced over at the other volunteers working alongside me, piling leaves and garbage, shoveling unwanted refuse from the streets. One guy in our group caught my attention. Clad in Carhartt pants, a heavy jacket, work gloves, and with the brim of a baseball cap pulled over his eyes, he leaned over to pick up the remnants of a Styrofoam cup, dropped it in the trash bag he carried at his side, and scanned the periphery for another article to collect. I could see his breath emerging from his mouth as he leaned over to grab what looked like an old T-shirt out of some briars by the sidewalk.

Following my conversation with Pastor Martin Smith, I rallied the leaders of my congregation to begin a partnership with his church. This was the first day of our bimonthly community cleanups, our version of Adopt-a-Block, where we picked up trash, cut and weeded yards, repaired fences, and secured roofing for members of his congregation, all in an effort to build trust equity with the community and begin to bridge the divide between white suburban or midtown churches and inner-city black churches.

On this day we had around thirty-five volunteers from our church working alongside another twenty from Martin's church. The seeds that had been planted during my conversations with Martin and Shaun were beginning to take root and grow. They were still unseen, still obscure, but reaching downward to form a stable foundation for a dream I hadn't believed could develop this soon—building a community center for underprivileged and at-risk kids and teenagers.

Martin had informed me that the mayor of Indianapolis had issued six focus areas where violent crime, drug abuse, and sex trafficking were running rampant. He had asked the faith community as well as civil service groups to begin jumping into these areas to fight against the generational systemic poverty that was causing the high crime rates. Martin's church happened to sit in the zone that ranked number one on all the scales—highest crime, highest rate of drug trafficking, and highest poverty levels.

When I shared my dream with Martin at coffee that day, he informed me that a community center where kids could channel their creative energies to more healthy outlets like sports, music, performing arts, and career skills training was much needed, but what was more important was that mentoring relationships be established between the kids and the volunteers stepping into their community.

"This isn't *Field of Dreams*, Davey," he had said to me. "You can't just build it and they'll come. They don't trust you yet. I grew up in this community and have only been back for two years now and they barely trust me. If you just build something with no relationship or trust equity it'll sit empty in a matter of months. The vacant, boarded up homes you see lining the streets of our community are indicators of something deeper—vacant and boarded up lives."

I intuitively knew it was true as soon as he said it. Any ministry program is hollow if it's not undergirded by relationships. Relationships are what bring color to life. They're what enable you to see past your own experiences and biases and begin to understand someone else's vantage point. Relationships can be messy, drama filled, and take time to develop. But the impact relationships have is far longer lasting than drop-in-the-bucket programs. Martin was helping me understand that both our government and many of our suburban churches have turned to *programs* to be the quick fix for the disrepair of the inner city—and that's exactly why nothing has changed.

A few years before, our church began a campaign called "ForIndy." Started as a way to rally our people to random acts of kindness for people in our city, ForIndy's message was one of love, acceptance, and servitude. We were tired of churches making a name for themselves by what they stand against, what they protest, and what they picket. We wanted to build a reputation around what we're *for*. We're *for* better schools. We're *for* safer streets. We're *for* better marriages. We're *for* stronger communities. We're *for* people. We're *for* Indianapolis.

Our first and—up to this point—only steps in our ForIndy campaign had been two seasonal pushes of random acts of kindness around our city. If you were to search #ForIndy on social media outlets you'd see tons of posts of people performing acts of good service to others and spreading it to inspire others. Amanda had especially taken to this campaign. She loved to do small, seemingly insignificant acts of kindness for people to make their day. Among many other things, I remember her buying a box of donuts for a cop who sat outside her favorite donut shop to thank him for working hard and putting his life on the line to keep our streets safe.

Amanda even designed ForIndy T-shirts for our church—the front of the shirt bearing a large outline of the state of Indiana with a heart in the place of Indianapolis.

While we had garnered some media attention that helped make ForIndy go somewhat viral, I began to feel like we weren't making much of a difference with the energy we were putting forward. At the same leadership retreat in Cincinnati where the "upper room" picture was taken, four days before Amanda was killed, I told our leadership team we needed to shelf ForIndy. It just wasn't having the impact I had originally envisioned.

And then Amanda was murdered.

Suddenly the heart behind ForIndy found its nurture. Suddenly it shifted from unfocused random acts of kindness to a focused effort to shine the light of the gospel in the darkest places of our city. Suddenly it shifted from just making someone's day to changing someone's life.

I began to uncover even more complexity in our push to get ForIndy going as I devoured any reading material I could get my hands on regarding the subject of urban ministry. I read one book called *Toxic Charity* by Robert Lupton, founder and president of FCS Urban Ministries and who has done ministry in downtown Atlanta for forty years. He wrote that prior to moving into the inner city he lived in the suburbs and attended a large suburban—and predominantly white—church. Every Christmas their church planned an "adopt-a-family" initiative where they purchased Christmas gifts for less fortunate families in the city. On Christmas Day they swept down into the city, rang the door-bell at the family's home, dropped off the gifts, took pictures that they could show their friends and congregation, patted themselves on the back, and drove back to the suburbs to enjoy the rest of their festivities.

For years he lived under the notion that this act of charity was helping urban families. But when he and his wife felt called to sell their home in the suburbs and migrate to the inner city, they quickly learned what they thought was *helping* was actually *hurting*.

He writes about sitting in the home of one of his urban neighbors one Christmas Day when they received a knock at the door. It was one of these suburban families who had "adopted" them for Christmas. He watched, almost as a fly on the wall, as the kids enthusiastically took the gifts and began tearing into them, while their father slinked out of the living room and exited out the back door, not to return until late that evening. After opening all the gifts, the kids looked at their mom and inquired where their dad was. "He had to go to the store for a minute," she responded.

All at once Lupton recalls the subtle lessons that were ingrained in these kids that day—Dad doesn't have the means to give us a good Christmas (thereby stripping Dad of his dignity), Mom covers for Dad's shame, and all shiny, new things come from white families in the suburbs. Lupton talks about how the initial gratitude these kids demonstrated eventually erodes into expectation and ultimately entitlement.

I looked up from my rake. Over the last thirty minutes I had collected a pile of leaves, mud, and garbage in front of an abandoned house, its front porch leaning and boards darkening its windows and entryways. For a second I stared, imagining the family meals that once may have been shared in the dining room, the bath time giggles that may have filled its hallways, the bedtime stories that may have been told. I imagined evenings where kids played in its living room as parents washed dishes in its kitchen. What stole life from this home? Could it have been a similar event to what stole life from mine? And could it all be reversed?

Shortly after my conversation with Shaun, I spoke with the Indianapolis director of Habitat for Humanity. We sat in Shaun and Kristen's home and discussed this new vision God was giving me for helping to restore our city's neighborhoods. I told him about the Riverside community and our new partnership with Pastor Martin Smith. The director informed me that they currently had no presence in the Riverside area—that it was the one focus area they were not doing rehab work in. When I pressed him as to why he said, "We have to wait for a spiritual pioneer to go in there. If we build homes before someone begins rebuilding lives, those homes will be vacant in a matter of years."

A spiritual pioneer, I thought to myself as I stared at this decaying home hunched over in front of me. *Could this be our role? I wonder if God has put us in this place for a time such as this.*

It was difficult even for me, the visionary of the group, to connect how cleaning up the streets and cutting people's grass each week was going to help us get to the ultimate goal, the one that had been planted in my heart on the side of the stage at the youth conference just months before. That morning before our group began working, I tried to motivate the team by reading aloud from Isaiah 61:4. As I read from the passage, "They will rebuild the ancient ruins and restore the places long devastated; they will renew the ruined cities that have been devastated for generations" (NIV), I couldn't help but feel intimidated by this daunting task we had chosen to undertake.

How do we go from serving people through manual labor to bringing spiritual vitality back into a community? How do we go from meeting physical needs to meeting the deeply entrenched spiritual needs that plague this community? The more I was learning about the complexity of urban ministry, the more disheartened I got. On the one hand I was fueled by an urgency to take back ground the Enemy had stolen when I found Amanda on the floor of my living room that morning. On the other hand I was realizing just how complicated the issues are that lead to systemic poverty, crime, and gang violence. My urgency was being met head-on by complexity, and I was beginning to understand there was going to be no quick fix in the process of restoring our city. It was going to take a lot of hard work... and a lot of time.

I finished scooping the pile into a trash bag, pulled the drawstring, and tied it closed. I pulled my hat off and wiped the sweat that had begun to form on my brow with my forearm. Even in the chill of the early spring with its gusts of wind, the couple of hours of raking and hauling had warmed my body. Little beads of perspiration peppered my face.

I placed my thumb on the underside of the bill to put my hat back on when something on the brim grabbed my attention. It was a bloodstain. A thumbprint from the morning I found Amanda. I hadn't worn this hat since the day I left the hospital with my mom.

Suddenly the image of Amanda's body face down on our living room floor flashed in front of my eyes. The blood surrounding her head. The credit cards scattered around her. A broken lamp lying beside her. I could hear her gasping for breath again. My heart began to race. My face grew hot. A thousand tiny knives pricked the back of my neck. My chest seized up as a surge of shock gripped my stomach. I began breathing quickly and deeply.

What's happening? Why can I see all this, hear all this so vividly again? It feels so real!

After what felt like several minutes of deep breaths, I snapped out of it. The images were gone. I was back on Rader Street in front of the vacant house. Now, however, I was sitting on the curb in a near fetal position.

I looked back down at my baseball cap and ran my thumb over the bloodstain a few times, trying to scrub it off the brim. It wasn't budging. Not even fading. It would be there for good. A thumbprint of blood. The only piece of Amanda's body I still had with me.

Look for the thumbprints, Davey. It was the voice. He seemed to be speaking more regularly these days.

Thumbprints? What about thumbprints? I directed my thoughts at the voice.

Look for thumbprints. The evidence that I provided and that led you to this. I'll lead you every step of the way through it—no matter how complex it may seem. Remember your meeting with Wendy Cooper.

I had nearly forgotten. Just weeks before this community cleanup I had been referred to one of the directors of the Indianapolis Housing Agency, Wendy Cooper. The director of Habitat for Humanity connected us and, after a few email exchanges, Wendy and I decided to meet up for coffee to discuss the Riverside area and how our church could partner with the city to bring vitality back into the neighborhood.

I sat in a booth at a downtown coffee shop waiting for Wendy to arrive. She was about five minutes late, and each time the bell in the doorway would ring announcing the arrival of another customer, I'd lift my head and glance over in that direction. If it was a woman, I'd wait for an indicator that she too was looking for someone she had never met. After several women entered the coffee shop, none making eye contact with me as they looked around the room, a petite lady in a black peacoat and scarf stepped into the shop. Before I could read whether she was looking for someone or not, she glanced over at me and immediately made her way to my booth. As she approached I noticed there was something strangely familiar about her.

"Davey, it's good to see you."

"Wendy? Um . . . yeah. Great to meet you. I'm Davey Blackburn," I replied as I got up from the booth and extended my hand to introduce myself.

Wendy gave me a congenial smile as she took my hand. "You don't remember me, do you?"

I searched her face, my hand still clutching hers, unable to figure out why this lady seemed so familiar. She obviously recognized me, and I was now embarrassed I couldn't reciprocate.

"I was your neighbor, two houses down from your Sunnyfield Court house. You and Amanda often hired my daughter, Iman, to do childcare for you when you first started the church in your house."

My eyes widened. I did remember! Though I had met Wendy only briefly as she was unloading groceries from her car one afternoon, Amanda and I shared many conversations with Iman, who I now realized was a twenty-five-year younger version of her mom.

"I was so glad when you reached out to me via email, Davey. I've been so touched by your story. I didn't know Amanda very well outside of a handful of conversations with her, but my heart is absolutely crushed for you and Weston. Amanda used to speak so much encouragement to Iman. She was a very special person. And I know God is going to use this situation in a mighty way to bring healing to many, many people."

This was the backdrop of my conversation with one of the main movers and shakers in Indianapolis housing.

Thumbprints, Davey. Thumbprints.

The voice snapped me back into present reality, sitting on the curb in front of the dilapidated, boarded-up house. The other volunteers had slowly made their way farther down the street to my left. I could hear an occasional laugh in the distance coming from the group as they continued to fill trash bags.

Just then, out of the corner of my right eye I noticed a figure standing on the other side of the street a couple of houses down, staring at me.

It was a boy. An African American boy.

He looked to be about twelve or thirteen years old and had two basketballs in his hands, one between each palm and hip. I met his gaze, and he darted his eyes but remained standing right where he was. My mind flashed back to sitting onstage at the youth conference a few months before, staring at another twelve-year-old black boy. I continued to peer in this boy's direction. He seemed not to pay attention but stood there as if waiting for someone.

I couldn't help but wonder what house this boy lived in, what his family was like, where he went to school, whether he was a good kid or a troublemaker. And then I couldn't help but wonder if six years ago, this could have been Larry Taylor—a seemingly harmless boy waiting on some friends to join him for some hoops.

And then the feelings surfaced again. All of them.

Fear. Anger. Hatred. Judgment. Prejudice.

Like a volcano waiting to erupt, I narrowed my focus on this boy and my heart rate quickened.

This time, however, I was better equipped. My conversation with Shaun had set a lens for my emotions. These feelings were normal, but that didn't make them right. I knew exactly what I needed to do.

I slowly rose to my feet and began to walk across the street. As the gap between this boy and me narrowed, I could see him nervously stiffen. His gaze met mine as I paused directly in front of him.

"What's up, man," I started. "What's your name?"

"Anthony," he spouted. His expression was cool and hard. "Anthony, you going to hoop with some friends?"

"Yeah."

"Where do you guys hoop at?"

"Riverside Park." Anthony remained expressionless.

"Wow, that's quite a hike down there, isn't it? They have some good courts?"

"Eh . . . they're okay."

"Well, Anthony. What if my friends and I put a couple hoops right here off this street. Would you guys use them?"

Anthony's face lit up. The callousness he previously displayed immediately melted. "Yeah! That'd be dope!"

"Cool. Would you mind if we came to ball with you too?"

"Naw! That'd be cool!"

"Awesome. We'll see what we can do." I extended my fist toward Anthony, the universal sign for offering "knucks." He lightly pounded my fist. As he was pulling away a voice boomed from the front porch of a house down the street.

"Anthony!" A teenager, probably seventeen or eighteen, strutted down the steps. His shorts sagged well below his waistline and the front of his T-shirt displayed multiple vulgarities. His eyes were squinty and his face cold and hard. He took a long drag from a smoke in his mouth, pulled it away from his lips, and flicked it to the ground.

"You comin'? We ain't got all day!"

Anthony spun around and began sauntering in his direction. I met the older teenager's glare as Anthony strolled away. Anthony glanced over his shoulder back at me and lingered for a moment before disappearing with the older one around the block.

I pulled my jacket closed as another icy gust swept down the street. I stood there for the next several minutes gazing past the building Anthony and this other boy had just ducked behind. I couldn't help but wonder which direction Anthony's life would take in the next few years and whether or not we could actually do something to influence it for good.

14

BACK TO GROUND ZERO

I STARED ACROSS THE VALLEY, WEAVING ITS WAY LIKE A DESERT snake through the landscape of the Judaean Mountains. The brim of my hat was nearly drenched from sweat, and the desert sun stung the back of my neck. Jerusalem's iconic Old City sprawled out in front of me like an old postcard.

The Dome of the Rock towered above every other building within the city walls. Its gold-embossed dome reflected the bright light and sent a blinding glare over the entire city. Through the haze, in the distance, I could see the Tower of David stretch into the sky. To my right, the noon prayer calls erupted from a Muslim minaret, clashing with the chorus of church bells chiming from the Basilica of the Agony behind me.

The taupe-colored stones that saturated the cityscape practically had me convinced I had stepped back into some distant time. I half expected to run into Jesus and His disciples around the next bend of the sidewalk.

We were at the top of the Mount of Olives, overlooking the Kidron Valley into the Old City of Jerusalem. I had been invited by Pastor Perry Noble to accompany him and forty other folks on a ten-day tour of the Holy Land. Visiting Israel had always been on my bucket list, and when NewSpring Church offered to cover my way, I certainly couldn't refuse. Now, I was experiencing a once-in-a-lifetime trip that, for me, was more timely and pivotal to my healing than I could have anticipated.

Since losing Amanda in November, I had been seeing life in one color—gray. It was the middle of April now, we were on day six of this trip, and I was already beginning to feel color being injected back into my life. There seemed to be a consistent theme that followed us with each stop we made: the powerful things God does throughout history to reverse evil's work in the world.

I was still ruminating over the experience I'd had in Caesarea Maritima three days before. We had been traveling from Tel Aviv to Galilee and stopped en route at the ruined site of Herod Agrippa's palace—along with the iconic gladiator arena on the shores of the Mediterranean Sea. The tour guide ushered us into a massive amphitheater, mostly still intact despite the centuries of battering it had endured from the salty ocean air.

My friend and fellow pastor Brad Cooper took on the teaching role that day. I had known Brad since college. He was part of the leadership of the Fellowship of Christian Athletes at Clemson University while I was pioneering our chapter of FCA at Southern Wesleyan. As former college athletes and enthusiastic ministry leaders, we formed an immediate bond. He and I would often get together at Dyar's, a local meat-and-three diner that quickly and aptly became nicknamed "Diarrhea's," to talk ministry, sports, and life.

Brad became a big brother to me. He left his role at FCA to lead the student ministry at NewSpring Church and it was largely his influence that connected me to a staff position there after I graduated college. It was also his office I sat in as I wept over the transition from NewSpring to planting a church in Indy.

He flew up to Amanda's celebration service and after that was a voice of wisdom and encouragement through some of the most difficult days. I was getting to spend a lot of quality time with him on this trip, which proved to be just the shot of spiritual adrenaline I needed. We all took our seats and plugged in our tour guide headphones as he began to teach.

"What you're sitting in right now is the very amphitheater where the apostle Paul gave his testimony to Festus and Herod Agrippa. You can read about it in Acts 25 and 26. This setting, the ruins of the ancient city of Caesarea Maritima, has powerful implications.

"Over my right shoulder you see the remains of Herod's Palace overlooking the ocean. When we walk down there, you're going to notice something. Herod was demonstratively ostentatious." Brad paused for dramatic emphasis, and I looked to the person next to me and grinned. We were all thinking the same thing: *Ostentatious, Brad? Really?* Brad was notorious for using million-dollar words. Everyone who had ever sat under his teaching knew it and often had their pocket dictionary handy.

He took a breath and continued, "In fact, he was so arrogant, he built a massive freshwater pool in the middle of the saltwater ocean. He ordered thousands of gallons of freshwater to be funneled in from inland via aqueducts just to maintain his pool. He made sure to establish his governance as a symbol of the power and might of the Roman Empire.

"What's important to note is that, according to the Jewish people, the Roman Empire represented one thing: *evil.* The extent of this evil is perhaps best demonstrated by the gladiator arena you see over my left shoulder." He turned in that direction. "As we walk into the arena in a few minutes, you'll see names carved in the rock of early Christians who suffered grotesque fates at the hands of the Roman government."

Gladiator arenas. The pure dominance and evil of Rome. This was beginning to sound all too familiar to me. I leaned forward to listen more intently to what Brad was saying, now curious to get a closer look at the two sites he had just described.

"As much evil as was orchestrated here in Caesarea Maritima, you also need to know there was another pivotal incident that occurred in this ancient city—one that shapes who you and I are today." We all held our breath to hear what he was going to say next. He paused for a moment, as if holding in a secret, and then said, "The first Gentile to receive Jesus's offer of salvation lived right here in Caesarea."

A bit confused as to why this was so significant, I cocked my head in Brad's direction as he continued.

"If you recall, at that time the Jews believed salvation and right relationship with God was available only to their own race— the Jewish people. They were God's chosen people of old. Jesus was Jewish, so naturally they considered themselves members of an exclusive club. But let me ask you something: Is anyone sitting in this group today Jewish?"

Everyone glanced around, looking at the group to see if anyone would respond affirmatively. No one did.

"No?" Brad continued. "That means we would all be labeled 'Gentiles.' Anyone not Jewish by ethnicity is a Gentile. So let me ask you something. If the promise of salvation was extended only to Jewish people, how have any of us experienced it? Each of you has stepped into relationship with God through the sacrifice of His Son, Jesus, right?"

Everyone nodded. "Then how do you suppose that occurred?" Brad asked.

I'm sure he noticed the blatantly inquisitive looks on all of our faces and decided to quickly answer his own rhetorical question. "Because someone went first. His name was Cornelius." We were all riveted as Brad continued.

"Cornelius was a Roman centurion, an official of the Roman army, stationed here in Caesarea Maritima. Ironically, he just might have been on a trajectory to become one of the commanders ordered to execute early Christians in the arena in front of you. But one day, Cornelius was told the good news that Jesus died for him so that he could have new life, and he received the gift of salvation and forgiveness of sins! And listen, folks, in the very place where some of the *worst* atrocities of all of history occurred, the gospel was made available to *all* people, not only the Jews. Cornelius was Patient Zero and you're sitting at Ground Zero."

I just sat there. Paralyzed. Overwhelmed. Here it was again. Out of the gravest of monstrosities, God once again brought forth new life. Could He really do this in my situation? This seemed to be a consistent theme in history, but is the God from history the same one who holds my circumstances too?

Brad pivoted on his right foot and motioned at the structure surrounding us. "This amphitheater happens to be the only Roman amphitheater that faces west. Every other ancient Roman theater faces a different direction. Here's what this means: Cornelius gets saved, opening salvation up to all people. Consequently the gospel gets catapulted westward, *boom!*"

Brad made an explosion motion with his hands toward the Mediterranean Sea to the west. "It was almost as if the gospel were amplified directly from the stadium where we sit this very moment. Sure, because of this place, hundreds and thousands lost their life. But also because of this place, you and I had the chance to respond to *new life* in Christ Jesus!"

Brad elevated his voice to emphasize his next point. "This city is a physical reminder of what the Bible says in Genesis 50:20, 'You intended to harm me, but God intended it for good to accomplish what is now being done, the saving of many lives.' How many of you are grateful today that God uses what the Enemy means for evil and turns it around for our good ... and in doing so brings others to faith in Christ?!"

People all around me began clapping. I sat there, stunned, as goosebumps crept up the back of my neck. I slowly turned my head and stared at the whitecaps crashing over the rocky shore. Here I was, a Gentile who knows Jesus because of what was done in Caesarea Maritima—because of the good news that was preached *and* because of the evil that took place. All I could think was, *A hundred years from now, how many people will possibly say, "I know Jesus better because of the evil inflicted on the Blackburn family, because of Amanda Blackburn's death?"*

Already my family and ministry team were receiving a barrage of messages, telling us how Amanda's story was touching so many. Thousands were writing in and sharing the impact it was making in their own life.

What the Enemy means for evil, God uses for good . . .

As the applause died down, Brad turned the floor over to Gilla, our Israeli tour guide. She escorted the group down the steps and across the walkway that led to the ruins of Herod's Palace. I remained pensive in my seat. Brad glanced back at me, noticed me staring out at the arena in the distance, and made his way to my side. He sat down next to me and put his arm around me. "What the Enemy means for evil, God uses for good, and for the saving of many lives. Davey, that was true back then and it's true today. The same God who did it back then is the same God who is walking through this with you, and He *will* do it in your life."

I stared in disbelief through tear-stained eyes. I didn't disbelieve that God *could* do it in my life. I was in utter disbelief and awe that God cared enough for me and for my situation to make sure I made it to Israel to be present for this moment. It felt like He had orchestrated it all just for me, like I was the only one in that amphitheater, the only one on this trip. It was as if Jesus Himself was guiding me to each site and whispering to me:

Davey, this world is much bigger than your world. History is much bigger than your lifetime. I know it's painful, but don't get so bogged down in your circumstances that you fail to miss the larger story of what I'm doing in history. You and Amanda always prayed to be a part of something much bigger than yourselves, and now you are. I know you would have never asked for this nor wished it on anyone else, and neither would I have, but I'm going to use this for good. What the Enemy means for evil, I mean for good ... and for the saving of many, many lives.

Now as I stared across the gaping Kidron Valley into the Old City of Jerusalem, I could still feel the lingering weight of that day in Caesarea Maritima. Other tourists bustled around me, nudging their way to the railing at the edge of the precipice in an effort to capture that perfect selfie with the Dome of the Rock peering through the background.

In the swirl of the hustle around me, all I could think about was just how God was going to turn this around for good. *I hear it, God. I just don't know if I can see it yet.*

I had no idea that what was about to happen next would begin to settle my quandary, bring clarity to my questions, and would forever stand out to me as one of the single greatest "God moments" of this entire journey.

15

FIGHT OR FLIGHT

"Okay, everyone! Let's go ahead and grab a seat!" Pastor Perry's voice was unmistakable. Standing at a towering six feet eight inches, he definitely stuck out in a crowd no matter where he was.

"We're going to walk down to the Garden of Gethsemane in just a moment, but before we do, I want to lay a backdrop for what you're about to walk into."

We all scurried to find a seat that would position us close to Perry. Listening to a teacher in these settings with all the hum of tourists—not to mention the bleating of camels—in the background was nearly impossible if you didn't get a seat front and center. There was probably not a person in that group who didn't consider Perry one of the best Bible teachers they'd ever heard.

I had spent the last twelve years sitting under his teaching and pastoring—four in college, four on staff at NewSpring, and every Monday morning of the last four, listening to his podcast as I recovered from what pastors often affectionately refer to as the day-after-Sunday "holy hangover."

Several weeks prior, Perry had asked me to join him onstage after we returned from our trip to the Holy Land to talk about what God had been teaching me over the last few months since Amanda's death. I agreed but couldn't help but be a little nervous. Don't get me wrong, I was accustomed to being onstage. I did it at my own church each week. But in my mind, there was a certain aura that accompanied a NewSpring stage. It had always been my dream to teach to the congregation that had played such a huge role in shaping me through college.

Now, here was my longtime mentor and pastor and friend, asking me to join him onstage. The thrill of the opportunity was dwarfed by the weight of the responsibility not only to be on that stage but also to be sharing Amanda's and my story. I couldn't help but wonder, *Am I ready? What will I say? How can I put words to my feelings and to what God is teaching me?*

What had me more anxious than these looming questions was the prospect of how public this interview could be. I knew there would be tens of thousands listening to us. Recently, we had learned several news stations wanted to cover the interview as well. One was even planning to live stream the entire service on their network website. I had this gnawing feeling in the pit of my stomach that this interview was going to open the floodgates for more requests to share the story.

I couldn't know for sure, but I had a feeling this was going to be more than just an interview; this was going to be the start of a whole new cross to carry—one I wasn't sure I was ready for.

On top of that, I was increasingly burdened by this new responsibility of being a single dad. Weston was growing up quickly, and a slew of questions plagued me: *How do I play the role of dad* and *mom? Will he be traumatized for the rest of his life because of losing his mom? As he gets older, how do I answer his questions about what exactly happened to Amanda? Will he become bitter toward God for taking his mother?*

"As most of us know," Perry's voice broke into my thoughts, "the Garden of Gethsemane is the place Jesus visited with His disciples just before He was arrested, put on trial, and killed. It was a spot He often visited with His disciples, but this trip was different than the others. Knowing His *body* was about to undergo extreme torture, this is where Jesus decided to put His *will* to death.

"You see, Jesus knew His purpose was to come and die, but that didn't keep Him from human emotions of fear and trepidation. In fact, Scripture illustrates to us just how anxious Jesus was when He knelt in the garden."

My mind flashed to the opening scene of *The Passion of the Christ* where a single beam of moonlight highlighted Jesus's agonizing face, eyes staring to the heavens, His hair matted with sweat and tears streaming down His cheeks. The notion that we were about to walk through the very garden where this iconic conversation between Jesus and His heavenly Father took place had me pinching myself.

Perry went on, "Jesus was so anxious about the thought of suffering and dying that He began to sweat drops of blood. This happens to be a viable albeit rare medical condition known as *hematidrosis,* where the body excretes blood from sweat pores because of mental and physical duress. Now, I've suffered with anxiety and had panic attacks, but I've had nothing compared to this!

"It's almost as if Jesus was already feeling the weight of the sin of the entire world on His shoulders. And in this moment we see a glimpse of Jesus's humanity. He tries to get out of the whole thing. He looks to heaven and makes a request, 'My Father, if it be possible, let this cup pass from Me.' In this moment He wants to skirt His assignment. He considers escape."

Escape . . . Yes . . . Escape sounds nice.

Escape is exactly what I wanted to do. I could identify with the notion of escape. This whole trip to Israel felt a bit like an escape. No one recognized me. No one stopped me while I ran errands. No one shared with me his story of pain. Inundated with messages from people all over the world, I was beginning to feel the crushing weight of pain—and not just my own but other people's as well. It was becoming too much to handle.

I can't hear one more story of pain, God! I have enough of my own I'm trying to deal with! I'm tired of carrying everyone else's!

Now halfway around the world from home, I was beginning to feel relief from it all. However, the thought of willingly stepping back into it—and with potentially greater volume than before—terrified me.

"This is a powerful moment in history, but to the Jewish person it would have held much more significance. You see, the Jewish reader would have understood the route Jesus and the disciples took that night to enter the garden."

Perry pivoted on his right foot and pointed off to the left side of the landscape spread out in front of us. "You see that building with a dome off in the distance to your left? That is the location where Jesus sat in the upper room with His disciples."

The upper room. My mind flashed back to the upper room in Cincinnati with Amanda and our leadership team. Each time I heard the term *upper room* now I couldn't help but be reminded of her prayer of surrender.

"They would have left that building and walked down into the Kidron Valley." Perry motioned with his hand as if he was tracing the trail with his finger. "Up this pathway to the Mount of Olives and on into the Garden of Gethsemane. This is the route history records for us. But it's not the first time someone took this route." Perry's inflection revealed something significant was to follow.

"The first time history documents this route is a thousand years *before* Jesus, when King David takes it in 2 Samuel 15 to *escape* his problems."

King David. My ears perked. *Geez. I keep hearing things about King David!*

"If you recall," Perry continued, "David was in one of the darkest times of his life. He lost one of his sons to murder, and the murderer—another son, Absalom—staged a coup to take over the kingdom. Now Absalom's troops were seeking to take David's life as well. David left his home—right next to the upper room—descended into the Kidron Valley, and marched up to the top of the Mount of Olives. The priest met him there and gave him a warning. 'David, if you leave the city, you leave the ark of the covenant.'"

Perry paused for a second to let the idea sink in for those of us listening. Then he continued.

"The ark of the covenant housed the very presence of God. What the priest was telling David on top of the Mount of Olives was this: 'David, if you run away from your problems, you'll be running away from God's presence and plan for your life. Sure, if you go back into the city, the problem may kill you, but there are hurting and enslaved people that need you to fight for their freedom—even if it requires your life.'

"Unfortunately, King David refused to go back into the city for fear for his life. He ran, straight into the Judaean desert." Perry pointed behind us. "But a thousand years later, a greater David—Jesus—was presented with a very similar predicament, only the repercussions of His decision carried far more weight: the salvation of *all* of mankind. He knelt in the garden, at a crossroads.

"Jesus knew that if He went back into the city, death wasn't just a possibility; it was inevitable. He could just run away and escape into the Judaean desert. He could go into hiding for a while. But then who was going to die to free humanity?"

Perry dropped his notebook to his side and considered the small crowd in front of him. "I want you to see this is a temptation for all of us. We are all tempted to run away from our problems—the difficult situations in our life. This is why men and women give up on their marriages, why people struggle to gain control of their finances, why folks never step into their true calling in life, why people become addicted to drugs and alcohol, why men walk out on their families—because it's just easier to *escape.*"

Why men walk out on their families. I remembered hearing a statistic that 85 percent of male inmates grew up without a dad. *Larry Taylor grew up without a dad. I wonder if Anthony's dad is present in his life. If the dad sticks around and embraces his role, rather than escaping, could we eliminate 85 percent of the crime in our city?*

Perry's voice interrupted my thinking. "We intuitively know that by stepping into the hard thing it will require us to die . . . to die to our self . . . our selfish desires, our comfort and convenience." He raised both of his arms as if embracing the audience in front of him and then stretched them to the sky and looked up. "But Jesus didn't run. He didn't try to escape. In fact, in a powerful moment of surrender, Jesus declares these words over His life: '*Father . . . not my will, but yours be done.*'"

I remembered Amanda's prayer again: *God, I want my agenda for my life to be Your agenda for my life.*

"So as we make our way into the garden, I want you all to spread out and think about this one idea: Maybe pain and problems in your life are the preparation grounds God uses to bring life and healing to others. The question you have to wrestle with is, Are you going to try to escape it, or are you willing to *embrace* it?"

With that, Perry dismissed us. Everyone stood and began to follow one after the other into the garden. I lingered behind, holding up the rear.

My legs felt like Jell-O, wavering at every step. I knew God was trying to speak to me about something, almost as if I was in the same predicament as King David, preparing to have my own conversation with God in the Garden of Gethsemane.

Davey, if you run away you'll be running away from My presence and My plan for your life. Sure, if you go back into the city it may kill you, but there are hurting and enslaved people who need you to fight for their freedom—even if it requires your life.

I reached the garden entrance, stepped across the threshold, and began walking along the dirt path that wove its way through the landscape. All around me olive trees spread their gangly branches across the path at nearly head height.

My tour guide earpiece crackled as Gilla said something about the significance of olive pressing. It wouldn't register with me until later what exactly she was teaching and why it was so profound. All I could think about was this ultimatum I was confronted with—go back to my city to embrace parenting Weston alone, pastoring Resonate, and carrying Amanda's story . . . or *escape*! I already knew which one sounded easier. I made my way over to a bench in the corner of the garden and sat down.

I began to talk to God.

I didn't ask for this, Lord! I don't want it! Sure, I'm grateful people are being impacted by this, but I don't think I can carry the weight of this whole thing. I just want to be Davey—a struggling church planter with Amanda, Weston, and Evie! I don't want this notoriety, I don't want this calling! Can You take it from me? Is there any other way to do this?

I noticed a girl I knew walking in my direction. I had spent a couple of meals socializing with Laura and her husband, Pali. The three of us had certainly connected on a surface level, but I wasn't sure why it seemed she was making a beeline to me at this moment.

"May I sit down?" she asked as she approached my bench. "Su-sure." I slid over to give her some space.

"Davey, I've been waiting for a moment to talk to you about this.

"No moment has felt right up to this point. But as I saw you across the garden I felt this nudge in my heart that I needed to do this now."

I turned my head in her direction, a little confused.

"My husband passed away eight years ago."

What? The words coming from her mouth almost didn't register with me. I tried to focus on what she was saying, but the surprise of what she had just said threw me completely off guard.

"I came home one day and found him dead. He had a condition where he suffered from epileptic seizures. Normally when an episode would overtake him, I would be there to help him, to protect his airway until the seizure passed. This time ... I wasn't."

Not one time at our shared lunches and dinners had Laura let on that she'd experienced anything like this. I had no idea Pali wasn't her first husband.

I'm sure she could read my face—jaw dropped and speechless. Sometimes you get so caught up in your own pain and your own predicaments, you forget that right there, under your nose, sharing a seat across the aisle of a tour bus with you, is someone with their own story of pain, someone with their own heartache.

"Laura. I'm so sorry," I finally managed to reply.

"Thank you, but I'm not telling you to dump my story of pain on you. I'm telling you this because I want you to know that, eight years later, I'm experiencing God's redemption and restoration in my life and my story. I want you to know there is *life* on the other side of death." Laura brushed her hair behind her ear and turned to face me.

"I want you to know how inspired I am by watching you walk through this. God has entrusted an enormous amount of pain to you. After my husband died, someone shared with me this quote: 'God gives His most difficult assignments to His most trusted soldiers.' At the time, I couldn't understand what it meant that God had *entrusted* me with this."

As she said this, I nodded. I had a similar reaction. *Entrusted? What does that even mean? I've always thought God entrusts good things like money, or possessions, or people, or careers. But pain?*

"Laura, I don't understand. I didn't ask to be entrusted with this. In fact, I don't want this. It's too much to carry."

"Davey, you need to understand something. Thousands of people are being impacted by Amanda's story—by *your* story— and thousands more will continue to be impacted as you step into this next season.

"God is doing something through this story unlike anything I've seen. I'm proud of you. *We're* proud of you. And I know Amanda is proud of you."

Tears began to well up in my eyes as she spoke.

"But you need to know something. You're not carrying this alone. *You can't.* When my husband passed, I tried to carry the pain by myself for a while, using excuses like, 'I need some time to figure things out.' It wasn't until the weight nearly crushed me that I opened up to people's help. God will bring people in your life to help you carry this if you'll be open to it. In fact, He probably already has."

Suddenly my mind began to race, reminded of all the providential relationships that had entered my life since November—giants who let me stand on their shoulders and borrow their faith.

I thought about my church family and leadership team, a group of people who in the midst of grieving the loss of *their* own friend hadn't left my side and almost daily spoke encouragement and faith into me.

I thought about Jake Baird, a pastor in Indianapolis who lost his wife five years ago. I remember him telling me his story over coffee right after we moved to Indy. I came home from that coffee and exclaimed to Amanda, "I can't believe his faith in the midst of his tragedy! He fully believes that God is still God and God is still good."

Jake was one of the first people who reached out to me when Amanda passed.

I thought about Bob Goff. He had certainly experienced his fair share of people taking cheap shots at him. I never understand how someone could hate someone whose primary message is: *love people*! He sat with me for two hours over sushi encouraging me that, if I'm doing the right thing, there will always be haters.

I thought about Todd Erb, a business owner in Indianapolis whose wife and daughter were both murdered two years ago. He attended Amanda's celebration of life service and then reached out to me a couple of weeks later when he discovered we buried Amanda in the same memorial park *and the same row* as his family. I thought about the coffee he and I shared where he spoke encouragement and life into me shortly after Amanda passed.

I thought about Pastor Levi Lusko—how strange it seemed that I'd hear his story just weeks before Amanda went to heaven and how timely our text conversation was back in December.

I thought about a lady I met at the Marion County Prosecutor's Office. After my first meeting with the prosecutors, as we were getting off the elevators for me to walk back to my car, she turned to me and said, "I want you to know our church has been praying for you. *I've* been praying for you. My husband and brother were both murdered several years ago. I want you to know there *is* life after death." *Wow . . . the same thing Laura just spoke into me.*

I looked back at Laura. I couldn't speak for fear I would lose it right in front of her. I simply nodded in agreement.

She smiled empathetically. "See, Davey, you've been carried this whole time. Sometimes by Jesus Himself, and sometimes by someone He sends into your life. He's been carrying you nonetheless. Don't ever buy into the lie that you're called to carry this alone. You're not alone."

I nodded and wiped tears away that were now streaming down my cheek.

"Now you get to be that for others. Davey, God has used my toughest test in life to be my greatest testimony. He's used my mess to be a message. As cliché as that sounds, I'm living proof that it's true! And it will be true for you. Just like people have helped you, you're going to be able to help many people who you'd never otherwise be able to relate to. If you can get your eyes off of your problem and allow your pain to minister to others, God will do a powerful healing work in your own heart.

"It's when people focus on their own pain that they get sucked into a vortex of despair and hopelessness. Helping others in the midst of your pain begins to mitigate your pain. God wants to give your pain a platform and a *purpose* to speak life and hope into others. I'm seeing you do it already and I know you'll continue to do it."

I looked back up toward the Old City of Jerusalem, its looming walls suddenly foreboding and ominous.

King David couldn't do it, but Jesus did. Jesus, if You're really in me, would You help me to do this? Would You strengthen me to embrace the difficult task in front of me, one day at a time? Not my will, Jesus, but Your will be done.

Five days later I stood backstage at NewSpring Church. It was just before the early service, the first of four scheduled for that day. I could already feel sweat running down my back, my palms clammy and hands shaking. I watched the television monitors as Perry addressed the crowd. "NewSpring Church, we have a very special guest today. Let's welcome our friend Davey Blackburn to the stage!"

Lord, this was Your idea. This is Your story. Now give me Your words and Your strength.

I pulled the backstage curtain to the side and stepped across the stage as the auditorium erupted in applause, the audience giving me a standing ovation. I pulled myself up on a stool and took my microphone.

Pain is a platform. Lord, help me to help people. I just want to help people.

I looked over the crowd and caught a glimpse of the tally lights of the cameras in front of me, having no idea that over fifty thousand people would be in attendance across all campuses and on the Web that day.

No turning back now. Lord, take this mess and turn it into a great message of hope and healing.

Sitting up on that stage that morning, I could have never predicted just how far this message would spread and what God was planning to unfold.

16

LIVING IN THE MESS

I STARED AT THE MOUNDS OF BOXES AND FURNITURE SPRAWLED OUT all around me. How was I ever going to get all this unpacked? How was I ever going to make this house a home?

I'd just returned home from South Carolina the day before and had forgotten what a mess I had left behind. Right before I left for Israel, I closed on a new house and moved everything from the old house on Sunnyfield Court, as well as from the temporary house where Weston and I had been living, to this new place. Now everything was stacked nearly floor to ceiling in this three-car garage.

Mattresses and box springs leaned against the wall. Two road bikes, one of them sporting a baby carrier, were propped on their kickstands. Boxes lay strewn across pieces of Amanda's old furniture, some of them finished, but many of them left undone. The entire garage was a glaring reminder of these two lives becoming one, and then that one life becoming half.

I thought about the time we moved everything from South Carolina to Indianapolis. The process was much more organized back then. Amanda had taken a couple of weeks before we moved to neatly box up everything and categorize them by room. My job was to haul them out to the truck. A sudden twinge of breath-stealing shock came over me as I was reminded how we worked together on nearly everything, each with our own strengths to complement the other.

She's really gone. She's never coming back. I can't believe it. This all has really happened. This is our new normal.

I swallowed a lump that had surfaced in my throat, scanned the garage, and mustered up a new resolve to put my life back together. I had gained new perspectives during my time with Dr. Walker and in Israel, and for the first time in months I was clear enough to give this my best attempt.

"Well, Davey, they're not going to unpack themselves," I whispered. I found myself doing this often—saying things out loud that I would normally have quipped with Amanda.

I decided to start in the front corner and work my way back. I squeezed my way past a row of lawn equipment and lifted the box at the top of a stack labeled Weston's Room. I hadn't noticed the piece of furniture the box was resting on until I lifted it and began to walk away.

The drafting table.

Suddenly I was taken back to the garage of our Sunnyfield Court house. It was a late September Saturday afternoon in 2015, and Amanda was returning from looting several garage sales for her growing business, The Weathered Willow.

She hopped from trade show to trade show all over Indiana and Michigan, held a booth at an antique store just outside Indy, and was now amassing quite a following on her Facebook business page. Any Friday or Saturday morning she wasn't putting on a show, you could find her pillaging other people's junk and throwaways to find a treasure. Before she named the business, I would joke with her that we should call the operation Trash to Treasure. She would just roll her eyes and say, "Leave it to the preacher to alliterate *everything*."

Ironically, it was her idea to call it The Weathered Willow.

"Oooohhh!! Who's alliterating now?!" I retorted sarcastically. She just giggled, punched my arm, and walked out of the room as I hollered after her playfully.

"The *Withered* Willow? A *Withering* Willow?"

"*Weathered!*" her voice boomed from the other room.

The truth was, I was so impressed at what she was doing and more proud of her than she probably knew. I thought back to our move to Indy from South Carolina and how she had refused to move some of the old furniture she had restored for our own personal use. Rather than cluttering the truck, she figured she would sell them on Craigslist. Even after using these pieces for three years, she turned a profit with each of them.

"Davey, I think I could do this for a living!" I had never seen her this excited about something.

"I don't know, babe. It doesn't seem scalable to me. I'm not sure you could find enough people to buy this junk for it to actually be profitable."

"Would you let me try? What if you let me borrow three hundred dollars. I'll buy whatever I can with that, repurpose and sell the pieces. Then I'll pay you back the money and keep the profits for myself. How's that sound?"

"Sounds all right to me." I agreed to it. Three hundred dollars seemed like a manageable investment, so I consented to her pulling the money out next time she went to the ATM. She spent the next two weeks scouring garage sales and bringing home some of the ugliest pieces of furniture I'd ever seen in my life. Two weeks later, however, she finished up her first show in Mishawaka, Indiana.

"Here you go, babe!" She handed me a wad of cash totaling three hundred dollars. The spring in her step and the tone of her voice told me she was pleased with what had just transpired.

"How'd you do?"

"I did all right."

"Just all right? You seem pretty pleased. How much is *all right?*"

"Twenty-five hundred dollars."

My jaw dropped. "Are you kidding me? That's amazing! You turned three hundred dollars into twenty-five hundred in two weeks?!" All of a sudden my gears began turning, and I simultaneously began considering how I could renegotiate the original agreement of her keeping the profits for herself!

A few years later, this seed of an idea had turned into a full-fledged operation that not only helped provide additional income into a struggling pastor's household but also allowed her to fulfill a dream of hers—to be a stay-at-home mom to Weston. I used to love walking into the garage while she painted furniture and hummed along with the country station she invariably had the radio tuned to. She was never more alive than when she was painting and restoring furniture.

I thought back to that September afternoon when she pulled into the driveway and stepped out of the Mountaineer, clad in athletic shorts, aviators, and a sweatshirt that fell off her shoulder revealing a light tank top underneath. Her blond highlights glistened as she tossed her head and shut the car door behind her.

"Right on cue!" She winked at me as I stepped out of the house to meet her. "You think you can help me unload this batch?"

I smiled and strolled around to the back of the SUV, pulled the latch, and looked inside. Side tables, lamps, desks, all finagled into the back of this car. I swear Amanda could have won a national Tetris competition with as much stuff as she squeezed into the vehicle. She always looked adorable driving around with ottoman legs hanging out the windows as if she had just stepped

off the set of *American Pickers*. I reached in and pulled out a
hefty wooden desk and began to lift it out of the car.

"Wow! This is a really cool piece! What is it? An old drafting
table?"

"Exactly!" Amanda was always enthusiastic when she came
across a rare find she knew would draw a lot of traffic to her page.
"I got it for fifteen dollars! Can you believe that?!"

Amanda was the best haggler. I would go to garage sales with
her and slink away, chagrined by her constant bartering. She
would pick up an item that was marked two dollars and offer one.
I would almost plead with her just to pay the full amount to save
me from the embarrassment. I'll never forget her reaction the
first time I tried to prevent her from haggling. You would have
thought I violated some secret code on a Pinterest board. "Are
you *kidding* me? You *never* pay full price for something!"

I remember making a mental note to do whatever I could to
never elicit that much disgust from her again.

I examined the drafting table, now sitting upright in the
driveway, "How much do you think you'll be able to sell this for?"

"Umm. I was thinking about two hundred."

I would have laughed at her had I not already witnessed what
kind of profit she was getting. I used to joke with her that she
needed to check with Chip and Joanna Gaines of *Fixer Upper*
to see if they needed an Indianapolis supplier. The truth was, I
wouldn't have been surprised if the Gaines family had called her
to fulfill some orders. She truly had a gift.

"What if I want to use it in my office?" I suggested as I
continued to study the desk. "I've always wanted one of these to
write messages on. I think it would be a cool piece."

We were actively looking for office space for the church. After
three years of each staff member operating out of his own house,
it was time to find a headquarters. Besides, with another little

one on the way, my home office was going to be transformed into Weston's room, while the new baby would move into the nursery.

"That would be okay with me," Amanda replied, and then her attention diverted back to the task at hand and she erupted with excitement. "Also, I got some things for Evie's nursery." Amanda pulled out a standing birdcage that looked like it had been retrieved from the set of an Audrey Hepburn movie. "Isn't it adorable?! I want to decorate the nursery in a bird theme!"

I smiled and wrapped my arms around her barely showing stomach, giving it a couple of smooth caresses before reaching in to pull another piece out of the Mountaineer. It was a dresser. But it looked like a piece of junk. Drawers were missing, hardware was hanging off, and it sat crooked. I couldn't hide my feelings.

"What is *this*?" I gasped.

"What do you mean? It's a dresser!" Amanda could tell I was displeased with this purchase, and I could tell she was offended. "What's wrong with it?"

"Amanda Grace! Are you kidding me? *Everything* is wrong with it! You'll never be able to sell this thing! It's garbage!"

She stared back at me visibly surprised and a little hurt by my lack of trust in her handiwork. "Davey, how many times have I told you? Trust me. Give me a little time and I'll turn this into something beautiful."

Suddenly, I was back in the present moment. "Give me a little time and I'll turn this into something beautiful, babe," I whispered, staring at the mountain of boxes towering in front of me. Somehow I was now sitting on the cold concrete floor of the garage.

I couldn't help but feel utterly discouraged, lost at where to begin this process, aching that Amanda wasn't there to help. Not just with the boxes but with life. I was torn. Part of me wanted to just throw everything away and start completely over. The other part wanted to leave everything in the boxes and push off unpacking into the distant future. Still another part of me wanted to arrange everything—furniture, dishes, silverware—just exactly as it used to be. Maybe then it would feel like some things were normal. The truth was none of this was possible. None of it would bring her back. Normal was now a thing of the past.

I sat there, wrestling, until the hum of a car engine diverted my attention. The car door opened and Megan stepped out.

Megan had just recently taken on the role of my personal assistant. She and I were on staff together at NewSpring for a couple of years. She assisted me in my role as a youth pastor and formed a level of friendship with Amanda many people never get to experience over a lifetime.

Megan walked beside us through the entire transition from NewSpring to Indy. The last week before we moved, she and Amanda had a slumber party on our back deck. They laughed about memories they'd made in Greenville, dreamed of the day we would one day do ministry together again, and wept over our imminent departure.

We stayed in touch with Megan over the years, always having lunch or dinner with her whenever we'd travel through Greenville. In May 2015 Megan told us she was moving to Indy to be a part of Resonate. She lived with us the month of August before settling into her own place. There were few people Amanda trusted more than Megan.

"Hey! Welcome home, friend!" Megan squealed, walking toward me, a pair of coffees in hand. "You did so great on Sunday! How was Israel? Oh, my gosh, we have so much to talk about."

Along with the rest of our church, Megan had tuned in to the interview I'd done at NewSpring the previous Sunday. As she walked toward me and saw my face, her tone shifted.

"You okay?"

"I guess. I'm trying to figure out where to start unpacking. I keep getting started, then I'll come across a piece of furniture or a trinket and get distracted by a memory of Amanda. It completely derails me."

"Well, maybe I can help." She set the coffee down on a stool at the edge of the garage.

"Really? Would you?" One thing I love about Megan is she is always able to help me take the big projects I'm tackling and turn them into bite-size steps.

"Absolutely! I'd love to!"

We began pulling boxes off stacks and shuffling through them together. After about five minutes, Megan looked at me.

"Davey, how much of this stuff do you want to keep?" she asked.

I looked at her. "This is the exact question I've been asking myself for hours."

"It's kind of strange," she said. "This whole thing is almost a metaphor for grief."

I looked up from the ratchet set I was poking through, confused. "What do you mean?"

"Well, think about it. You're in a new house. The old stuff doesn't fit in the new house. As much as you want it to feel like normal, it *can't*. There's a *new normal*. Isn't that what they always say about loss? That *new normal* begins to set in? It's kind of like your life. You're different, Davey. You're a new you. This whole thing has changed you. You carry a weight, a humility, I've never seen in you before. You interact with people differently. You love people differently. You preach differently. It has come from being gutted, but I can tell it's built you into a stronger, sturdier person. Now some of who you used to be doesn't quite fit. As much as you want it to, it can't."

Stronger? Sturdier? I certainly didn't feel stronger. I felt like the slightest breeze could topple my emotions at any moment.

"Of course you can't throw out all of who you used to be," Megan continued, "because all of those things laid the foundation of who you are now. You'd no longer be *you* if you completely threw out who you used to be. Your life with Amanda helped form you into who you are today. But at the same time, you can't remain the same. Some things about your old life have to go— some by default, and some by choice."

Megan scanned the scene as if looking for an example. Across the garage Weston's crib leaned against the wall, disassembled, dusty, and tired.

"Amanda and I talked about how she was going to use Weston's crib for Evie when you guys moved Weston to a big boy bed. So now you have this crib, but you don't necessarily need it. That was part of your old life. So what do you do with it? How do you give it purpose?"

"Give it purpose?" I wasn't sure how it could serve any other purpose than being a baby crib.

"Some of the things in this garage can be repurposed by using them in your new home in a *different* way. And then some can be given a *new* purpose by giving them away, to someone who needs them and who will cherish them because of the sentimental value they hold. I think part of grief is making the choice between what you hold on to as sentimental, what you repurpose, and what you let go of."

I took a sip of coffee, eyes fixed on Megan, as she continued.

"You know, there are some parents who lose a child and they'll keep their child's room set up the same way for years.

They're terrified to touch it. Like if they disassemble the room, it's somehow dishonoring the memory of their child. But what's really happening is they're now being held hostage by the memory. They're unable to find purpose in the pain. They're unable to *re*purpose and move forward in the midst of pain."

Megan stood up and walked over to a table that had previously sat in our dining area at Sunnyfield Court. She grazed her hand across the vintage finish as she continued. "That's what Amanda did with each piece of furniture in her business. She repurposed it. She gave it value again. She took what was regarded as trash and was discarded by the rest of the world and she made it into something beautiful, something of value, something useful."

"That's interesting you say that," I commented. "Before you pulled up, I was just sitting here thinking about how she used to say to me, 'Davey, trust me. Give me a little time and I'll turn this into something beautiful.'"

"I know. She used to tell you that all the time! Remember, you told Pastor Perry to talk about that at her celebration service. And that's exactly what the Lord is saying to you now. *Davey, trust Me. Give Me a little time and I'll turn this into something beautiful.* I believe He has already begun to do so."

I turned my head and gazed out the garage bay door to the driveway and yard. The spring buds had now begun to open into a warm array of color, speckling the neighborhood drive. A red-crested cardinal perched on a tree whistling a melody just outside the garage. In every direction I looked, signs of new life were beginning to stir, overtaking the remnants of the harsh Indiana winter.

Megan continued, "I know we can't see it right now, but I have to believe that when God says, 'He makes all things beautiful in His time,' He means *all* things. Even this. Davey, Romans 8:28

promises us, 'And we know that for those who love God all things work together for good, for those who are called according to his purpose.' That means God is repurposing this mess . . . and He is calling you to partner with Him in that. He's calling *all of us* to partner with Him. That's where the painful part of unpacking and sorting comes in, and I don't mean boxes."

"So what you're saying is I essentially need to unpack my grief?"

"That's exactly what I'm saying. And not just you. We *all* do." Megan paused for a minute. "There are things in these boxes I'm terrified to look through too. But I know I need to. Then I too need to decide what to keep, what to repurpose, and what to let go of."

Megan and I both sat in silence for a minute, letting the weight of her words sink in before she spoke again. "Do you know the reason I came over today, Davey?"

I hadn't considered it but, now that she mentioned it, it did seem odd she had just stopped by unannounced.

"I didn't come over to help you unpack. I came over to show you something. You know how you asked me to start transcribing Amanda's journals in case we wanted to publish them one day?"

I nodded.

"Well I've been going through them and I found an entry that may encourage you."

She shuffled through her purse, pulled out a small, thin, brightly colored notebook adorned with spring flowers, birds, and butterflies, and handed it to me with her thumb marking a page.

"You need to read this."

I glanced down at the pages filled to the margins with Amanda's handwriting:

Jesus,

Thank you for Davey. What an incredible man he is. Thank you for growing him into an even better man than he was. I am so lucky to have a husband that is always trying to be better. I love him more and more b/c of that.

Thank you so much for blessing my life with him.

Tears immediately began to flood my eyes. Oh, how I missed the affirming words of my wife, letting me know she was proud of me and I was doing a good job. I took a breath and gathered myself to continue.

I just want to pray for him. The more we get into this church thing—the larger we get, the more our team works, the bigger we pray and dream—the more I'm realizing how desperately we need you—but even more so, how desperately Davey needs you. Father please place your hand of blessing on him. I've been reading through Genesis and Exodus and seeing how your blessing was so sought after and that it's ok to ask for it. So Father I want to pray for that. Lead Davey through every step and stage of this. Show him what the best way is to reach these people here. I pray that his time with you would be very intimate and that his relationship with you would deepen every day. Give him your vision for Resonate and give him the boldness and courage he needs to do whatever you lead him to do in order to carry out that vision. Show him how to be a leader. I'm so proud of him already for how he has been leading this team. He has such a good balance of compassion and sharpening. Please show him how to lead each person as well as the team as a whole. I pray that your Holy Spirit would speak heavily to him as he prepares, writes, and speaks messages. Give him words to say that will speak directly to the hearts of people. Lead him personally, Jesus. That he would be a man of such integrity. That people would talk about and admire his integrity.

I looked up at Megan barely able to see the next words on the page through the tears in my eyes. It seemed as if Amanda's prayer was reaching beyond the grave to speak to this very moment—this new season of life.

"Keep reading. It gets better," Megan motioned toward the journal.

Jesus—I know you can do unimaginable things if people would be willing [to] do whatever it takes. Father I want him (and us) to be a part of the unimaginable and the supernatural. I know he wants that and is dreaming of numbers I can't even comprehend. But Father, I absolutely want you to use Davey in that way and I want you to know that I'm willing to do whatever it takes as his wife to make that happen. It makes me fearful to pray that, because I know that "whatever it takes" means some extremely difficult times and circumstances [lay] ahead. But I also know it's necessary and worth it.

"It's necessary and *worth it*?" I repeated out loud. I was sure I didn't agree with that statement.

"Davey, keep reading."

So Father, protect our hearts and our lives. Help us to stay strong in you no matter what happens. Thank you for giving me Davey. I know my life won't be wasted with him and I love that. I love you.

"Davey, this was the most beautiful and yet eerily prophetic thing I've ever read. Amanda knew her life *wouldn't be wasted* with you. She knew her story wouldn't be wasted. God doesn't waste pain, and He invites us to partner with Him in the repurposing of our pain."

"But Megan, *necessary* and *worth it*? How could anything ever be worth losing her?"

"Davey, Scripture tells us in Second Corinthians that this suffering is *light* and *momentary* compared to the *eternal weight* of glory we'll experience in heaven with Jesus. I don't know how, but I have to believe that one day we'll look back on all of this and say it was worth going through it—for the reward we'll receive in heaven, for the thousands who will join us there because of it, for how much nearer we now know Jesus. Second Corinthians also says our suffering is *producing* for us glory. Almost like a mother who, immediately after enduring labor pains, holds her baby skin-to-skin and whispers, 'it was worth it.'"

I grimaced at the thought of ever saying this was worth it. Megan must have noticed. She lowered her voice to soften the words.

"Do you think when Amanda stepped into heaven, and Jesus revealed to her His perspective on this—all that would come of it—*she* thought it was worth it?"

I looked up at her. I hadn't considered it. All the wrestling we did with God calling us to Indy, convinced He had called us, but recognizing that calling was a fate we would have never chosen for ourselves. Prior to November, I lived under the assumption that we were almost invincible. That tragedy doesn't happen to people like us, especially because we were doing God's work in this world.

Megan opened a box labeled books and pulled out a Bible that happened to be sitting on top. "Davey, Amanda asked God for blessing. And God promises to bring blessing as we follow in obedience to His calling, but oftentimes that blessing is preceded by a massive burden—even brokenness." She opened the Bible and began flipping through the pages.

"It's like in Hebrews chapter eleven—the 'Hall of Faith'— where the author lays out all the people who received God's blessing because of their obedience. Then, toward the end of the chapter, it says: 'others ... were tortured, refusing to be released so that they might gain an even better resurrection. Some faced jeers and flogging, and even chains and imprisonment. They were put to death by stoning; they were sawed in two; they were killed by the sword.' And yet considered it *worth it* because of the reward they would receive in heaven." Megan kept going.

"Davey, it also says *the world was not worthy of them*. I truly believe this world was not worthy of Amanda."

Just then, an image came to my mind. *Like John the Baptist.* The Barbarian Way. I thought about Amanda's journal entry from when she was eighteen years old. She talked about how she wanted to sacrifice *everything* to follow Jesus—even unto death. *Amanda really did take* the Barbarian challenge. She followed Jesus even to death. Into something more. Into something greater.

This thought suddenly emboldened me, strengthened me, almost as if Amanda's prayers were jumping off the pages and permeating my soul. As if connecting the dots of God's hand in this whole story suddenly gave me a renewed sense of ownership in my part in the drama—discovering and uncovering the purpose in all of this.

I suppose there really can be purpose in pain, even in pain this deep. In fact, as I thought about it, it seemed that in God's processes, the greater the pain endured, the greater purpose He employs. Could all of this really be working for my *good?* Could everything that happened to Amanda—as brutal, bloody, and senseless as it was—actually have some sense? Could it be repurposed for a greater good? Could we actually, one day, look back and say it was all *worth* it to know Jesus more and to see more people know Jesus?

My mind traced back to sitting beside Amanda's hospital bed—Elevation Worship's music echoing through the cold, sterile room, my heart strangely warmed by the poignant and timely lyrics. *Nothing is wasted. You work all things for good.*

I looked around at all the boxes left to be unpacked and turned my attention back at Megan. "Okay, I think I'm ready."

Megan looked at me, tears forming in her eyes. "Me too, Davey. Me too."

The next two months Derek, Ashley, Weston, and I lived in a construction zone. The subcontractors ripped up our floors to put new ones in. Tarps were hung over all the entryways. We breathed dust and renovation residue incessantly. We had no floor to walk on, no kitchen to cook in, and no place to gather in the evenings. I found myself, at moments, losing hope in this whole thing, losing sight of the newfound purpose I had kindled that day in the garage with Megan.

The environment surrounding us became a perfect image of the environment of my heart—messy, unsettled, under renovation. With no true floor to walk on, I began devising a plan to put life back together, to lay a new flooring for our life. I was determined to sit in the driver's seat of the "new normal."

What I didn't understand at the time was that part of sitting in the driver's seat is knowing when to press the gas pedal and when to push the brakes. Part of reconstructing life and owning your grief is admitting when you need to step back, rest, and take care of yourself. I'd soon learn this lesson the hard way.

PART 4

WALKING WITH A LIMP

17

FINISH STRONG, FINISH WELL

The bass from the Bose system hanging from the catwalk suspended across Washington Street thudded in my chest as I glanced over the sea of more than forty thousand runners surrounding me.

"Runners! We're nearing the start time for the 2016 Indy Mini Marathon. Good luck to everyone!"

The official announcement from the emcee echoed off the buildings in the middle of downtown Indianapolis, over the people neatly organized in corrals, and was then swallowed up by the cheer erupting from the crowd. The music surged and would inevitably end with a perfectly timed drop of a beat and the firing of the starter pistol to signal the start of this iconic race.

The Indy Mini had been a tradition for Amanda and me since we moved to Indianapolis. It gave us a reason to get out and enjoy training runs together; and it kept us both healthy and active. Its route weaves through downtown Indianapolis, includes a lap inside the Indianapolis Motor Speedway's two-and-a-half-mile oval track, and finishes at the entrance of Military Park.

Our love for running began when Amber, James, Amanda, and I joined a group in San Diego in 2009 for the San Diego full marathon. After four months of daily 5 a.m. training runs, the four of us made the trip out to sunny California and participated in the event. Amber, Amanda, and I spent the entire twenty-six-point-two miles chatting while we ran, crossing the finish line nearly arm in arm. After that race we were all hooked.

During that time, I fell more in love with Amanda than I ever thought I could. She was tenacious and gritty when she trained, meeting every challenge head-on, full of courage and determined to finish. Amanda's last Indy Mini was in 2014 when she ran and completed the race while six months pregnant with Weston. She was a fighter and consistently lived up to the childhood nickname given to her by her dad, "Junk Yard Dog," a name she also proudly donned on all of her race bibs.

This year, however, instead of having Amanda smiling at my side, her sister Amber and I stood together in the middle of a crowd, feeling as if we were the only two running this race. We were alone in a sea of thousands of people.

Our eyes, red and bloodshot from fighting back tears, were a stark contrast to the grins of the other runners and spectators, and neither one of us spoke a word.

As Amber and I stood anxiously awaiting the starting gun, all I could think about were the countless memories of running with Amanda. This year's Mini had taken on a whole new meaning for our church family. We had forty runners all clad in matching orange T-shirts. On the front of the shirts was a logo Amanda had designed for the church's ForIndy campaign a couple of months before she passed. Our church worship band was part of the en route entertainment, and I had been training to set a personal record (or PR) during this race—all in Amanda's memory.

My stomach formed a knot as I reflected on the magnitude of the moment, a gripping reminder that she and I would never enjoy running side by side again on this side of eternity. I stood there pensive, remembering runs with Amanda.

There was nothing I enjoyed more than running with my best friend, and I always loved her pace. Sure, I could have run faster if I had pushed myself, but something about running her pace felt even better than posting a PR. It was comfortable and familiar. It was as if *this* was the way my legs were designed to run, like we were meant to run together.

As we ran, we would download our thoughts to each other, plan for future vacations, encourage each other through tough ministry conversations, externally process our frustrations, and dream about what our family was going to be like. More arguments were settled, more dreams concocted, and more of our friendship was forged in those runs than in any other setting. We could go out for an hour, run, and talk, and she hardly ever wavered from her pace.

She would hit nine-minute-mile splits on long runs, every mile for ten miles. No fluctuation. Steady.

That's how Amanda operated life. If there were two words that defined Amanda they were *wisdom* and *balance*. Over and over in her journal she prayed that she would be "steadfast and immovable." She loved life to be balanced. No extreme fluctuation. No polarizing roller-coaster rides of emotion.

I, on the other hand, am the complete opposite. I've always been the kind of guy who will run Mach 6 until my hair is on fire and everything (and everyone) around me is burning down. I'll go, go, go and then crash. She was steady and consistent. She taught me how to run at a slower pace to enjoy the little things of life. I loved running with her.

Still, in every training run, we would get down to the last mile or two, and she would turn to me midstride and say, "Babe, if you feel good, run on up ahead. Finish strong at your own pace." Sometimes I'd stay with her because I was enjoying our conversation so much. But most of the time, I'd take her up on the offer to leg it out. I'd kick it into another gear and run the last mile or two at a seven or seven-and-a-half-minute pace, arrive back at the house, run inside to grab us a couple of waters, and be back out in the driveway by the time Amanda would finish.

A thunderous crack in the morning air and a sudden lurch of the crowd interrupted my thoughts. The runners in front of us were beginning their surge forward, squeezing toward the starting line. The starting gun had fired and our corral was inching forward for our official start time to begin.

Amber and I followed suit and met them stride for stride.

The pace quickened around us and I felt a sudden urge to pee. This always seemed to happen at the beginning of a race. I don't know why—nerves, excitement, the realization that for the next two hours it would be impossible to find a place to relieve myself. I shrugged it off and secretly hoped I would just sweat out any body fluid that needed to be released. I was *not* deviating from my pace this race. This one was for Amanda.

Amber and I cut a quick glance at each other as we saw the starting line stretched out in front of us. Now the runners to our left and right were nearing their race pace. Our eyes said to each other everything that needed to be said, *I really wish Amanda was doing this with us, but I'm glad we're not doing this alone.* Amber had agreed to run at my pace, which would be a personal record for both of us and would make the race much more enjoyable.

We crossed the starting line and stepped into our stride, jumping up on the sidewalks and weaving around people who happened to be slower in front of us. Nothing was getting in our way of finishing this race strong. I saw a clearing in the road ahead, stepped off the sidewalk and for the first time—about a half a mile into the race—settled into my seven-and-a-half-minute pace.

I let my thoughts pick up where they'd left off. *Davey, if you feel good, run on up ahead. Finish strong at your own pace,*

Amanda would say. The significance of this wasn't lost on me. I was convinced when Amanda stepped into eternity she crossed the finish line and heard her heavenly Father say, "You've fought the good fight, you've finished the race. Well done." Now I could almost hear her soft voice whisper in my ear, "Babe, if you feel good, run on up ahead . . . Serve more people. Help more people. Build Jesus's church. Make something of this. Don't waste it . . . Finish strong at your own pace."

That's exactly what I seemed to be thrust into—a faster pace. After speaking at NewSpring with Pastor Perry, my calendar was quickly filling up with more opportunities to share my and Amanda's story—sometimes in front of big crowds. I was staring down the barrel of a summer full of airports and rental cars, spreading the message of hope and healing in the midst of trial at churches around the country. I felt, at times, like I was running, trying to keep up with the pace of things—like running on a treadmill notched at level ten, desperately reaching for the hand grips to keep me from falling.

We skirted the one-mile marker, not even stopping for a drink from the attendants passing out water cups, and a thought hit me. *Amanda would have hated this pace. She would have hated this breakneck speed of ministry.* I'm not sure how you hurt and smile at the same time, but in that moment I found myself simultaneously in those two worlds.

Just then, I thought about a massive argument Amanda and I had had just one year prior, in May 2015. For the first time in our ministry I was receiving requests to speak at youth camps and conferences and I wanted to say yes to all of them. I just *knew* we could figure out a way to make it all happen. Amanda, on the other hand, vehemently opposed it. She wanted to ensure balance and practicality in our lives, especially as we kept to Weston's sleep schedule.

After a couple of days going back and forth, I finally convinced her. "Babe," I said, "I remember growing up seeing the camp speaker there *with* his family. It made him seem more personable, more transparent. And I always looked up to ministry couples—they were like *power* couples. That's what we are! That's what I want us to always be!"

These words must have been the tipping point for Amanda because she finally agreed to say yes to the requests, and she and Weston traveled with me. What ensued was arguably the greatest summer of our marriage. We enjoyed the thrill of seeing new places, loving people, encouraging hearts, and growing closer together in the process.

I'll never forget driving back to our hotel after speaking at a youth conference in Greenville, South Carolina, in August. Amanda had spent an hour or so after the message praying with young girls in front of the stage. I still have such a strong memory of her arms around these girls, her whispering life into their ears. I can't forget the way each girl's countenance visibly changed after her encounter with Amanda. In the car that night, Amanda looked at me and said, "Davey, that was one of my favorite nights of my life."

Even furniture restoration couldn't compete for Amanda's heart when it was put side by side with *people* restoration.

That's your calling, Davey. People restoration. As we wove our way past the zoo and out of downtown, I thought about the possibility of Amanda restoring furniture and decorating mansions in heaven. Why wouldn't we have purpose in heaven? Why wouldn't we have a job, an assignment that gives us direction and joy? God told Adam to work the Garden of Eden *before* sin fractured the universe. If ministry isn't necessary anymore when we get to heaven because everyone knows Jesus fully, Amanda is surely restoring furniture. She's probably even requested to distress the streets of gold to give them more character!

My thoughts drifted to a journal entry she had written back in June at a camp I was speaking at:

I just had this vision of our church being 300 people and what a massive difference that would make. The way Davey preaches and the energy and enthusiasm he can feed off a larger crowd makes such a big difference. I've never heard him preach like he has the last two nights. And I mean preach. It is awesome. I know it's more difficult to do that at Resonate. He literally tries to create energy while he's preaching to our people because they just don't have it yet. Anyways, it gave me such an excitement and anticipation for our church to be that size and our culture to become that way. Davey seems like he truly comes alive when that happens . . .

Thank you that I've gotten to be along for the ride. Thank you for how you have provided this as well. You are good, Father.

Show us what we need to do to grow our church. Show us how to lead our people in this next season.

Now our church was experiencing explosive growth for the first time in its short history. People from all over the city were coming to see how this little church plant was standing tall after such a tragedy. Hurting people were flocking to our doors to get a taste of the hope they saw in us. A few thousand people were tuning into our services each week online, clamoring to hear God's truth in the midst of their own trial. Already hundreds had made first-time confessions of faith in Jesus Christ. Little did Amanda know her death would be the very catalyst for this growth.

But, why did it require her life, Lord? My breathing quickened and I could feel my legs tighten as I continued to ruminate.

It's almost like it took her dying before our church could have life, before it could experience the growth she had begged for.

Just then a thought hit me. Like a tracker following a scent, I let the thought lure me in. Jesus once said something about this in John 12:24 (NIV): "Unless a kernel of wheat falls to the ground and dies, it remains only a single seed. But if it dies, it produces many seeds." The recollection of the verse nearly caused my knees to lock up midstride. *It takes the death of something to produce new life.*

I thought about how many old habits of mine had to die in order to produce new healthy habits. I thought about how I've had to choose to die to my own selfish desires and agendas in order to offer life and hope to people. I thought about how Jesus had to die in order for us all to have eternal life. I suppose this principle is true, albeit nearly impossible to accept. Amanda's life was a seed, a seed that was planted in the ground by the master Gardener so that it could bear a plentiful harvest of new lives. At the end of the day, wouldn't that be the most fulfilling way to live life? To give up your life in order to produce life for others?

As I ran, I wondered if the same was true for me, if now I was called to die as well. Die to my agenda. Die to my desires. Die to my sorrow. Weep without wallowing in my grief. All the while working the ground so more lives could be infused with hope and healing.

We crossed mile two.

It's one thing to maintain a quicker pace with the help of a life and ministry partner, but what about now? What do I do when there's just one of me? How could I possibly run this pace as a single parent? I didn't know how to be dad *and* mom to Weston, let alone be a pastor to everyone else. I remembered back to what Pastor Kevin Myers from 12Stone Church in Atlanta had said to me, right after Amanda passed. "If you're going to make an error with time, err on the side of spending *too* much time with Weston," he'd told me.

It made sense. But how? Between preparing messages, pastoring people, setting vision, carrying Amanda's story outside of the church, and fathering Weston, I felt tugged in a hundred different directions. I was spending a considerable amount of time with Weston, but I felt the increasing strain of giving myself to so many different demands that I couldn't give myself fully to any one of them—including my son. How do I reconcile this calling God had placed on my life, this story He'd stewarded to me, and this little boy He'd tasked me to raise, nurture, and develop?

Mile three.

I thought about how, prior to Amanda's passing, my calling had been so clear: Be a great husband to Amanda. Be a great father to Weston and Evie. Be a great pastor to Resonate Church. But now what? Everything was more complicated than it was before, more confusing.

I kept putting one foot in front of the other, keeping in step with Amber and with the pace we had set for ourselves. As I ran, I felt God say to me, *Davey, I'm not giving you a* new *calling, but I am asking you to* shift *your calling. Here are your new directives: Be a great father to Weston. Be a great pastor to Resonate Church. Carry Amanda's story.*

Mile four.

Shortly after Amanda and I started dating long-distance, I received a phone call from her one day in February. Her voice seemed weighed down and a little shaky.

"Davey, I need to talk to you about something."

"Okay, this sounds serious."

"Well. It's pretty important. My youth pastor spoke a message tonight about sacrificing something for the Lent season in order to foster personal spiritual growth. He talked about cutting something out of your life—even something good—and how this can pave the way for growth. Like when you prune a tree and it grows back stronger and healthier than before."

"Oookaaay," I responded slowly, wondering where this was leading.

"I wanted to give up something like chocolate, or coffee, but the more I prayed about it the more I felt like God was asking me to give up something that would hurt even more than those things. I think He's telling me to give up talking on the phone with you for the Lent season."

I was dumbfounded. I couldn't even respond. Here we were, in this new, exciting dating relationship that *depended* on phone conversations and she wanted to give that up? No talking for forty days? I was sure this was some new Christian-girl way of breaking up: "It's not you, it's me." Or, "I just need some space."

"I don't know what to say," was all I could squeeze out.

"I'm sorry, Davey. I just know I have to do this. It hurts so badly but I have to be obedient. I'll talk to you in forty days." Before she hung up the phone, she added, "I'll be counting down the days."

I sat at my college dorm room desk in shock and feeling abandoned. That shock quickly turned to offense and outrage. I picked the phone back up and dialed my cousin, Mark. He was a missionary in the Czech Republic at the time. I wasn't even sure what time it was on the other side of the globe there, but I had to vent to him. He, of all people, would see the absurdity of this and let me sulk in my misery.

"Hello?" the voice on the other end said.

"Mark! I have to tell you something." I didn't even give him time to respond. "You'll never believe what Amanda just did!" I spent the next couple of minutes spitting out the words about

Amanda's irrational decision. When I finished, there was a long pause on the other end of the line and then a deep sigh.

"Davey, what have you always told me you want in the girl you'll eventually marry?" Mark asked.

I knew exactly what he was talking about but I didn't want to say it out loud. He and I had shared many conversations dreaming about our future wives. "Mark, now is not the time to be spiritual. I'm really ticked off!"

"Just answer the question."

"Fine." I waited a few seconds before practically whispering what I knew was true. "I used to say I need a woman who loves Jesus more than she loves me." This wasn't the way I had envisioned this conversation going.

Mark paused for a second and then shifted his tone, "Sounds like you've found your girl."

Mile five.

As I ran, I thought back to that moment—right as I hung up the phone with Mark—and how I *knew* I was going to marry Amanda. She was my girl. I wanted to spend the rest of my life with someone who loved Jesus that much. The forty days of separation were hard, but it was *separation* that paved the way for our *sanctification*—our spiritual growth. Ever since that short season of forty days, the foundation of our relationship had been predicated on one thing: Jesus—the one who would always be first in both of our lives.

A wave of sadness came over me as I thought about Amanda and how we were separated again. How was I ever going to spend the next forty *years* of my life not being able to talk to her? Not able to share with her my hopes and dreams? Not able to disclose to her my fears and frustrations? Am I now forced to wander this wilderness, seeking the Promised Land but never entering it?

Mile six.

I looked over at Amber, who glanced down at the watch on her wrist and then smiled at me, an indication we were still right on track. A thought struck me. I may not be running this race with Amanda, but I have others by my side now—her family, my family, my *church* family. As Laura told me in the Garden of Gethsemane, I wouldn't have to do this alone. No one has to. I gave Amber a thumbs-up and we kept running.

The truth is I was starting to feel tired. I wouldn't have told Amber that, but she probably could have guessed. This is always the point in the race when you start to wonder how you're going to keep your pace all the way to the finish line. But thinking of Amanda—about my separation from her and how much I missed her, and how I couldn't stand the thought of all that pain being wasted, kept me putting one foot in front of the other.

I thought about everything that was coming up in my schedule and how I was going to have to do it all without Amanda. Then, suddenly, this thought came to me: *Over my dead body am I going to let this be wasted.* I felt a sort of coldness creep over my heart, even though my body was about as heated as it could be, running and breathing heavily. A strong resolve, almost anger, stronger than I'd ever felt before overtook my senses, and I kicked my stride into a new gear.

I *thought* I knew what I was doing. I thought this was a good thing.

It felt like this might be the push I needed to keep this pace I was running to honor Amanda, to make the most of all of this pain. What I wasn't thinking about at the time—what I couldn't have known yet—was that it was never my job to make sure Amanda's life wasn't wasted. And if I kept trying to do it alone, I would never make it.

We were nearing the entrance of the Motor Speedway, and up to this point everything had seemed a blur. I had been lost in my thoughts. I glanced over at Amber. "You feeling good?" I asked. She nodded and smiled. Usually she spent the entire time we ran talking, while I would listen. Not this time. Something was different.

Just then something seized up in my left calf muscle.

A streak of fire ripped up the back of my leg, from my ankle to the back of my knee, and I nearly tumbled to the ground.

I immediately pulled up and slowed to a walk as I clutched my left side, hobbling next to the curb, unable to put pressure on my leg. "Davey! Are you okay?" Amber turned around and rushed over to me.

"I don't know. I think I pulled a muscle or caught a really bad cramp! *Agh!!*"

The pain throbbed with every ounce of weight I placed on it. *What happened? Have I not been drinking enough water? Did I not stretch well enough?*

I tried limping back and forth as waves of runners went by.

"Amber, I don't know what this is. I've never had this happen to me before!"

"What do you want me to do, Davey?" I knew she would stay with me if I asked her to.

"You go on. You're running an excellent pace. I'm sure this will loosen up in a second and I'll try to catch up."

But it wouldn't loosen up. And I wouldn't catch up with her. In fact, I wouldn't even finish the race. There was so much I needed to learn from being hurt. A lesson I'd never be able to fully learn if I had been healthy.

18

THE BLESSING OF A BROKEN HIP

I SPENT THE NEXT TEN MINUTES LIMPING BACK AND FORTH, JUST inside the entrance of the Speedway. I found a medic tent to see if they had anything that would take away the pain enough for me to finish the race. Unfortunately no such product existed, and the medics nearly laughed at me for being naive enough to think there was. It's funny how we think there is some sort of instant cure for pain—how panicked we get when we can't fix something overnight.

After several minutes of watching me hobble around the sidewalk, one of the medics approached me. "Let me take a look at it." He bent over and ran his hand down my calf. "Son, it's extremely tight. The longer you've been here, the more it seems to be tightening up. Is that accurate?"

I nodded at him, grimacing a little.

"If you try to keep going, you're likely to tear something and cause permanent damage. I think you should call it quits for today."

I felt my heart race and my breath quicken as he said that. I thought about telling him the whole story—everything from the moment I walked in and found Amanda lying there, so helpless, to the moment I held her hand at the hospital, to how she and I had *always* run this race together, and now she wasn't here.

I looked back to the race pathway, where I couldn't see Amber anymore. I thought about explaining to him why I couldn't possibly quit now, how this race was for *Amanda*, and how there was no way I could possibly let all of this go to waste. Instead, I just shook my head.

"I think I'm actually okay. If I just try to stretch it out, I'm pretty sure I can get it to loosen up."

The medic put his hand on my shoulder. "Son, sometimes it's okay to admit when you're too hurt to finish."

Too hurt to finish? I wasn't too hurt to finish!

"There will be other races," he went on. "At least, there will be if you don't try to keep going. Quit this one and live to race another day, or keep going and risk never racing again. Your choice."

I lingered there for a moment considering what he was saying. I knew he was right. I did. I didn't want him to be right. I felt like such a failure, like I was letting Amanda down again. I felt so powerless over the place I was in—like there was just no way I could possibly fix it. I nodded.

"You're right," I said. He nodded at me and I turned back, beginning the slow walk back to the starting line. I don't know why I felt I had to go back to the beginning, but I did. With each step, I limped, my head hanging as healthy runners passed me.

I once again passed the six-mile marker—this time going the opposite direction.

I was literally the farthest out from the starting line I could possibly be. Six and a half miles into a thirteen-point-one-mile race. Really? Why this? Why now? I was furious at myself, at the race, at the runners who passed me, at life, and honestly, at God. *This was supposed to be a race in honor of Amanda, and I couldn't even finish it?! Why would You let this happen?*

Just then, the still, small voice, a faint whisper.

Davey, I want to show you something.

Show me something?

I trudged forward, each step shooting searing pain through my left side. *Okay, Lord. I'm listening. What do You want to show me through this?*

I quieted my heart and waited for a nudge. After a few seconds and a few more slow steps I suddenly heard the medic's words echo in my mind.

Son, sometimes it's okay to admit when you're too hurt to finish.

Am I too hurt to finish? I asked God. *Is that it?* Here I was plotting out this new race I had been assigned to run. Planning how to carry Amanda's story and not waste any opportunity. Was Jesus telling me I couldn't do it? That I needed to wait? That I needed to slow down?

Suddenly I remembered another time this had happened with my calf—on a training run a few weeks before, in Israel. I felt a twinge in my calf and instead of paying attention to it I pushed through it. After all, isn't that what I've been taught to do? Push through pain? Coaches had taught me to push through pain in order to get to the next level of strength and endurance. I suddenly realized I was transferring that principle over to my emotional pain. *Push through the pain.*

Of course, on some level, I was forced to. I had responsibilities—a son, a church, people depending on me. I had to push through pain to carry everything effectively. But there is a stark difference between pain you can push through and pain that will injure you—that will take you out if you keep pushing. As I walked, I thought about the difference between the two. Emotionally, I realized I was in the midst of a pain that would injure me, that would cripple me for life if I didn't properly heal from it. This pain could keep me from finishing my race.

Just then the rest of the medic's words came to me.

There will be other races. At least, there will be if you don't try to keep going. Quit this one and live to race another day, or keep going and risk never racing again. Your choice.

That's it, huh, Lord? That's what You wanted to teach me? Mile five.

I hobbled past a stream of runners coming from the other direction, dropping my head sheepishly. I was embarrassed to be injured. I couldn't help but think people were staring and judging me. *He must not have trained properly,* or *He's not in good shape,* I was sure they were thinking.

I wondered to myself if that was what it felt like to be hurt and walk into most churches in America—nearly hobbling through the door, tentative, insecure, wondering what others are thinking of you. *She must not love Jesus enough,* or *He's made some really poor choices,* they must be thinking. It wasn't the first time I had empathized with someone walking through the doors of a church for the first time—but it was the first time I really *felt it.* It was all making so much sense. This pain, this slowing down, this being the injured one—it has so much to teach us, if we let it.

I kept walking toward the starting line. Actually more like hobbling than walking, realizing slowly that this might take a while. Healing always takes so much longer than we want it to. While I walked, I talked with God.

What else, Lord? What else are You showing me?

Look at your hand, the voice prompted.

I glanced down at the newly formed scar on my right hand. With the searing pain in my leg, I had almost forgotten about the blisters and rips that were just barely starting to heal on my hand.

In the process of training for the mini marathon, I had also begun training at my local CrossFit gym. A combination of power lifting, high-intensity metabolic conditioning, and gymnastics, CrossFit was providing me a healthy outlet for the grief, anger, and frustration I was feeling. But just a few weeks before, during one of the workouts, I ripped the skin on my right hand while stringing together multiple sets of gymnastic pull-ups, leaving the flesh bleeding and moist and raw.

One of the CrossFit trainers explained to me that to keep from ripping my hands in the future I needed to regularly shave all calluses off my hands. *What?* That didn't make any sense to me. In baseball and golf, you wanted to *build up* calluses on your hands. Tougher hands meant a stronger swing. But in CrossFit, it turns out, the opposite was true. *Tender* hands, not tougher, mean more strength and endurance in the workout. The gymnastic moves in CrossFit are so unique and intense they require malleability in order to sustain the duress.

The voice whispered again: *Davey, life is often so unique and intense that it requires malleability in order to sustain its duress. Your heart needs to be tender, not calloused.*

I knew it was true. I had witnessed many people undergo something traumatic, who then allowed that circumstance to cause their heart to grow cold and calloused. I recognized the same temptation in my heart. It was easier to wake up every day in callousness. It was easier not to allow anyone to see the pain I was going through. It was easier to just push through the pain. I wanted to think that because I had experienced a perspective change that my healing process was finished. But that was the furthest thing from the truth. My perspective change needed to extend to a *heart* change.

I stopped walking and glanced down at my hand again. It had begun to heal, new layers of skin forming over the dried-out wound.

Healing happens over time and in stages.

We want healing to come in *poof.* That's what Dr. Walker had said to me. Instantaneous. But there was no way to take away this pain immediately. Sure, I could try to numb it for a bit with medication, alcohol, drugs, relationships. But by doing so. I'd do more damage in the long run. The thing I was realizing is that numbing pain also means numbing its antithesis—joy. You can't selectively numb. If I tried to numb the pain now, I would be taking myself out of the race in the long run. True, deep, unadulterated healing comes in stages, feeling the depth of each layer as the new flesh forms around the old.

God, what does healing look like? I asked.

I thought back to when I initially ripped my hand—how I didn't even realize it at first. I didn't feel it all in the moment. In fact, I was able to finish my workout, and it wasn't until I saw the blood smeared all over the bar that I started to see something was wrong. The adrenaline—it kept me from feeling the pain.

But for the next few days, the pain was almost unbearable. Trying to use my hand was futile. Every time I attempted to carry on normal life activities, I would open or close my hand, and searing pain would cause my whole arm to flinch. I was *constantly* reminded of the rip, of the incident that had torn open my hand.

Over time, as you let the wound be exposed to fresh air, it will begin to heal, I heard God tell me. I looked down at my hand and realized how I was now able to open and close it with virtually no pain. I was able to use my hand again for nearly any function. Healing happens if we slow down and let time do its work. Of course it might leave a scar. But unlike a flesh wound that brings unmitigated pain with every use, a scar tells a great story of healing.

Immediately I thought about when I found Amanda lying on our living room floor. Adrenaline and shock kicked in. I was able to perform functions, talk to the media, and believe with a faith that was beyond my own capability to muster up. But when the adrenaline subsided, and the real pain set in, that's when I lost the ability to perform even the most trivial of tasks without the constant reminder of the pain, of Amanda's absence. I was nearly paralyzed.

There were times when people close to me tried to caution me when they discerned I might be pushing through pain, striving instead of resting. My heart was too calloused to listen. I'd blow them off, hiding my wound behind the bandage of ministry, coercing calluses to form so I wouldn't have to feel it.

But over time, as I exposed my wound to air—Levi Lusko, Laura in the Garden of Gethsemane, Dr. John Walker, my congregation, so many others—my heart was healing. As much as I wanted to suppress the pain, keep it in the dark, bandage it up, close myself off, not talk about it, I didn't. In fact, the more I exposed the pain to the light, the more God used others' faith and perspective to breathe a healing wind over the wound.

I thought about how one day this pain might be a scar that would allow me to live in a new normal and tell the story of God's healing.

You're healing, however, is not over, the voice reminded me as I limped.

I glanced down at my hand, crouched over, and grabbed my calf muscle. I knew there were a few things I needed to do. I needed to admit that I was hurt, first of all. Slow down, heal in stages, be intentional about shaving the calluses from my heart when I begin to lose tenderness. I decided right there I was going to get back on the gymnastic bars, and one day I was going to return to PR the Indy Mini.

Mile four.

The last few runners passed me as I continued to limp in the opposite direction. Four more miles to the starting line, then a couple more blocks on to the winner's circle. Over the last two miles of walking and talking to Jesus, I felt the callousness being shaved from my heart and fall away, like cataracts being removed from my eyes.

There was something still gnawing at me, however—a question I had asked a thousand times before. It was the question of *why*.

Each time I tried to ask *why*, I seemed to get the same answer. *Davey, if I told you why, you wouldn't understand.* It reminded me of being a child and asking my parents, "Why," and their reciting to me, "Because I said so." As a child, this response frustrated me and even caused me to resent my parents at times. But now as a parent myself, I understand. What that really means is: "There are several very good reasons, none of which you will understand, so you just need to trust me."

Now, as I walked alone and talked with God, something told me I needed to ask again. Something made me feel like my heart was tender enough to hear the answer, even if it was going to be tough to stomach.

"Lord, can You tell me why? Why this pain? Why me? Why Amanda?"

I trudged forward expecting to hear the familiar, *You won't understand if I tell you.* But it didn't come. Instead the still, small voice whispered something else to me.

Because I want to bless you.

What? He wants to bless me? Maybe this was a bad idea. Maybe I really wouldn't be able to understand. This certainly didn't feel like a blessing. It felt like the exact *opposite* of blessing.

I want to bless you, the voice said. *But first I have to allow you to be broken.*

I halted right where I was, halfway between mile five and mile four. The Indy Mini course now deserted of runners, empty water cups strewn over the ground in front of me. *Blessing. Brokenness.* I had heard this before.

My mind flashed back to a conversation Amanda, Derek, Ashley, and I had with my friend, Brandon Berry.

It was February 2013. The four of us were staying with Brad Cooper in Anderson, South Carolina. Brandon and his family had stopped in to visit on their way from Charlotte, North Carolina, to Atlanta for a wedding. Brandon was about to plant a church in Charlotte and was asking us questions about Resonate. I'm normally skeptical of what the church world calls a "prophetic gifting," meaning a person who has the ability to speak truth into a situation that points someone to the future. I've seen people claim to have the gift and abuse it. Brandon is one of a few people I know who legitimately possesses a prophetic gift.

He stopped in the middle of his questions, almost as if he had lost his train of thought, and asked us, "What's the name of your church again?"

"Resonate Church," I responded.

He looked at us as tears began to well up in his eyes. "This is going to be really good," he said. "God is going to use you greatly, but first you'll be wounded deeply. His blessing will be preceded by brokenness. Just stick together through it all and it will turn out for good."

This left all four of us stunned. None of us wanted to ask for clarification. We loved the idea that God was going to use us greatly, but the thought of walking through a wounding season? Frankly, that scared us to death. Maybe if we didn't address it, we thought, we could keep that wounding season at bay.

It also wasn't lost on me the quote he was referring to when he said, "you'll be wounded deeply." The great theologian A. W. Tozer wrote in his book *The Root of the Righteous*, "It is doubtful whether God can bless a man greatly until He has hurt him deeply." [3]

I had heard this quote from a preacher one time. In fact, this preacher had proposed that the level of hurt you experience in life is directly correlated with the level of influence God wants to give you.

Church planting had brought some level of pain in our lives, and naturally Amanda and I accepted the pain as a pruning process in order for our church and our lives to produce fruit. During one particularly trying season of church planting, when people were leaving in very hurtful ways, Amanda wrote this in her journal:

Jesus, we are so overwhelmed and just helpless. We feel like we have done everything right. We feel like there's nothing we would have done differently. We have stuck to your vision and done our very best to listen to your voice and not compromise on truth. Which is why in our earthly minds none of this makes sense. Why can't people stay? Why can't we gain some momentum?

Why at the time we feel like we're going to experience a breakthrough is it the exact opposite?

Jesus, this is the hardest thing we've ever done. Not only is it hurtful but we don't even know how to deal with most of it. My mind keeps going back to what Brandon told us in SC in Feb.

That "God wants to use us greatly but He's going to have to wound us deeply first." Ouch! I'm just wondering if all this is part of that.

It is only because of you, Jesus, that somehow we have hope. That we're not going to quit. Only because of you that we still have an inner peace that we are doing the right thing. Jesus, I know it is and it will all be worth it.

Tears came to my eyes as I walked along the race route that day, remembering these words—"it will all be worth it." I was perfectly content with a nominal level of pain. I did not, however, see *this* level of pain coming. How was it possible for something to hurt this badly? There was much more to this journal entry, though—a resolve in Amanda that I was now feeling:

Jesus, I've never doubted your faithfulness and your plan. I know you are with us. Father, to be honest I'm scared about this "wounding deeply" part. It's not that I don't know and believe you will bring us through it. It's that I don't know what's coming. And I don't possess the strength to get through it. When I'm such a "forecaster" and trying to mentally prepare myself for something this season is hard for me.

But, Jesus, you know I've always wanted to be used greatly by you. I still do, with all my heart, want to do your work and what you have called me to do. I never want to quit, Jesus. I truly want to see this thing through to the very end.

And I'm not ignorant in that this is just the beginning for us. There's going to be a lot more problems. A lot harder problems. Father please just give us your strength to work through every single one. You are greater. Help me and help us to dig ditches through every storm so we can soak in all you have for us.

I swallowed hard, parched from all the running and the walking and the limping, the sun beating on my brow. I wiped a layer of dried sweat salt away from my eyes. I wasn't sure I wanted to ask any more questions. This was too much to take in.

The voice, however, didn't let me catch my breath. *Remember Jacob*, it whispered.

Jacob? The Bible character, Jacob?

My mind raced, remembering the story of the boy who grew up the son of Isaac and younger twin brother of Esau. Although the older brother was promised blessing in the Jewish tradition, Jacob's ambition in life wouldn't allow him to take the backseat to Esau. He earned the name "Heel Grabber" when he came out of his mother's womb holding on to the back of Esau's heel. He spent his life manipulating and deceiving, grasping at the allure of a blessing from God.

In fact the name Jacob means "deceiver" or "trickster."

It began when he manipulated Esau into handing over his birthright for a cup of stew. It continued when he tricked his father into giving him the blessing of the firstborn and culminated when he manipulated his father-in-law out of over half his flock, which would equate to hundreds of thousands of dollars. Jacob was witty, talented, intelligent, and ambitious. God wanted to use him for great things. God wanted to bless him. In fact, throughout history, Jewish people have referred to the God they serve as the God of Abraham, Isaac, and *Jacob*. God wanted to bless Jacob and bless an entire nation *through* Jacob. And Jacob desperately *wanted* the blessing.

One night while Jacob was on the run from his brother, Esau, and his father-in-law, Laban, God met him in person and began to wrestle with him. Jacob fought hard and wouldn't let go until God handed over the blessing. His whole life of wrestling for a blessing had culminated in this point.

That's when God touched his hip and broke it. He changed his name to Israel, meaning "he wrestles with God." And then God blessed him.

Jacob's blessing was preceded by a broken hip and a changed identity.

Amanda and I had spent much of our lives begging God for a blessing, begging to be used greatly by Him. Now limping along the mini marathon route, I knew the last several months had broken me . . . and begun to change me.

"Why must brokenness precede blessing?" I again asked out loud and braced myself for the answer.

Because otherwise, you'll think you had something to do with the blessing. You'll walk with a swagger in arrogance. I want you to walk with a limp in humility.

A limp. A limp that shows off weakness. A limp that tells the world I had nothing to do with the blessing. A limp that proves God is strong in the midst of my storm and that He works best not through my talent and strength but through my weakness— not through personal records but through surrender.

I now began to realize that I had been trying to operate much of my life in my own strength. When we faced challenges with the church, in marriage, in parenting, instead of kneeling before God to beg for Him to move, I would muster up a can-do atti- tude and plow through with a solution. Before losing Amanda, I would step onstage and preach to impress. In the most recent months since returning to preach, the only thing that gave me the strength even to walk onstage was not a desire to impress people but a newfound ambition to *help* people.

God was now using my brokenness more than He could ever use my talent. He was using my weakness more than He could ever use my strength. And *He* was getting the glory for it, not me.

While my attitude had been "over my dead body will I let this be wasted!" Jesus was reminding me of His heart.

No, Davey, I'm the one who won't let this be wasted. Not over your dead body, but over My dead—and resurrected—body will this not be wasted. I can actually work this whole thing out better than you can imagine or fathom.

Brokenness before blessing.

"So where's the blessing?" I said aloud indignantly. "This still feels like brokenness. I'm ready to experience the blessing."

You misunderstand blessing, Davey. The voice was clearer now than ever. *Blessing isn't something you receive for your benefit. It's something produced for the benefit of others. Jacob's blessing wasn't what he received but what he gave to others. True blessing is being a blessing.*

Being a blessing. It was making sense now. My life was being wrung out for the refreshment of others. My cup was being poured out to quench the thirst of others. My body was being broken for the healing of others. This is what Paul meant when he called himself a drink offering poured out for others (see Philippians 2:17). This is what Jesus meant when He blessed the bread, broke it, and distributed it, and told His disciples it was a symbol of His body being broken for them (see Matthew 26:26). Out of Amanda's death, God was producing something in me that would be a blessing to others.

I had one more question—one more unsettled thought. Something I needed to know before I took one more step in this whole thing. I blurted it out, this time a little more soberly than the last. "Okay, Lord. Last question. What are You trying to produce in me? What are You trying to do through me?"

As I asked this question, I passed the mile-three marker and felt a shift in the air. A cool breeze washed through my T-shirt. A slight shiver shot up my spine. What I would hear over the next three miles from the Lord would completely change the trajectory for how I viewed tragedy—in my own life as well as in the lives of others.

19

THE VALLEY OF THE
SHADOW OF DEATH

WHAT ARE YOU TRYING TO PRODUCE IN ME? THE QUESTION LINGERED. The stillness on the street created an eerie overtone despite the rapidly climbing sun. I followed a slight zigzag on Michigan Street and crossed over Holmes Avenue.

As I did I could feel the stiffness in my leg setting in. My underarms were tender from the dried sweat rubbing against my shirt like sandpaper scraping with each swing of my arms. All moisture had escaped my lips, leaving them dried and cracked, aching for a balm or healing drink to quench their thirst.

I waited, listening, eager to hear what the voice would whisper next. Nothing came. Had He grown silent? Had He gotten frustrated with me asking so many questions? Was He tired of this wrestling?

I made my way up a slight incline, the three-mile marker now well in my rear. A lonely concession table was still set out and covered with small Gatorade cups, filled with water. Now that every runner had been by the table, it sat deserted. I hobbled over and reached for a cup, dying to wash down the cottony feeling in my mouth.

Out of the corner of my eye, a dilapidated church sign caught my attention. I normally love seeing these signs, bemused by the way they attempt to capture audiences with their pithy phrases.

But this one was different, almost as if it had been written solely for my benefit. It read: The Lord is my Shepherd, I shall not want.

Psalm 23. I knew this passage well. In fact, of any passage in Scripture other than John 3:16—"For God so loved the world, that he gave his only Son, that whoever believes in him should not perish but have eternal life" (ESV)—this had to be the most well-known and oft-quoted psalm in all history. Most Christian homes have a coffee mug or a picture frame with this passage stenciled onto it.

Not to mention, Psalm 23 had become a particularly relevant psalm to me in the past few months, not because of the beginning of the passage but because of the middle. Verse 4 reads, "Though I walk through the valley of the shadow of death, I will fear no evil, for you are with me." I had read this psalm dozens of times and held on to it for dear life since I'd lost Amanda.

To be honest, before Amanda died I would read King David's writings and feel confused. One minute he would speak of God's closeness, saying basically, "God, I feel You so near to me, Your breath is on my neck, Your comforting touch on my shoulder." Then, the very next passage, David would be screaming at God, "Where are You!? You've abandoned me! Left me to die at the hands of my enemies!"

I used to think David needed medication. He was bipolar, schizophrenic, and needed a prescription for Prozac.

Then *I* went through the valley of the shadow of death, and suddenly I understood where he was coming from. Perhaps David needed medication, but if he did, then so did I.

I understood what it was like to feel closeness to the Lord in the midst of abandonment from others. I understood what it was like to feel a peace that I couldn't explain in the midst of a tumultuous storm. I understood what it was like to stand in the midst of adversity and death and declare the goodness of the Lord in the land of the living.

I also understood what it felt like to long for my own death—to feel utterly abandoned by God. I understood what it was like not to be able to fall asleep for fear of the nightmares that laid siege to my mind. I understood what it felt like not to be able to pull myself out of bed in the morning because I couldn't see a reason to live. I understood what it felt like to secretly plot how I could end my life.

I finally understood the waves of sorrow described in many of the psalms, and David didn't seem so crazy to me anymore. *The Lord is my shepherd, I shall not want,* the still, small voice suddenly chimed in.

Verses 1 through 3 of Psalm 23 are uplifting verses. In fact, I used to think these verses described the life of someone following Jesus closely, doing His kingdom work. *The Lord is my shepherd; I shall not want.*

It's an incredible feeling to know that when I surrender my life to Jesus's leading, when I yield to Him as the boss of my life, I will lack for nothing. There have been many times in my life when I have felt that kind of contentment with the Lord, as if nothing else could fill the void in my heart like He could.

"*I love verse 1,*" I whispered to myself as I thought about verse 2. "*He makes me lie down in green pastures. He leads me beside still waters. He restores my soul.*" Jesus gives me rest, and refreshment!

Amanda and I always kept a regular day off for rest together—a Sabbath—as part of our weekly rhythm. We'd drop Weston off with Amanda's grandmother and spend the entire day reading, lounging, talking, listening to Norah Jones radio on Pandora, watching movies—and doing what married couples do. There were seasons when these Fridays were the only thing that got us through to the next week together. They were a chance to reconnect, refresh, and rejuvenate. The Lord always restored our souls during these rest days.

"Verse 2," I sighed, remembering Fridays with Amanda as I chucked the empty cup to the ground. I began to walk again, my steps more laborious now. I was unable to flex my ankle and, with each step, landed on my left side flat-footed. But I still had some distance to go to get back to the starting line. Verse 3. *He leads me in paths of righteousness for his name's sake.*

I thought about how God had led Amanda and me in paths of righteousness since calling us to start the church. He taught us to listen to His voice and direction as we begged Him to reveal to us whether or not we were supposed to move. He taught us to cry together and hurt together when, as happens in most church plants, the occasional person left the church in a mean and ugly way. He taught us to communicate more intimately with one another during times when our schedules weren't lining up and we failed to connect with each other.

He taught us to trust His provision when we didn't know how we were going to pay the bills some months. He taught us how to trust Him with everything when we emptied our retirement accounts to keep the church afloat. He taught us how to be content with the small ministry He had given us when the church didn't take off immediately—and when it still didn't take off after three years of hard labor.

Since Amanda and I first met, the Lord had changed us from the inside out. He had radically transformed us since we first stepped onto Indianapolis soil. I was a different person now. Amanda was a different person the day she was killed.

The day she was killed. The thought sent a wave of shock through my system that abruptly took my breath away and caused me to gasp.

Look at verse 4, the voice suddenly cut in.

I didn't want to. I knew what it said. I didn't want to consider it. Up to this point I assumed verses 1 through 3 were true of the life of a believer if they followed Jesus closely. I thought that, as long as Amanda and I were doing the work of God, we would be invincible, impervious to Satan's schemes. Sure, I knew we'd walk through difficulty, but I also knew we could walk through anything as long as we had each other. Part of me felt that this valley I was walking through alone was some sadistic sort of punishment for past sin in my life or failing to follow Jesus as closely as I should.

I don't want to, I answered in my thoughts.

Look at it, Davey.

Finally, I turned my heart. *Even though I walk through the valley of the shadow of death, I will fear no evil, for you are with me . . .*

Good. Now look again at verse 3.

What? Why?

Davey, look at it. What does it say?

"He leads me in paths of righteousness for his name's sake," I said aloud.

Now again at verse 4.

"Even though I walk through the valley of the shadow of death, I will fear no evil, for you are with me."

My mind's eye shifted back and forth between the two verses. And then it hit me, like a rush of reality, a truth salve to the crevices of my heart.

What if one of the paths of righteousness God leads us in *is* the valley of the shadow of death? What if we don't fall into the valley because we've lost our way or because we made a misstep? What if the valley isn't *punishment* for something we've done wrong? Instead, what if it's *preparation* for a greater potential in our life? The thought nearly took my breath away again. My heart began to race, and almost on cue the voice chimed in:

Davey, there are some things you can't be taught in verses 1 through 3. There are some very necessary components to your righteousness that must be infused in you but can be accomplished only in the valley. In those valleys, I'm doing something in you *so I can do something even greater* through *you.*

It was beginning to make sense. I had spent years telling people that unless they endured some sort of trial they could never experience true triumph. There are some muscles that can't be built unless put under strain. Faith is a muscle too. Unless faith feels the pressure and duress of trial, it can never be strengthened, let alone perfected.

"Okay, Lord! I get it. But *what* are You trying to do through me!" I was fed up. Ready for the answer. That's when it came— swift and cutting, simple but profound, the answer I had been looking for.

Mile two.

I'm making you dangerous.

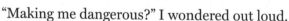

"Making me dangerous?" I wondered out loud.

What does verse 5 say? He responded.

I rifled through the first four verses to prompt my memory as to what came next:

"You prepare a table before me in the presence of my enemies."

That's it! Dangerous! How dangerous of a dude do you have to be to sit and dine in the presence of your enemies? I thought about every major battle scene in all the epic war movies I had seen—*Braveheart, The Lord of the Rings, 300.* I thought about what it must feel like to be surrounded by enemies on all sides and in that moment pause, sit down at a table, take out a fork and announce, "Before I open up a can of you-know-what on you, I'm going to open up a can of Chef Boyardee right here!"

That's dangerous! It's like Liam-Neeson-in-*Taken* dangerous! You can't touch a dude like that!

I thought about the apostle Paul and what he said toward the end of his life: "To live is Christ, and to die is gain" (Philippians 1:21 ESV). In other words, "If you let me live, I'll preach Jesus. If you kill me, I get to spend eternity with Him. Win-win."

What do you do to a guy like that? How do you stop him? The religious leaders of his day couldn't! They tried to silence this guy who was relentlessly spreading the good news of Jesus everywhere he went.

"Let's arrest him," they conspired.

And then Paul started a prison ministry from the inside, and all the jailers became Christians.

"Let's flog him," they decided.

When they did, people watched in awe as Paul walked in triumph to and from his flogging. Everyone who watched wanted the hope that Paul possessed. He got to share Jesus with more people because of it.

"Okay, if those won't work, let's kill him."

Well, then you make him a martyr and more people come to know Christ.

You see, Davey, I will accomplish My purposes. I will get My gospel out there, no matter what Satan tries to throw its way. And I use dangerous people to push it forward.

This was happening to me. I could see it in myself. I was becoming dangerous. I no longer feared death. Suffering didn't terrify me. I was no longer held hostage by what others said or thought about me. My life was committed to one purpose and one purpose only: make heaven more crowded. And when I die, I know I will not lament leaving earth. I will be grateful to be with my Savior and with my bride for all of eternity.

Davey, I want to wield you as a weapon to accomplish My purposes.

Wield as a weapon. I stopped in my tracks. A weapon. A sword. Immediately my mind flashed back to Valentine's Day 2008.

Amanda and I were engaged and set to get married the following August. I had purchased her a sword from the movie *Braveheart*. I know, most guys do chocolates and flowers, but I'm not most guys, and Amanda wasn't most girls. She was special, and each special occasion I felt the urge to do something special for her. Something that would top the last.

This one took the cake.

She was going to school in Pensacola, Florida, at the time, and I was in South Carolina. I found a website where you could order a commemorative edition, full-size *Braveheart* sword, so I had it shipped to her college dorm. With all her girlfriends standing around her as she removed it from its awkward oblong box, I imagined them raising their eyebrows in dismay.

"A *sword*? ... How romantic!" I could picture them remarking sarcastically.

The next thing she would pull from the box, however, would be an epic poem called "The Fight" I had written on a papyrus scroll.

The poem went like this:

Valentine's Day has always been a holiday of cute hearts and cutout shapes of love. Fleeting notes and candy seem to idealize

the Valentine experience. We feast on the luscious array of choco-
lates and flirtatious phrases until we've gorged ourselves so obese
with infatuation that we miss the truth behind love.

And the truth is that we fight. We fight the crowds to be noticed,
to be sought after, to be something more than just a number on
this populated planet. We fight for significance ... because it's in
this significance that we can lie awake at night and dream.

It's in this significance that we can endure the present hardships
because the hope of tomorrow is deep within our clutches. It's in this
significance that we can stand alone on a promise even though we
look out at a sea of seated, apathetic souls. It's in this significance
that we find our battle, a war that wages where we cannot see.

Only few dare to venture into this other world where warriors
lay slain and their corpses strewn over the hillside. To set foot in
this world is to sell your soul to one side. It's a world of signifi-
cance. Know this today, for this is a declaration that I make not in
haste but in earnest resolve. I will fight. I will fight for this calling.
I will fight for the world unseen. I will fight for your love. I will
fight for this relationship. I will fight for your respect. I will pick
up my sword, even when everyone has laid theirs aside. I will
stand in the face of all danger and peril to win your heart ... for
I could never fight enough to receive a reward as valuable as you.

But I will fight ... and I ask you one thing:

Will you take up this sword and fight alongside me, and
through this raging battle, stand victorious . . . my Warrior
Princess?

As I thought about the memory, I imagined Amanda pulling
that sword from its sheath. I imagined her reading the poem. I
imagined the look on her face as she decided if she wanted to join
me in the fight. I imagined the way she looked on our wedding
day, how soft and beautiful and brave she looked walking down
that aisle.

I also thought about where that sword sat now—in my bedroom, where I was keeping it as a reminder since her passing. I thought about where Amanda sat now, a true Warrior Princess, through and through. Tears welled in my eyes.

A sword is a weapon that when wielded properly can claim territories, defend nations, and protect the defenseless. But if a warrior is going to use a sword in battle, he must ensure that it's strong enough to endure the stress it will inevitably undergo. It needs to be resilient enough to flex under strain and immediately return true.

Because of that, every sword goes through a careful shaping and refining process.

A blacksmith—or more specifically a bladesmith, whose trade is to shape blades—will put the sword in a fire heated to upward of twenty-one hundred degrees Fahrenheit. The metal is then taken out of the fire, placed over an anvil, and repeatedly struck with a hammer or mallet in order to shape it into a strong, durable weapon.

If we were to personify feelings onto this sword, we could say it's undergoing a lot of pain. Such intense heat and hammering cannot be comfortable for the sword. But without each of these things, the sword remains a piece of metal that cannot be used. It remains purposeless. It must undergo some sort of "pain" to be forged into a weapon.

This same shaping process occurs in us when we undergo pain and hardship.

Doesn't it seem that the most trying times in our lives have also been the most developmental? Rather than these trials shaking our faith, God uses them to *shape* our faith, if we let Him.

The old adage "no pain, no gain" seems trite to insert into seasons of life where senseless tragedies overtake us. But I guess no matter the degree of the pain, the principle is still true. Not that we have to go seeking out pain in life, because pain will inevitably find us in some way, shape, or form. We don't get to choose *if* we're going to walk through pain, just *how* we walk through it.

In fact, I wonder if the degree of the intensity of the pain we undergo directly correlates with the degree of the impact we will eventually have on others. So the thing that Satan did that was meant to devastate me, destroy me, and deter me from moving on was actually the very thing that God uses to make me a *dangerous* weapon of love to push back darkness in this world.

Davey, the voice interjected, *the key is not to let your pain define you; rather, let it* refine *you into something that is more useful, purposeful, and helpful to others.*

I stared ahead at the road stretched out in front of me. Less than two miles to go. It might as well have been a thousand. I couldn't help but remember our wedding and longed to be transported back to that day, leaving this entire struggle behind.

On that day, Amanda and I carved out a time before the pictures and the ceremony to do what was called a "First Look." I know a lot of couples do this. We closed all the doors to the sanctuary, and I stood in front of the stage as the sound guy cued a compilation of our love songs. Our photographer peeped through the small windows on the sanctuary doors, attempting to capture the moment. I stood there, waiting in breathless expectation to see my bride for the first time.

As the double doors at the back opened, my heart stopped. She slowly stepped through the threshold, the most beautiful smile I've ever seen. Her luscious white dress and veil settled softly on her bronze skin in a way that made my stomach do flip-flops and my heart flutter in rapid syncopation.

My eyes scanned her perfect frame as she waltzed toward me.

I was so distracted by her radiance that I didn't even notice she was holding her arms behind her back, suspiciously. But as she approached me, she brought her arms around and presented me with something so familiar to me, I lost my breath. It was another *Braveheart* sword—one she had purchased for me. "Davey," she said. "Today I'm joining you in this fight. Until the day I die, I'll fight for you, for us, and for people who are far from God."

And she did.

God had made her dangerous. She pushed back darkness until the day she walked down that heavenly aisle and got her "first look" at her true groom, her first love, her savior—Jesus.

Now He was doing the same in me. He was forging me into a ferocious warrior, wielding me as a weapon, shaping me with significant purpose. In William Wallace fashion, my purpose was now to push back darkness; seek revenge on my true enemy, Satan; and fight for the freedom of God's people. And now two *Braveheart* swords stand in a corner of my bedroom to spur me on each day.

As I trudged along I wondered to myself, *Was that it? Was that all He was doing in me?*

Just then I heard the voice cut through my thoughts, *That's only verse 5, Davey. There's more. Keep going.*

20

MIXING THE INGREDIENTS

I KEPT WALKING DOWN THE STREET, NOT A SOUL IN SIGHT NOW. I could almost see the one-mile marker ahead. This was taking longer than I expected it to, but I was still having this private moment with God.

This could possibly have been the longest conversation I'd ever had with Him in a single setting. It reminded me that we really can communicate with Him if we'll posture ourselves to listen, if we'll take the time to open up. This road I was walking was a road of healing. Even as I limped along.

You anoint my head with oil; my cup overflows.

"I'm not sure where this is going, Lord," I admitted as I played over and over the passage in my mind. The language of this part of the verse seemed a little confusing to me, but I kept listening, furrowing my brow as if that would help me hear better.

Davey, the second thing I'm doing is increasing your capacity.

"Increasing my capacity, God? But how? And what on earth does that have anything to do with this verse?"

The voice prodded. *Anointing oil, what do you know about it?*

I had grown up in a church where anointing oil was used on babies for dedications and used to pray for the sick who needed healing. The oil itself contained no magical or mystical quality but was powerful because of what it symbolized. It represented the idea of calling. When a king was anointed in the Bible, oil was poured over his head. This oil signified God's hand of special purpose on that person's life. David, who wrote this psalm, would have known this well. He was called to be Israel's second king and anointed by the prophet Samuel after each of his older, statelier brothers were passed up for the same role.

What always baffled me about David's life was that he was anointed—or called—when he was a teenager but didn't become king for almost fifteen years. In fact, the day after he was anointed as the next king, he found himself back out in the sheepfolds, tending to his father's flock as a shepherd boy. Nothing had changed externally in his life, just this internal sense of God's unique plan for his life.

I began to think about how God has a unique plan and calling for everyone's life. The book of Jeremiah says, "'For I know the plans I have for you,' declares the Lord, 'plans to prosper you and not to harm you, plans to give you hope and a future'" (Jeremiah 29:11 NIV).

This is true of each one of our lives. God has uniquely and distinctly designed each of us with a purpose and a calling—a special story that He is writing in our lives. Often we look at our tragedy and pain as an *interruption* to our story, but God sees it as something else, an *invitation* into a greater story—His story.

That was true of David. It was brokenness, tragedy, pain, and hardship that prepared him for his destiny to be king. David had to undergo a fifteen-year pressing before he eventually sat on the throne.

That's it, Davey, pressing leads to purpose, the Whisperer continued coaxing.

Just then I remembered what Gilla had been trying to teach us on top of the Mount of Olives in the Garden of Gethsemane—when I was too distracted to fully listen. Scattered throughout the entire garden were olive trees. The garden was historically

MIXING THE INGREDIENTS   297

a place where olives were pressed to make olive oil. In fact, the word *Gethsemane* in the Greek means "the place of pressing."

But what's even more fascinating is the garden was called something slightly different in Aramaic, the common language spoken in Jesus's day. It was called "*Gadsemane*," which means "the place of ascension."

Two diametrically opposed concepts, each the namesake for the same location.

Pressing and Ascension.

Down and Up.

Humility and Elevation.

You see, God has an *ascension* plan for each of us—a plan to take us to new levels in life. In our relationships, in our calling, He has a plan to take us places we would otherwise not be able to go on our own. But, we don't get ascension without pressing. We can't have calling without crushing. They always go hand in hand. Why? For the same reason God had to break Jacob's hip: humility.

Can't you see, Davey? I'm broadening your calling. Increasing your influence. But before I can do that, I have to make sure your life speaks of humility.

I crouched next to the sidewalk. The stiffness and pain in my calf had become too unbearable to continue without more stretching. I placed my left toes on the edge of the curb and put my weight on that side to feel a full stretch. "Okay," I said out loud, "I get that. But what about my cup overflowing? That seems like a stretch." I hadn't intended the pun, but I winced as pain shot up my calf. "It seems more like my cup is being emptied."

That's precisely right, Davey. Your cup is being emptied. Sometimes I have to empty before I can fill.

"What? Why?"

Because sometimes there are things contaminating your cup. Pride is the worst of these contaminants. And in order to strip you of pride, often your life must be stripped of other things, even good things. I want to serve up My food and drink in clean dishes. I need to clean you up and make you humble. If your cup isn't clean when I fill you up, it will muddy up anything I pour into your life.

I thought about people who bounced from place to place, church to church, relationship to relationship, contaminating everything in their wake, always blaming their dissatisfaction on others and never realizing that they are the common denominator of the wake of destruction they leave. As I heard a preacher once say, "Where you go, there *you* are. You are your own worst enemy. No one has lied to you, deceived you, tricked you, and hurt you more than *you!*"

You see, Davey, there is a deep cleaning of your motives and your desires that can happen only through emptying. I'm emptying you of you.

"That sounds about right. I feel pretty empty now, Lord. Is that the *point? Is that what You wanted?*"

No, son. This is the first time in this conversation I could feel the fatherly affection coming from the voice. *I always empty you with the plan to expand your cup and fill it back up. I will restore what has been taken from you, but I don't just fill to the brim. I do more than that. What does verse 5 say?*

I sighed. "My cup overflows."

That's right. I fill you so full, it overflows. And you know what happens when your cup overflows? It fills other people's cups. It blesses and refreshes others. That's what I want for you.

I slipped my toe down the side of the curb and back onto the road, where I began walking again, my calf now a little looser than before. I started to think about the idea of my cup being expanded, my capacity being increased and overflowing into the cups of others. I could already see it occurring in my life. I now had a broadened and crystal-clear vision for our church and its role in our city. I was becoming a better communicator. I was being given opportunities to encourage more people. I was becoming a better leader because, as I made decisions, I could now see what was truly important in the light of eternity and what wasn't.

I was also becoming a more caring pastor to people. Before Amanda passed, I didn't understand people in pain. I could barely sympathize with them. Now I do more than sympathize with them—I hurt with them, I make sure I'm present with them, I cry with them, I pray with them, I *understand* them. I've moved along the spectrum from sympathy to *empathy*. And more than just throwing out trite theological phrases to "fix" people's problems, I understand the power of presence, of just *being* with people when they're hurting.

You see, Davey. I am increasing your capacity.

I *could* see it. It was difficult to admit—even to myself—that it had taken this level of pain to see this level of growth occur in my heart. But I was beginning to understand. I was beginning to see how God was working this for my good.

My good, I thought. *Hmmm. I used to believe that everything worked for my good.*

My mind flashed to another familiar verse in the Bible that had carried me through another difficult season.

I was seventeen years old and my parents announced to my brother and me that my dad was resigning from the church where he had just spent the last ten years doing ministry. This meant we would be moving. It was the summer before my senior year of high school, and now I would be starting over—a new city, a new school, new friends, a new baseball team.

That summer, I played on a completely new travel team, and before each game, I pulled a pocket Bible out of my bag and set it on the dugout bench. It was dog-eared to Romans 8:28, and I would read that verse before every game—unwittingly, leaving out one important word.

And we know that for those who love God all things work for good, for those who are called according to his purpose.

I've often looked back at that year, which should have been the toughest year of my life to that point, and reflected on how everything good in my life came as a result of the move—being called to ministry, playing baseball on a full-ride scholarship at Southern Wesleyan, meeting Amanda, joining the staff at NewSpring, and starting a church in Indianapolis.

What now didn't make sense to me was how one of those *good* things could be taken from me and how my life could still be called *good.* In my mind, the *good* of Romans 8:28 had been rendered void. It seemed His promise was no longer true for my life. *Bad* had now overtaken the *good.*

Hobbling down White River Parkway, past the zoo and the one-mile marker, I told the still, small voice just that. And before He responded to me it seemed He stood silent and let me grumble, let me spout off my complaints, all of them—verbal punches I threw out blow by blow. He absorbed them and then He continued.

This is the last thing I want to show you, Davey. I'm not done yet. I'm mixing the ingredients.

Amanda used to bake the best chocolate chip cookies. Move over Pepperidge Farms, Amanda's would make you, as they say in the South, "slap your grandma!"

Any time we had guests over, Amanda would bake a batch of her homemade cookies, much to the delight of all our friends. I remember four of us eating two dozen cookies together in one night. They were the precise texture you want, just chewy enough, without being so soft that they would come apart in your hands. They were the exact right amount of sweet—just perfect.

They were also from a secret recipe. Amanda refused to give away the secret to anyone. I once asked her what the difference was in her recipe and other cookie recipes. She looked around and lowered her voice to answer me—double-checking that we were alone in our living room.

"I double the sugar," she whispered.

Of course! No wonder they were so good!

The voice interrupted. *Isn't that what everyone wants out of life, Davey? Double the sugar?*

I thought about it for a second. I suppose that was correct. I sure wouldn't mind double the sugar out of life. I love the sweet seasons of life. Don't we all?

But what about the other ingredients? it pried further.

I thought about what else Amanda would put in her cookies. Salt.

I definitely wouldn't eat salt by itself.

Raw eggs.

No way, Rocky Balboa!

Baking soda.

Ugh! How bitter!

Flour.

Not a chance. Talk about drying you out! It would make a funny prank or old youth group game—"How much flour can you eat in a minute without taking a drink? Ready go!"—no thank you!

The voice again spoke: *I know you'd never eat each of these ingredients by themselves. But can you agree with Me that they are each necessary for the end product?*

I didn't want to admit it, but He was right. They were necessary. In fact, I could even see the purpose in each one of them. Salt is good for seasoning and preservation, baking soda and flour for rising.

Look at the verse again. You've missed a key word there, He said.

This time I pulled out my phone, opened my Bible app, and plugged in Romans 8:28 (ESV) to get a good look. "And we know that for those who love God all things work together for good, for those who are called according to his purpose."

There it was. I had missed it. Completely left out the most crucial word in the verse.

Together.

Like a baker mixes the sweet ingredients with the bitter and dry ones to make something beautiful and tasty—like my sweet Amanda mixing together her cookies—the Lord stirs *together* the sweet seasons of life with the bitter and dry seasons to produce something beautiful. And in the process He even redeems the purpose of each ingredient I wouldn't eat alone.

What the Enemy means to use to dry me out, like flour, God will use to raise me up. What the Enemy means to make me sick and break me down, like eggs, God means to use to build me up. What the Enemy means to use to make me recoil with distaste, like salt, God means to use to season and preserve my life. He is mixing all the ingredients, both the good and the bitter, to make something beautiful.

I wiped the sweat from my mouth and squeezed a newly formed tear from my eyelid. "So what You're saying is, even in this situation, I'll look back and see the good in it one day?"

That's exactly right, Davey. Just like you looked back to your senior year of high school and have seen the good produced from that trying season and over the last ten years, I'll do the same for you over the next ten years and beyond. Trust Me, give Me a little time, and I'll turn this into something beautiful.

I could almost hear Amanda's voice echoing: *"Trust me, give me a little time, and I'll turn this into something beautiful."*

I hit Lock on my phone and shoved it back into my pocket.

One more thing, Davey. Psalm 23. The last verse.

"Surely goodness and mercy shall follow me all the days of my life, and I shall dwell in the house of the LORD forever."

Goodness and mercy will follow me. I reflected on that for a moment. As I did, I looked up and realized I was on Washington Street, back at the starting line. The streets were clear, and two blocks away, I could hear cheers mixed with the public announcer beckoning runners to push hard on the last leg, to finish strong.

I sat down for a moment . . . in the middle of the street.

That's exactly what you can't do in all this, Davey. You can't sit down. People sit down in their grief. They stall out. They get lost in it. Remember the first verse. I'm your Shepherd. I will guide you through this. If I called you to it, I'll see you through it. Don't stop walking behind Me. As you follow Me, goodness and mercy will follow you.

"But I can't see goodness and mercy following me in this, Lord." I wasn't sure how to reconcile what appeared to be a promise from God with my present reality.

The voice came back again, this time in a loving whisper. *Of course you can't, My son. You don't know something is following you until you look back. Look back at all the markers in this journey since November. I've never once left your side. I'm with you always.*

I thought about when I walked into the house to find Amanda on the floor. I thought about the song "Nothing Is Wasted" playing over Pandora in the hospital room. I thought about my meeting with Pastor Martin Smith, my week with Dr. John Walker, my trip to Israel, my text conversations with Levi Lusko. I thought about walking back into the Sunnyfield Court house and running toward the roar. I thought about how every time I needed an encouraging touch from Amanda, one would confront me in the pages of her journals.

And then, in the stillness of that moment I realized something. Something incredible. Something that sent a warm shiver through my veins. Like a fleece being wrapped around my shoulders, it invited me into a nearness I'd never felt before. I realized the voice the psalmist uses in Psalm 23 to refer to God changes mid-passage. Verses 1 through 3 are in the third person:

"*He* makes me lie down . . ."

"*He* leads me beside . . ."

"*He* restores my soul . . ."

But in verse 4, in the valley, everything changes. The voice shifts. He addresses God personally—in the second person.

"*You* are with me . . ."

"*Your* rod and *your* staff . . ."

It was true. In the mountaintop experiences of life, before all of this happened, I tended to merely know *about* God, like He's some distant being, an acquaintance I acknowledge. But this valley is where I've really gotten to *know* God personally. Connected. Close. Intimate.

In the six months following Amanda's death, I had experienced a nearness to God I'd *never* before experienced in my life. He had never once left me. Sometimes His provision and direction was in the form of His comforting Spirit, and sometimes it was in the form of someone else's encouragement. Regardless, He was with me every step of the way.

And no matter what, I'll stay with you—just keep walking behind Me. I'll see you all the way through this valley.

And with that, He was finished.

I knew this wouldn't be the last I'd hear of the voice. In fact, I was sure I'd hear Him even more regularly now than before, because now I was listening. I was waiting to hear from Him— the still, small voice that would never leave my side.

"Excuse me, sir! You're missing the party!" A voice broke through my thoughts and startled me to my feet. "The finish line is two blocks up that way." The gruff-looking man held a broom in his hands and was sweeping the strewn confetti to the edge of the street.

"Oh . . . right . . . sorry about that," I nodded, pulled myself from my seated position, and slowly hobbled up West Street two blocks toward the finish.

As I turned the corner to New York Street, the finish line emerged in clear sight. The celebratory screams of the crowd and the electronic beats of the winner's circle music faded into the background, and I fixed my eyes on the clouds above the finish line banner. I had only one final thought.

I can't wait to cross the finish line.

But I also knew that was for another day. My finish line is still in front of me. Today I keep walking, running when I can, and maybe at times, hobble.

The rest of my story is yet to be written. So is yours. But we each have a race marked out for us. We don't get to determine *when* we'll finish the race, only *how* we'll finish. One day, I'll cross the finish line of this life and meet Amanda in the winner's circle. I picture it a glorious reunion, an epic rejoining of two hearts destined to beat as one. We'll have so much to catch up on. We'll have so many scars to show each other, so many stories to share, so many new relationships to regale each other with. Maybe, just maybe, we'll go on another one of those long runs together, this time through heaven.

I imagine her taking me by the hand and showing me all the places she's already explored in this new world. She'll show me the pieces of furniture she's restored and the mansions she's decorated. She'll talk about all the things we still need to do together, places we need to see, and how we now have eternity to accomplish them. And then she'll introduce me to Evie, whose mother's blond highlights by this time, no doubt, will have begun to show in her hair as well.

Then Amanda will look at me and say, "Davey, I have to introduce you to someone else. You've heard His voice for a long time, but just wait until you meet Him face-to-face. All those questions you have—the same questions I also once had—they'll be answered the moment you see Him. He's magnificent, Davey, He is truly magnificent." And then she'll walk me into the halls of the most beautiful palace I've ever laid eyes on. There, seated on the throne of heaven, will be the Master Storyteller, the one who called Amanda and me to live out this great, epic adventure together—King Jesus. He'll stand before us both, His eyes gleaming with delight, and say to us, "Well done, My good and faithful servants."

Until that day, my race is yet to be finished. So is yours. Another mile marker has passed, another chapter is closed and closing, day by day. A new chapter begins. No matter the trials we endure in life, the hardships we face, the valleys we find ourselves in, I'm more determined now than ever that we don't face them alone. The still, small voice walks beside us, carries us, guides us, sees us through all of it. And one day He'll pull the veil back from my eyes and show me the countless lives and stories that have been altered because of my story.

Maybe you're one of those lives. And what I know to be true is He'll pull the same veil back for you. In that moment, we'll all see what we've been hoping for and believing all this time—that goodness and mercy have followed us all the days of our lives and that truly nothing has been wasted.

I absolutely believe all of this will happen on the other side of eternity. But a few years later I would get a glimpse of redemption unfolding in my story here on earth ...

PART 5

THE END OF ONE CHAPTER, THE BEGINNING OF ANOTHER

21

REDEMPTION

The pew-like wooden bench at the front of the gallery felt cold and stiff despite my racing heart and clammy palms. A nervous knot was entangling itself inside my stomach, causing me to almost shake. I'd been sitting in exactly the same spot for the last three days, shifting uncomfortably back and forth as trial proceedings played out in front of me. It was the last week of September 2022, nearly seven years since Amanda was murdered. After seven or eight trial continuations, a global pandemic that shut down everything for nearly a year (not excluding jury trials), delays associated with a new judicial building being constructed in Indianapolis, and, most recently, two mistrials earlier in the year, we finally had come to the moment where a verdict was about to be declared.

I stared straight ahead with bated breath, waiting for Judge Grant W. Hawkins to reemerge from his chambers. This particular courtroom had somewhat of an unorthodox layout. Lining a panel directly in front of me sat both the prosecution team and the defense, their backs facing the gallery and their attention fixed in the same direction as mine. The prosecution took up the left side of the table, while the defense occupied the right. To the farthest right end of the table was the defendant, Larry Taylor, clad in a wrinkled button-up shirt and dress slacks, shackles on both his wrists and his ankles. Out of my right peripheral I could see an empty jury bench along the wall, a glaring reminder of the crazy journey this whole legal process had been for us so far.

Amanda's case had been covered off and on over the last seven years in every local media platform, even touching several national and global outlets, allowing anyone who so desired to have an opinion about her life, her death, my healing journey, and our family to give their input. For the most part, people had been wonderful—the large majority of believers and unbelievers alike had responded in overwhelming kindness, empathy, consideration, and condolences—save a few loud voices who still desired to tout conspiracy theories of my involvement in the crime. A handful of these voices even began mailing packets that outlined their theories to any church or organization I was being requested to speak at. Perhaps they had some personal vendetta from an unresolved injustice or abuse they'd experienced in their own life and were projecting onto our story. Or perhaps they had good intentions but were grossly misled. Whatever the reason, to them this seemed like another true-crime drama case they could help crack— but I wish they could see that to our family, it was the most agonizing thing that has ever happened to us. Nonetheless, it seemed that our grief had become their entertainment.

It now seemed strangely ironic to me that her case would come down to a bench trial, where only *one* voice would make a determination about the parties in question. It was a fitting allusion to the worldview I had chosen to adopt through the whole journey—that in the end there is only one opinion that matters, and that's God's. That He is the ultimate judge and arbiter in all cases of injustice that we experience in life. That He is the one who will exact revenge. He is the one who will levy punishment and grant mercy. He is the one who will make all things right. He is the one who will, as J. R. R. Tolkien said, "render all things sad untrue." And He is the only one who judges the true heart of a man.

The two trials before this one were declared mistrials before they even got through jury selection. They were mistried as a direct result of tainted jury pools, largely due to the high-profile nature of the case. After the second mistrial the defense had allegedly gotten so fed up with the state's inability to collect a strong jury, they filed for a speedy trial—even after nearly seven years of dragging their feet.

As we waited there for Judge Hawkins to reappear, I couldn't help but think about how we were warned years before that this could be a long process and that we would need to "settle this" in our hearts long before the case was settled in court. Over the last seven years I'd found my heart on multiple occasions vacillating between the spiritual realm and the natural one. On most days I'd tell you I'd come to a deep and genuine acceptance of what had happened and that I trusted God with justice, while other days I grew impatient feeling like the only sense of closure I'd get in this would be the case finally going to court and Larry Taylor being locked away for life.

Now all of that was about to come to a head. It would either be resolved with a guilty verdict or the whole landscape would get completely upended with a declaration of "not guilty"—something I would have been entirely unprepared for. Sitting there now, anticipating Judge Hawkins's arrival, I was barely holding up, even with 99 percent assurance that Larry was the true perpetrator.

The week had been a bit of an emotional whiplash. I went into it with the understanding that we had an "extremely solid case," that the prosecution was "confident that Larry is the right guy," and that we'd get a guilty verdict by the end of the week. So rather than expending emotional energy in that direction,

I focused on what I was going to feel when, for the first time, I finally stepped into the same room with the man who killed my wife. I don't believe there is any way to prepare yourself for that moment.

For me it was buffered by a law called the "separation of witnesses." According to Indiana law—and most states, as I understand it—once you're subpoenaed for court you can't discuss matters of the case with any other witness, suspect, or courtroom player other than your legal representation. In my case, it meant that I would miss opening arguments and the testimony of the head EMT who was the first responder on the scene. Thankful that I'd be spared from hearing in detail his account, I entered that week and that courtroom with one thing on my mind: the apprehension of looking in the eyes of the last man who ever saw Amanda alive and conscious.

So while the trial finally got underway, I found myself sitting outside the courtroom in a long hallway lined by large windows, facing the cityscape of Indianapolis on the horizon. My dad sat right next to me, opting to forgo the opening arguments to be present with his son. A weird tension hung in the air as we sat there—not between us, rather in light of the fact that we were finally here. As he and I tried to talk about anything other than the looming moment occupying both of our thoughts, I couldn't help but think about frantically dialing his number nearly seven years before as I knelt by Amanda, her breathing shallow and labored. I couldn't help but think about the morning in February he drove me back to the house to confront "my demons" there. And here he was now, sitting by my side during this pinnacle moment of this journey. I choked back tears as I looked at him. "Thank you, Dad. For everything." Somehow nothing more needed to be said. We both understood. Somehow beneath my stoic exterior, I knew he recognized that if I said any more I might just lose control and wind up a weeping, blubbering mess in that hallway.

"We're ready for you, Mr. Blackburn." The head prosecutor's voice felt abrupt as he peeked his head out of the courtroom and motioned me to come on in. My legs were like jelly as I stood and began walking toward the door.

I entered the courtroom and could immediately feel all eyes on me; the room seemed to hold its collective breath, all except for Larry Taylor, of course, who presented a certain rigid callousness. The way the courtroom was arranged he was facing Judge Hawkins, and all I could see was the back of his head and his short, stout frame seated at the end of the defense table. I had to walk right past him from behind to get to the witness stand. I glared at the back of his head and felt a sudden rush to my face. Like a camera reel on fast-forward, the image of my wife gasping for breath, the blood on my hands as I held the back of her head, the doctors informing me about the gunshot wounds—all flooded my mind. A terrifyingly dark and rageful thought slinked up my spine. *I wish someone would put a bullet in the back of his head.* I felt like I could pass out as my vision began to blur, my thoughts racing as my body had to will me forward. I nearly brushed him as I squeezed by the narrow opening between the defense table and the enclosed jury area. Larry could have stuck his leg out and tripped me, I passed so close to him. If he had, I'm not sure I would have been aware enough at that moment to do anything but tumble to the ground. I felt completely disoriented.

As I climbed the single step to the witness stand and turned toward Judge Hawkins to be sworn in, I don't remember much of what he said, or what I said in response. I was so distracted by what I knew was about to happen next. I was going to look my wife's killer in the eyes for the first time. I took a deep breath and exhaled.

This moment had haunted me for seven years. Ever since seeing Larry's face on the news for the first time, I dreaded the moment that I'd have to sit in the same room as him. Sometimes a moment can become magnified in your head, almost like the fear of the thing is bigger than the thing itself. As I took my seat I tried to remind myself of what had happened when I finally looked Jalen Watson in the eyes during a hearing over a year before. When I told him I had chosen to forgive him, something broke at that moment. As the words "I have chosen to forgive you" left my mouth, I felt strength and fortitude surge through me, such that I had never experienced before, and what could only be explained as someone other than me taking over.

"Jalen, look me in the eye," I had said. "I have chosen not to hold this against you." *Where did that strength come from? It was so liberating! So empowering!* The entire room could feel it that day. Like a collective sigh, a tension broke. Jalen immediately slumped in his chair, pulled his orange jumpsuit over his face, and began weeping. I walked away from that day with a little more courage to face Larry whenever it finally came because I had *experienced* the truth of "He who is in you is greater than he who is in the world" (1 John 4:4 ESV).

Although I wasn't addressing Larry Taylor directly, I knew this moment could have a similar outcome if I looked at him. Eyes are telling. I was convinced that, like with Jalen, something would break both in me and in the spiritual realm if I could meet his gaze. I slowly lifted my head and looked directly at Larry, not knowing what to expect or what would be staring back at me.

As I quickly scanned his face, I was taken aback. I didn't see sorrow or remorse, nor did I see smugness. I didn't even see angst or concern. I saw a sort of blank stare. He was looking in my direction but seemed to be staring right through me, like everything was dead inside. All at once I was reminded of my conversation with Pastor Smith at Starbucks years ago, and the thought popped into my head, *What kind of terrible things has happened to his kid that would compel him to do something this atrocious?* And my heart melted. Rather than bitterness, rather than callousness, rather than anger, much softer emotions began to flood me. Was that compassion? Pity? Hurt? I wasn't too sure what it was at that moment. All I knew was that my heart had almost instantaneously softened. Rather than the warrior spirit I had approached this whole thing with for so long, I felt the heart of a big brother, a father even. And looking back on it now, that would set the tone for what happened next.

Questioning from the prosecution team began precisely as they had prepared me for it. I turned my attention to Emily Snyder, the counselwoman lofting questions to me, all the while seeing Larry's face blurred in my periphery. I didn't want to show emotion. For some reason it felt weak to do so, and at the same time it seemed to me calloused and inhuman *not* to. All I really wanted to do was get this part over with and then hide in my seat in the gallery.

I held my composure well until Emily offered up a question that she hadn't prepared me for. "Why did you call your dad after you called 911?"

It stopped me. Abruptly. They had not prepared me for this question, and I hadn't considered an answer. Rather than just factual, this felt visceral. *Why had I called my dad?* I had circled that question for the last seven years, dismissing it when no quick explanation came to me, but in this moment it became clear.

A lump formed in my throat and I tried to choke back the tears but couldn't. It was all so clear now. Here sitting in front of me was a young man whose dad hadn't been there for him. He was fatherless, and the wake of that had ransacked my whole world. Generational sin had mounted on itself and, like a wrecking ball, pillaged my life. And that generational sin threatened to invade my story if I didn't decidedly put a stop to it, if I didn't choose forgiveness over bitterness. If I didn't override my desire to run away from the difficult task of shepherding Weston's heart even through this horrific thing that marked his life. Sure, my trauma may not result in perpetuating harm or hurt toward others intentionally, but I could easily see myself disengaging, dissociating from the difficult tasks of life. I could imagine neglecting my kids because my own hurt was too much to deal with.

It was my dad's example, on the other hand, that had given me some kind of anchor of truth to tether to. He had been there for me through so many ups and downs. He'd tell you he wasn't a perfect dad (although he was near enough to it), and he never really tried to solve my problems for me, but he was always *present.* And, whether he was consciously aware of it or not, his presence had set a precedent and laid a foundation for an even greater presence in my life—my heavenly Father's.

Even in that moment sitting with Amanda dialing my dad's number, a haunting, empty feeling had come over me: *My dad can't do anything about this. The only one who can is my heavenly Father.* And now, looking back on it, as I choked out the response through tears, "My dad's always been there for me," the dual nature of that statement hit me with such an emotional ferocity. *He* had always been there for me. *He* had walked with me through the valley. *He* was right by my side as my story was playing itself out. And *He* was working to redeem it one moment at a time.

Judge Hawkins motioned for a courtroom attendant to bring me a box of tissues, and after a few moments I was able to regain my composure and finish my portion of the questioning. Once I stepped down from the stand and took my seat (again walking right past Larry), I breathed a sigh of relief knowing my part was over and now I could just watch as the prosecution secured the case. But over Monday and Tuesday of that week, the tension in not only my heart but our entire family's tightened as we heard a litany of evidence be discarded, one after the other, as unsubstantiated. We watched in disbelief as the prosecution revealed that there were no fingerprints, no eyewitnesses (or at least who could describe facial features in detail), and no DNA left on the scene. If you had asked me at the end of Tuesday what my confidence level was in the case, I would have said 30 percent. It seemed to all of us, Amanda's family included, that it could have gone either way and, to our horror, this case might be in jeopardy of being dismissed.

It wasn't until Wednesday that the picture of what happened on the morning of November 10 began to come into focus. Between the sworn-in testimonies of the two accomplices, Jalen Watson and Diano Gordon; a piece of DNA found on a sweater left in the stolen getaway car, cell phone triangulation technology; and recovered texts and Google searches that had been deleted from Larry's phone, the investigation pieced together an incredibly precise case, and the prosecution did a masterful job of unveiling it. Early in the morning the three men—Larry Taylor, Jalen Watson, and Diano Gordon—had left a friend's apartment on the east side of Indy, broken into an apartment in the same complex, stolen a car there, and driven across to rendezvous with Jalen's girlfriend at an apartment complex just outside of our neighborhood. When she didn't wake up to their early morning knocks, they decided to break into a house three doors down from mine. The residents were out of town, so their forced entry went undetected. They backed the stolen car into the garage to load up the stolen goods from the house. Larry Taylor sat in the driver's seat and watched me pull out of my driveway as I left for the gym on a "normal Tuesday morning."

So there we all sat, anxiously awaiting the verdict, me mulling over the details of that day. As the minute-by-minute rundown came into focus, I was again haunted by what seemed like the sheer misfortune of the whole morning. *Why did I leave for the gym later than I originally intended that morning? Why didn't I go earlier? Why didn't I go later? Why did I even go at all!?* It seemed like ten minutes earlier or ten minutes later would have changed the entire course of that morning and the last seven years of my life. *Amanda would still be here with us.*

As if on cue to quell my anxious thoughts, a hand from my left reached over, the fingers interlocking with mine, and gave a little squeeze. I glanced down, my eye catching the sparkle of an oval-cut diamond and wedding band overlapping mine. I raised my head to meet her deep brown eyes. This lovely dark-haired woman gave me a reassuring look through her slightly puffy and tear-stained almond-shaped eyes. In that moment I couldn't think of another person I'd rather be sitting next to given the circumstances, and in an instant I was teleported back to the moment I first laid eyes on her exquisite features.

It was September 2016, not even a year after Amanda had passed away. I watched this enchanting and mysterious dark-haired, brown-eyed girl walk through the doors of the CrossFit gym where I was working out. I'm not even sure when I learned her name was Kristi, but she had my attention from the moment I saw her. Though I was sure I was being furtive with my glances in her direction, she would tell me later I was being far less discreet than I hoped.

At the time I had just started writing this book. The process of putting emotions and memories to paper was bringing me a lot of healing, so much so that I began to feel like I might be healthy enough to poke my head up and be open to God bringing another woman into my life. I knew that for many people this seemed a bit soon and, trust me, it did to me as well. But my healing journey is unique, as is everyone's. I was beginning to realize that when you lose a spouse, whether you want to or not, you wake up every day confronted with the reality that you've lost your best friend and soulmate. Other friends and family aren't forced to grieve that progressively, so they will often be slower to accept a new season and more resistant to welcoming someone new in the widow or widower's life.

At one point one of my aunts had told me that statistically, those who had a great first marriage tend to get remarried sooner after losing a spouse because they understand the power of two becoming one. There were a great many factors that contributed, but regardless, I was feeling open to sharing life with someone new again.

As it turns out I found out quickly I wasn't ready. And neither was Kristi.

I had decided I wouldn't pursue anything with anyone no matter who it was until after the one-year anniversary of Amanda's death. I knew this is what God put in my heart, and I was going to stick to it. In fact, I kept my wedding ring on until November 11, 2016—one year to the day. Our worship team and I had gone on a writing retreat earlier in 2016 to write some songs about the grief journey and how God was meeting us in our pain. We had scheduled November 11 as a night to "take back territory" from the Enemy by recording a live worship album featuring those songs at Amanda's home church—the same church her dad now pastored and in the same auditorium where we had our double wedding in August 2008.

So from September until the beginning of November, I just observed Kristi. We said maybe a dozen words to each other, mostly cordial hellos, but things got interesting when she showed up to my church one Sunday in October. You see, prior to her coming to church I only *suspected* she loved Jesus. I had overheard a conversation with her and some other girls in the gym about a Christian rap concert they went to. *Okay!?* I thought, *this girl has good taste in music and maybe she loves the Lord!* (Prerequisites: music connoisseur and Jesus-lover, check.)

So when I saw her walk into my church for the first time, drop her daughter off in our kids ministry, sing during the worship time, take notes during the message, pick her daughter up, and leave—yes, I'd kept an eye on her—something stirred in me. It was apparent that church was important to her. As a pastor I can tell right away if church is a priority for someone. There is a certain intentionality they approach it with, and this woman demonstrated that. So when I saw her do this week after week, I was more and more determined to find out her story.

For several weeks I tried to "naturally" run into her in the atrium and ask her a bit about herself, you know, in a very noninvasive, pastoral way. The problem is, she was so elusive! I'd find myself in a conversation with someone, watch her walk across the atrium, and hope she'd linger, but by the time I concluded my conversation she was gone.

Truth is, for much of 2016 I had been a bit wary of the single women, particularly single moms, who showed up to our church. There seemed to be an influx after Amanda passed. I hoped it was because they felt especially connected to the story and not for ulterior motives, but at the time I knew I was in a vulnerable place and couldn't really trust everyone's motives. I hate disclosing that now, thinking of the genuine females who came to our church during that season and may have felt a coldness from me, but at the time I couldn't be too careful.

Kristi, however, conducted herself in a much different manner. She not only didn't go out of her way to talk to me after each service, she seemed to *avoid* me. And it made me want all the more to learn about her!

One day in early November I was working at our ForIndy adopt-a-block in the Riverside neighborhood when Kristi showed up. Now she had my attention. Who was this charming mom from the suburbs who walked into my church like a New York fashionista, donning the latest trends and high heels, clutching an actual Bible (this seems to be a lost practice in the modern church era), presenting herself with poise and confidence, and now wearing old jeans and a sweatshirt with a shovel in her hand? She wasn't afraid to get her hands dirty and seemed to have a genuine heart for helping people.

I just had to get to know her more that day. So I asked Derek's wife, Ashley, to round up a bunch of folks for lunch after adopt-a-block and be sure to invite Kristi. She said yes, and I finally saw the path toward a match made in paradise—or at least a way to see if there was any spark between us.

The problem is, she stiff-armed me the entire lunch. She practically sat with her back to me the whole time while chatting with a couple of other volunteers. Each time I'd ask her a question she'd barely turn, give me a curt answer, and then turn back around. *Wow*, I thought, *I must be a little rusty on this charm thing.*

I didn't know much more about her after that day, but the message was loud and clear. It was a dead end. There would be no getting to know her, let alone her reciprocating my interest.

Oh well, I thought, *it's probably for the better*. What I didn't know is that the Lord still had some work He needed to do on my heart before I could truly pursue and love a woman other than Amanda. Widows and widowers often ask me when you know you're ready to meet someone and get remarried. I tell them when you're not just trying to fill a void of loneliness, but when you're truly ready to love someone else sacrificially. Through November, December, and much of January, the Lord revealed to me very clearly that I *wasn't* ready.

On top of this, I didn't know Kristi's story, but I was sure it included some kind of pain. She was thirty-one at the time, with a three-year-old daughter. I knew she had a backstory, and I guessed it was in my best interest not to get involved with someone who was carrying something into the relationship. I was bringing quite a bit of baggage myself, you know—recovering from losing a wife to murder, a two-year-old son, an internationally known story, and the inevitable reality that whoever stepped into a relationship with me might feel like they were living in Amanda's shadow, not to mention under the scrutiny of everyone following the story. In fact, when I gave it any considerable thought, it seemed an almost impossible hurdle to overcome. For that reason, I occasionally felt downright hopeless about finding true love again.

For the next several months after that dead-end lunch with Kristi, I worked heavily on the book. I was looking toward the live album recording on the first anniversary of Amanda's death, Thanksgiving and Christmas were approaching, and I faced the daunting task of writing a book with the January deadline my publisher had given me. Most difficult of all, the more I immersed myself in elements of Amanda's and my love story as I wrote the book, the more hopeless I grew that I would ever find a love like that again.

In my naivety and immaturity, I began imagining what it would be like to find someone like Amanda: blond, blue-eyed, an "exact fit" in the family to fill this empty void, and maybe even a long-distance dating stint to cap it off. It seemed perfect. I could just recreate the love story that I had lost. But it soon became apparent that no one would or could ever "fill the void" that Amanda left—and to attempt to do so would be downright foolish. Besides, God doesn't *rewrite* carbon copy stories. He's in the business of doing *new* things and writing *new* stories to redeem the broken ones that haunt our past.

I'll never forget driving in the car one day and weeping uncontrollably for thirty minutes as I headed back to my house. It all felt impossible. Everything. The story I was carrying. The pain buried deep inside. The feeling of being stuck in it and not knowing if I'd ever reemerge into a "normal" life. The hopelessness of never finding a love like I'd had with Amanda.

And yet through it all, in the back of my mind, I still found myself wondering about Kristi.

One night early in January of 2017, I was working intensely on finishing up the first manuscript of this book. I was writing every day from 7 a.m. until about 7 p.m., breaking only for lunch. The owner of my CrossFit gym was kind enough to give me a key to the gym so I could break a little sweat in between writing stints. On this particular night I headed to the gym for a little after-hours workout. The last class of the evening was finishing up when I arrived, and as providence would have it, Kristi was in that class.

I decided this was the moment I was going to work up the courage to engage in conversation with her, even if I had to step in front of her to do so.

"Hey!" I said, trying (to no avail) to play it cool. "You've been coming to my church for like four months now, and I know almost nothing about you." And of course to keep it pastoral I added, "What's your story? How did you come to know the Lord?"

She must have known she was cornered because slowly she began to tell me her story. For the next thirty minutes or so we stood there as she regaled me on her upbringing and past. I was a little surprised that she didn't spare many details. She was very up front about her story, even with some of the rough edges. I'll let her tell you her story if and when she ever decides to. Let's just say that she informed me later she was trying to scare me off by giving me the gory details.

What's funny is out of everything she told me, I homed in on the four years she spent studying abroad and on the mission fields in Mexico, Cambodia, and Brazil. "Oh!" I replied. "So that's why you've been serving in our inner city a little bit. You must have a heart for missions."

"Yeah," she said with some hesitation, "but also my family lives in that area."

"Wait, by choice?" I blurted out, thinking of how dangerous the area was.

"Yeah." She kept her poise. "My stepdad has lived there for seventeen years and my mom with him for ten. They feel called to that area as their life's ministry. In fact, that was one reason I chose to attend Resonate. Everything you guys talk about with your ForIndy vision and initiatives in that area is what my family has prayed for for years."

"Wow. That's really amazing!" I said. *So her family has a heart for ministry.* That'd always been important to me because a ministry lifestyle isn't a normal one. Ever since God called me to ministry I'd wanted a wife whose family understood the sacrifices God often calls us to. I had that in Amanda's family and definitely desired it in my next wife.

I continued, "Yeah, you know ever since Amanda passed I've felt this huge burden for that area. She and I used to run by that neighborhood and pray for it while training for half marathons. Much of what we do as a church comes out of our story and the burden it's placed on me."

"It's truly amazing how you guys have walked through this, Davey," she responded. "Obviously I've been following your story since it happened, considering you guys were friends with my old pastors. Also a good friend of mine is a physician assistant, and she was on duty on the hall below you in the hospital the night you were there with Amanda. She texted our whole small group saying, 'You wouldn't believe this family! They're praying and worshipping right here in the hallway! It's like a revival breaking out here!'"

"Wow. So you've been closely connected with our story for a while then, huh?" I peered at her with heightened interest.

You see, several months after Amanda passed I wrote something in my prayer journal: "Lord, if you ever bring me another wife here's what I ask for, that she loves you more than she loves me, that she loves me, that she loves Weston like he's her own, *and that she loves Amanda.*"

I knew that last one was going to be crucial, because the way life was unfolding seemed to be propelling me into carrying Amanda's story and sharing about my journey through trauma and tragedy. It would take a special woman to step into that calling, a secure woman, someone who was grounded in her own identity with Christ and who wouldn't merely be "okay" with me carrying the story but who help me champion it.

"Um, yeah," Kristi said. "I'm connected in some other ways, but I don't think you'll want me to tell you that." She shuffled her feet a little and looked around the room.

"What is it?" I was intrigued and a little apprehensive, especially at how awkward she had suddenly become.

"Well. Um. Davey, my stepdad is one of the chaplains for the Marion County prison system." She paused as if to let what she said set in for a second. "And he has regular conversations with the men that killed Amanda."

I felt all the blood rush out of my face and the room begin to spin. "What?!" I was dumbfounded. *What are you doing, God? This girl that I've been interested in for a couple of months has this close of a connection to my story?* Here I was coming to the gym trying to decompress after being buried all day in writing the manuscript and asking the Lord to show me the redemption in my story, and this happened?

I couldn't help what came out of my mouth next. "You want to go grab some dinner with me?" No sooner had the words left my lips than I immediately regretted them. I couldn't be seen out in public with a woman! Everywhere I went in the city I'd regularly get stopped by people who knew my story. What would people say about the pastor whose wife was murdered a year ago who was out on the town with random women?

She and I both decided it wouldn't be a good idea, so we chatted a little more at the gym and then each headed out.

The next several months was a game of trying to get around Kristi. I had to uncover what God was up to. So, naturally, I used our kids as the angle to spend some time with her. Despite her reluctance, she and I would coordinate when she was bringing her daughter to CrossFit so I could bring Weston and they'd have a buddy to play with while we worked out. I wish I could say my motives were altruistic. I really just wanted to be around her any moment I could.

In fact, I would drive thirty minutes (past the CrossFit gym, which was ten minutes from my office) to pick Weston up from his Mamaw's house and drive twenty minutes back to CrossFit to keep my end of the bargain. It was ridiculous, but it felt good to have butterflies and romantic feelings again. That part of my heart had been dormant for a long time, and feeling it reawaken was both bitter and sweet.

One night we took the kids to Chick-fil-A together. As we walked through the doors, she took both kids to the back where they were making balloon animals, and I hopped in line to order food. As soon as I'd ordered, a random lady came up to me. "Davey Blackburn? Oh my goodness! I can't believe it's you. We've been following your story and praying for you! Can we get a photo with you?"

Now, normally I'm grateful and humbled to run into people impacted by our story, but this night was different. All I could think about was that I was out in public with another woman! Looking back now, it probably wasn't that big of a deal, but it sure seemed like it at the time. Despite this awkward moment, Kristi and I remained at Chick-fil-A with our kids. In fact, we closed it down! Three or four times the kids came out of the play place complaining they were tired and ready to leave. "Just a little while longer, kids!" we'd say as we shooed them back in. Both of us were riveted by our conversation. It was about the time the Chick-fil-A employees started mopping the floor around our feet that we got the hint it was time to leave.

One afternoon in early March, I wound up in a three-hour text conversation with her. Now, I'm usually the one haranguing teenagers for not picking up the phone and making a voice call, but on this particular day I found myself giggling as I typed miscellaneous emojis. In this text conversation I discovered that although she'd chosen the route of sports her whole life (softball, track, cross country, and volleyball), she was extremely into ballet. Immediately I looked up when the ballet was going to be in Indy next. This was my opportunity to ask her out on a date!

That same night at CrossFit I walked up to her and opened with, "Hey, what are you doing on March 31?"

She looked puzzled as she answered hesitatingly. "Uh, I don't think I have anything planned. That's a long way off though."

Her bewilderment didn't faze me one bit. "Will you let me take you to the ballet?"

All of a sudden her eyes widened and a broad smile stretched across her face. "Really? Yeah! That'd be great!" I found out later that she didn't know I was asking her out on a date, but that she was so obsessed with ballet she practically would have gone with anyone. Oh well, I was in.

But on March 31 it wasn't me taking her to the ballet. We had received some counsel from some mentors that it would be a good idea to stay under the table with this budding relationship until after Amanda's trial (which was set for May of 2017 at this point). So instead of taking her to the ballet, I paid for her and the wife of one of the elders in our church to go to a nice dinner and the ballet while I took her daughter to Chick-fil-A and Build-A-Bear. We still tell people this was our "first date."

When May arrived and we realized Amanda's trial was going to be delayed yet again, I called the prosecutor and asked how it would affect the case if my relationship status changed. "Not at all," he answered. "You have to do your best to move forward with your life because you never know when this trial will actually happen." (This was a truer statement than he even knew at the time).

At that point Kristi and I felt the freedom to go out in public on dates, and in mid-May we did just that. It was incredible. It was the freest I'd felt since Amanda's passing. Certainly it was bittersweet to be dating again, but the budding connection with

Kristi seemed at times to lift the cloak of sadness I felt with Amanda's absence.

After a few months of dating and as things began to get a little more serious, we decided it was important to involve more people in our relationship. Because of the complexity of being with me, we wanted to focus on the two of us first. Then from there, we wanted to make sure our families felt good about this: hers, mine, and Amanda's. So in August of 2017 we spent a week with Amanda's family in Elkhart, Indiana, and then a week with my family in North Carolina. With Kristi's family being in Indy, we'd already had some time with them.

We approached those two weeks knowing it was make-or-break for us. We knew we had this sense that we'd either come back and hit the gas pedal on our relationship, or pump the brakes, or even screech to a halt altogether. On the last day my mom sparked a marriage conversation that led us down a road of topics we had not yet let ourselves entertain. We returned to Indy and tried to date as normal, but all we could think about was a future together.

While both of us still had some apprehension, our hearts were quickly melding together.

One night in September, I was asked to share Amanda's and my story at a fundraising event on a rooftop penthouse overlooking Indy's downtown cityscape. Kristi came as my plus-one. At one point I was standing in front of this group of donors seated at banquet tables, the sun fading behind the skyline in the background, and I glanced over at my date. She was looking up at me, eyes beaming with pride. It was at that moment I knew I wanted to spend the rest of my life with her. Here was a woman in whom God had used a painful past to shape such a strength that I was confident she could stand next to me as He continued to write my story, and that, in the process, both of our stories would find redemption—together.

You see, a couple of months after we began dating I'd read one of Kristi's favorite books, *Redeeming Love* by Francine Rivers. It's the story of the biblical character Hosea in a modern adaptation. Before reading the book I was asking God, "Lord, what are You going to do to redeem *my* story? How are You going to make all this right? How will You bring justice for Amanda, another wife into my life, and another mom into Weston's?" While reading *Redeeming Love* I sensed God telling me, *I want to redeem your story, Davey. But maybe I also want to use you to redeem someone else's story. This is about more than just you and your story.*

Very quickly I was discovering that Kristi was that someone else. The next few months were filled with marriage conversations and consulting wise people in our life. We both believe that "plans fail for lack of counsel, but with many advisers they succeed" (Proverbs 15:22 NIV). By October we knew we were ready to commit to marriage.

So on November 8, 2017, almost exactly two years after Amanda's death, I took Kristi back to that same rooftop penthouse, got down on one knee, and asked her to be my wife.

The next month was a flurry of wedding preparations and layers of announcements—to my congregation, to friends and family, and to the world. Mostly met with overwhelming positivity and congratulations, our journey was now public, and there was no turning back. As daunting as blending these two pasts and stories seemed, we forged ahead *knowing* that God was in it.

One major hang-up from Kristi, however, was that she wanted a small, private, and quiet wedding. You see, part of her past is that although she now had a very loving and involved stepdad, her biological father hadn't been in her life since she was in college. Because he suffered through years of serious mental illness, she often feared for her safety with him. He eventually chose to walk out on the family when she was nineteen, and she hadn't seen him since. For that reason, she never envisioned herself walking down an aisle, so a quiet, private wedding felt safer and touched far fewer childhood wounds.

I, on the other hand, knew there were dozens, if not hundreds, of people who had been so personally involved in my journey, both with Amanda and me and since her passing. I couldn't imagine not having those people celebrate the start of a new chapter with us. Then one day the Lord's message hit me again: *My redemption story would usher in Kristi's as well.* So I convinced her to let us go through with a bigger wedding and told her to leave the "walking down the aisle part" to me.

On a chilly, rainy, magical December day in 2017, we gathered friends and family in a castle—well, a local venue that looked like a castle. Although almost nothing about our stories was fairy tale–esque up to that moment, we certainly felt like we were living one that day.

We squeezed as many people into that wedding hall as possible, an upstairs nave at the end of a dark wood, baroque grand staircase. The sea of people clad in winter evening cocktail attire and the touches of greenery around the room provided a pleasant contrast to the stark white walls of this upper room. I stood at the front with Brad Cooper, who was officiating the wedding, waiting for the doors to open, knowing that what was about to ensue would have us all in tears.

"Claire de Lune" began playing softly. *Here she comes.* I shifted nervously, hoping that everything would go as planned. The doors swung open and everyone in the room stood to their feet. There she was, standing alone, a magnificent beauty, delicately resplendent in a fashionable white gown with lace sleeves, clutching a bouquet of snowy flowers. I could see the hesitation on her face as she began to step forward. Almost immediately, Lee, her stepdad, eased out of the back row to meet her. She smiled at him, politely accepted his arm, and they proceeded. Step-by-step she walked to me, and I could feel my composure cracking. She looked ravishing.

Just then, Lee stopped and, by default, she froze with him. He leaned over, kissed her on the cheek, and whispered in her ear, "This is where I leave you." Stunned and unsure what to do next, she looked up at me. At that moment, Phil, Amanda's dad, got up from his seat and walked to her, gently taking her arm in his and escorting her the next several steps. You could almost feel the entire room gasp as seemingly everyone was choking back tears. Phil led her another third of the way down and then, right on cue, my dad got up from his seat and walked her the last bit. As she stood directly in front of me in her radiance, Brad asked the iconic question, "Who gives this bride to be with this groom?" "We do," the three declared in unison from behind Kristi.

It was a storybook moment, and it wasn't lost on either of us. Tears filled both of our eyes as we looked at each other, two broken puzzle pieces about to fit and stitch our crazy lives together to display to the world a picture of God's redemption—an unordinary family.

"All rise!" The bailiff's booming voice shook me from my flashback. Judge Hawkins had just opened the door leading to his chamber and ambled over to his chair. This was it. I stood up and glanced down the gallery bench to my left. From there Amber, James, Phil and Robin, and I exchanged concerned looks as nearly simultaneously all of us breathed in, exhaled, and braced for the next words that would come from the judge's mouth.

22

ANOTHER DEATH, ANOTHER RESURRECTION

"You may be seated." Judge Hawkins looked solemn and stalwart. I caught Phil's eye as I took my seat. His face told me everything I needed to know about where he was at this moment: *this is it*. I could tell he was forcing a reassuring smile my way.

The judge took a few seconds to collect his thoughts.

"I want to thank the gallery for being so patient and professional through this whole process. Cases of this nature are almost guaranteed to stir the deepest of emotion, and it can often get elevated in the courtroom. I want to thank you for conducting yourself with the utmost decency."

I turned to scan the people in the gallery behind me, most of them representing Amanda and our family. My eyes bounced from one to another, taking a moment to look them in the eye as a way of expressing my heartfelt gratitude too. They'd stood by me this whole time, through all the ups and downs.

One particular grouping, though, directly over my left shoulder, caught my attention. Megan Griffith was sitting beside Cameron and Karissa Sprinkle. Seeing this juxtaposition sent a sudden pang through my heart. You see, Megan represented so many in our church who had walked with me during the first months and then years of my healing journey. But unlike Megan, most of the others were *not* present in the courtroom.

Not because they didn't want to be but because their lives had transitioned, taking many of them to new geographical locations, and essentially out of my life—Derek, Ashley, and the rest of the Resonate community.

Cameron and Karissa, however, represented a new ministry I was now leading, appropriately called *Nothing is Wasted*. The irony of seeing a picture of my old life seated right next to my new life wasn't lost on me. This pairing reminded me of the second-most agonizing transition and loss I had experienced since Amanda's passing: the loss of the little church she and I had planted—Resonate Church.

It was the end of 2018, and Kristi and I were nearing the one-year anniversary of our marriage. That first year of trying to blend our family under the public eye, Kristi finishing up PA school, and us trying to figure out how to lead this church into a new season had been tough, but we were battle-tested and felt like we could forge ahead. As fairy-tale as our wedding had been and as deeply as we felt about each other and God's work in our relationship, we quickly realized that blending families after trauma and tragedy is not for the faint of heart. It's downright difficult. In fact, what I know now is that "blended" families is completely misleading terminology. It should be called "slow-cooked" families.

On top of that, pressures at the church were mounting. Through much of 2016 and 2017, God had done remarkable things in people's lives through Resonate. Hurting individuals came from all over our city and found a church home that wasn't afraid to talk about pain and trauma. Looking back now, I can see that it became a healing oasis for so many who couldn't find a safe space within the church to unpack their painful pasts.

But just as quickly as Resonate burgeoned with growth and potential, it seemed to stall out and stagnate. Our church didn't have a healthy leadership infrastructure necessary to transition people into the next season of mission—a critical phase for a grieving congregation to undergo in order to find long-term vitality. Much of our staff and leadership were close friends of Amanda and me when she passed away, and the combination of the toll of grief and leadership responsibilities was wearing on all of us.

Amid these pressures, one of the things that was feeding my soul was a podcast that we had started as a side project called *The Nothing is Wasted Podcast.* I was having conversations with people all over the world through comments on my blog and over social media who just couldn't understand how I was still holding up after losing Amanda. I tried to convey to them all of the amazing people I had encountered along my healing journey who breathed hope into me, but nothing seemed to translate—until I finally put a microphone in front of some of those people and let them tell their own stories of pain and trauma and, most importantly, how God showed up for them. We would sit for hours and talk about healing from trauma and tragedy, and, unbeknownst to me at the time, it was facilitating a critical part of my own healing—finding purpose in helping others through their pain.

Things at the church, however, continued to steadily dry up. Key staff members and close friends transitioned out. We saw an alarming decline in attendance and giving, the venue we were renting doubled their rate as a "polite" way to force us out, our office building got sold and we were served an eviction notice, and despite a solid amount of reserves in the bank we were hemorrhaging money each month. It seemed like there was so much sideways energy going toward very little spiritual return.

The most painful part for me, however, was watching my entire community who helped me survive the loss of Amanda slowly exit my life. I wish someone would have warned me of the harsh reality that relationship transitions tend to accompany grief. It's an almost inevitable downstream effect of loss: some people were not meant to join you in your next season and will exit your life—often not graciously. The only way I can describe it is a group of friends went through war together, survived, and were so intricately involved in battling together, but when they returned home, they didn't know how to live in "normal" civilian society as a unit. It felt like a very painful divorce.

The only thing that remained thriving and steadily growing was *The Nothing is Wasted Podcast*. People were tuning in to these healing conversations, and lives were being transformed. Later a mentor would tell me that I was in a season where God was shifting a grace in my life—intentionally putting favor on one area and drying up another.

One night in late November 2018, a board member of ours suggested to Kristi and me that it seemed like God was transitioning us into a new season. Others had hinted at this over the last few months, but I refused to entertain the thought. After all, this beautiful church family that Amanda and I had labored so long to birth and that had grown under the shadow of the agonizing tragedy could *not* die. I wouldn't let it. I had promised Amanda. But something about the timing of my conversation with that board member that night caused both Kristi and me to pause. *Could this be? Could God be calling us into something else? Could He have another plan?*

The very next week, on a gloomy Wednesday night, Kristi and I sat in our executive pastor's office. We were talking about how to restructure things and stop the bleeding.

"Davey," he pivoted the conversation. "Can I take off my employee hat for just a second and put on a friend's hat?" I looked at him inquisitively yet apprehensively and nodded.

"I have been wrestling with this for months now. This is going to be really tough to hear, but it's even tougher for me to say out loud. As I've been observing what's going on, it seems like God is drying up Resonate Church."

I looked at him stunned. I couldn't believe he was saying this. The person tasked to help me carry this vision forward despite any opposition. His discernment, however, was absolutely correct.

"Hear me out," he pressed on. "I watch what God is doing with your story and with *The Nothing is Wasted Podcast*, and I think He's got something else for you and Kristi. I think these conversations of pain and trauma need to be fostered in the church abroad right now because, for the most part, they aren't. It seems like God is putting His breath on *Nothing is Wasted* for a time such as this, and maybe trying to force you two into that by squeezing you out of pastoring a local church. If I'm you, I'm asking the question, 'What is keeping me from doing *Nothing is Wasted* full time?'"

Kristi looked at me as if she'd seen a ghost. This executive pastor had no idea of some of the recent conversations we'd had. He had no clue that we'd been clenching our fists and white-knuckling things, refusing to relent to what was seeming to be inevitable. After all, we dreamed we'd baptize our kids in this church. We dreamed we'd be pastoring it for the rest of our lives. Kristi had resolved to carry the baton that was left when Amanda passed away.

But God had other plans. He was writing something new.

After a couple of weeks of painful conversations and seeking counsel from mentors in our life, we realized that, in fact, God *was* calling us away and that Resonate Church would need to be dissolved. It had been purposed for a season, that season was done, and now it was time for the new thing He had in store for us.

Letting go of the little church Amanda and I had birthed was beyond agonizing—a debilitating death in itself. But, as I was learning about any grief journey, I had to mourn it, accept it, and step forward. "Weep well without wallowing," as Dr. John Walker had told me.

Immediately after closing the church at the beginning of 2019, Kristi and the kids and I spent three weeks at an intensive counseling retreat, trying to process much of what had just happened. Between the death of my wife and unborn child, Kristi's previous marriage ending in divorce, and now shuttering the doors of our church, loss seemed to touch every aspect of our lives. And yet, as we'd seen time and time again, that loss was a seed for new growth. We knew exactly what our mission was as we left counseling—to help others navigate pain and trauma.

I began traveling and speaking, sharing our story. At each speaking engagement a long receiving line would come up to talk to me. The first time I was thrown off, thinking that each person was merely coming to offer condolences or say they'd been praying for our family. Surprisingly, one after the other, they would share their own stories of pain and trauma, almost as if it was the first time someone had given them permission to talk about it. After this happened a few times, I decided I needed to try to do something about it, so I began coaching people one-on-one, trying to help them navigate their pain and find healing and wholeness.

Out of that coaching, we developed a curriculum called *Pain to Purpose* and began offering it as a self-directed study online to try to meet the demand of people asking for help. Soon pastors and church leaders began requesting to offer this as a group study curriculum in their church. Simultaneously, the need for one-on-one coaching grew, and with a budding new ministry, my capacity was shrinking. With the help of a few key players, we developed a coaching certification program and began enlisting coaches for targeted pain points—everywhere from widowhood to child loss, divorce to sexual betrayal, childhood trauma to abuse, abortion regret and recovery to addiction, and more. By 2022 I couldn't believe how God had shaped and grown a podcast into a full-fledged ministry that was having this much impact as we launched a healing curriculum in churches, college campuses, and correctional facilities around the world.

Cameron and Karissa Sprinkle had appeared on our podcast during a series on sexual betrayal and shared their story of addiction, infertility, betrayal, and restoration. Their episode is still one of our podcast's all-time most listened to episodes. Soon after that Karissa became a certified coach for us, helping women far and wide through similar situations of betrayal.

During a fifteen-minute recess taken just before Judge Hawkins was going to read the final verdict, Cameron had pulled me aside. "Man, I can't imagine how you're holding up right now. All I can think about as I hear the details of what happened to Amanda is how in the world has this awful, tragic moment in her life and yours become a seed of restoration for *my* marriage? I just can't reconcile it. I want none of this to have happened to Amanda, but if it hadn't, we wouldn't have the friendship we do with you and Kristi right now. It's been your friendship that has really helped us get through this next phase of our recovery journey. I don't want to sound cliché, but truly, Davey, as difficult as it is to wrap my head around, *nothing is wasted.*"

Now, sitting on that hard wooden bench scanning the gallery behind me, I caught Cameron's eye. He leaned forward and gave me a reassuring pat on the shoulder. I remember reading somewhere Elisabeth Elliot saying she would never have asked for her husband to die on the mission field but that she also wouldn't trade what it taught her for the world. At that moment I thought of the thousands of lives that had been completely altered because of Amanda's faithfulness, her legacy, her steadfast love for God. I thought about all the marriages that, like the Sprinkles', had been restored, all the people who would spend eternity in heaven, all the addictions broken, all the hearts mended, and all the stifled dreams and paralyzed purposes that would break free and come to fruition as a result of Amanda's life—and death.

The work God has invited us into now to help people become whole after their tragic stories was growing into a massive tree that was providing healing, shade, protection, and hope for thousands. *If a single seed falls to the ground and dies . . .*

For a moment, the thought of the impact of Amanda's life distracted my mind from what was looming in front of me. I felt caught up in a different realm, a realm where justice and mercy were not mutually exclusive. A realm where something seemed to overshadow my nervousness that there was still a possibility Larry Taylor might not be convicted, that there was still a slight chance he could walk. In that moment I didn't have this haunting fear that we didn't get the right guy and that he's still somewhere at large. Or that we did get the right guy but he would be let off the hook on some kind of technicality. Or the more likely possibility that he would be convicted but not sentenced to the amount of time I thought was fair or just. How much time did I think Larry *should* serve? I hadn't thought of anything other than life in prison. In that case, would any number satisfy my pain? Would any length bring Amanda back or satisfy retribution for what he stole from all of us? Was there any worldly institution or governmental policy or legal proceeding that could put back together what was fractured in our story? Would Larry ever express remorse? From what I saw in him that week, he couldn't care less about what he'd done to Amanda. To him this was a flippant, evil act in an effort to prove his place in some gang and with hopes that he might get a new pair of shoes as a bonus.

What about Jalen or Diano? Did they feel remorse? And do I even want them to be shown any compassion or mercy? For that brief moment just before Judge Hawkins spoke his next words, all of these questions that had been swirling in my head suddenly stood still, and a clarifying epiphany interjected. Any scenario I played out that could occur right then and there felt at best transactional, a feeble attempt by the justice system to assuage the inconsolable pain we'd endured. Suddenly I knew no verdict could fully mend the rupture, but there was something that truly transcended my desire for punishment or consequences here on earth—and that was full *restoration*. I wanted things to be fully restored, and I knew that nothing this judge could say would do that. After all, this has been a seemingly inexhaustible journey with the justice system, and even the best systems in this world will fall short in the end.

My mind flashed back to December a year earlier, when I'd received a text message from one of the prosecutors thirty minutes before I was to report for the scheduled jury trial. The text said, "Davey unfortunately it was a mistrial. I will call you in a bit." I was in the car halfway to the courthouse and, flabbergasted, our entire family decided to continue anyway to meet the prosecutor in person and hear what had caused the mistrial. We all stood in a clumpy semicircle dumbfounded that things had been delayed yet again, imploring the lead prosecutor to give us some answers. Confused himself, he humbly responded, "I can't imagine how upsetting this must be for you guys. I'm just as taken off guard by this as you are. But I promise you," he leaned in and declared, "I will see this through to the end."

I walked away from that moment in December feeling a little more reassured, but a few months later that prosecutor took another job role and transitioned off our case.

As I sat there now, anxiously awaiting the next words that would come out of Judge Hawkins's mouth, I realized there was only one person who could truly say with all authority, "I will see this through to the end," and that is Jesus. After all, isn't He called the Wonderful Counselor? That term *counselor* had now been broadened for me. Of course He's the best *therapist* one could ask for. Of course He is the only one who can heal the wounds of the heart, who can restore us from trauma, but now I could see that He was the Wonderful Counselor—as in Wonderful *Attorney*. He is the mediator between us and the true judge and arbiter, God. And I knew I could trust that no matter what conviction was declared over Larry Taylor in this next moment, Jesus would one day declare a final conviction over all death, all evil, all wrongdoing, all injustice, and all pain. In the end there will be no mistrials, no statutes of limitation, no loopholes, no corruption in the system. Instead, there will come a day when, because of the finished work of the cross of Jesus, justice *will* prevail and all things will be restored. And forgiveness in its simplest form is me not taking it on myself to hold Larry or Diano or Jalen accountable, but to trust God that *He* will, and in a perfect way that judges the heart.

I was reminded in that moment of God's promise that the ingredients of goodness and mercy He was mixing together behind the scenes would one day eclipse any hardship or disappointment I would face here on earth. That in *His* time, *He* will make all things beautiful, no matter how grim they may look right now. I was reminded that forgiveness and wholeness find their roots in trusting all of these questions to the Lord, knowing that placing my hope in any human institution or process will only lead to disappointment.

I felt a hand pat my leg. I looked at the man sitting to my right. It was Kenneth Wagner. My best friend in the world. The one I had hung the phone up with when I walked into my house to find Amanda that awful morning. With sweaty hands, a clenched jaw, and tears welling up in his eyes he gave me a nod as if to say, "I'm here for you no matter what." Here it was, on my right a picture of God's faithfulness and loyalty in Kenneth, on my left the representation of His redemption with Kristi, and behind me, a testimony of how He melds our past and present to propel us into a divinely purposeful future with Megan, Cameron, and Karissa. He truly had me surrounded this whole time.

Just then the judge's voice pierced the silence, "On fourteen of the sixteen counts brought before the court in the case of the *State of Indiana vs Larry Jo Taylor*, I find the defendant ... *guilty!*"

An audible exhale enveloped the room. For the first time all week, and perhaps in seven years, I burst into uncontrollable tears of relief. It was over. Amanda's murderer had been brought to justice. The case was closed. I couldn't believe the finality of it. How long we had waited, agonizing over the process, trying our best to move forward with life, all while the legal side of things remained unresolved. How many times it had been rescheduled and mistried—and in one fell swoop, it was finished.

It didn't seem real. I felt such closure, and at the same time, I didn't feel any different. Almost as if through the whole seven years I'd been walking in a different realm, like I'd been invited to rise above the way we would naturally think about these things, and instead been given a glimpse into God's view. People had asked us about the trial and would say something like, "I can't wait for this whole thing to be put behind you." I never understood that phrase. "This whole thing" will *never* be put behind us. We will always carry it. It will be a weight we wake up with every day. But we'll learn to carry it. We'll grow stronger as we go, so it won't feel so weighty, but it won't disappear. And now I could feel that truth. Now, with a guilty verdict, I understood it even more. Nothing on this side of eternity could make any of this right or take away the pain.

But one day, I'll stand in front of Jesus, the only one who can truly deliver on the promise that *He will see this through*, that He will carry it out to completion, and in that moment it will all make sense. Everything will be set right. All my questions will find their answer in Him, and He will wipe away every tear. And then I imagine I will hear His voice, and though I'll never have heard it audibly up to that moment, it will sound so familiar, as if it's been speaking all along, and it will say, "Well done, good and faithful servant." And then, as I imagine it, He'll turn and gesture to me to enter into my reward, and as He does, Amanda will walk up. And she'll look at me, her blue eyes glimmering in the light of the Son, and she'll say, "Davey, I'm so proud of you."

Five days later I sat in that same courtroom again, this time in the back of the gallery, for Diano Gordan's sentencing. Diano, like Jalen, had taken a plea agreement with the state to testify against Larry Taylor. As long as he followed through with that testimony commensurate with the prosecution's expectations, he was guaranteed to get a lesser sentence.

Kristi and I sat in the back of the gallery as we entered the courtroom. The first two rows were taken up with Diano's family members—his mother, his grandmother, aunts, cousins—all women save for one young man.

Like at each of the sentencing hearings, I was asked to give a statement on behalf of Amanda and the family. That statement typically was for the purposes of bearing witness to the toll, cost, and fallout the crime had inflicted. It was to demonstrate to the judge what you think he should consider when sentencing. I chose to carry a message in my statement different from the other victims, though I don't fault them in the least. One by one the other victims of that terrible day shone light on how their homes being broken into had violated their sense of security; had catapulted them into an impossible journey through mental unhealth, depression, and anxiety; and how they hope each of the men would "rot in jail" for the rest of their lives.

For each of the statements I would read to the three perpetrators, I followed a pattern that differed somewhat from those others'. That day, I walked to the witness stand and read this aloud to Diano and to the judge, first looking in Diano's direction:

Seventeen years ago this coming Saturday I met the most amazing girl I had ever had the pleasure of knowing up to that point. It was very unlike me to get swept off my feet by a girl, but those who knew Amanda Blackburn—then Amanda Byars—will easily see how even the most unimpressed of individuals could be absolutely struck by her. She possessed every quality one might say it's impossible to wholly possess—beauty, kindness, intelligence, quick-wittedness, steadfastness, conviction, grit, principle, balance, and self-control. She always demonstrated an unassuming humble confidence that drew you in. She wore a smile that warmed your heart and lifted your spirit. When you interacted with her, you felt like the most important person in the room—and to her, you were. Because she always made sure her life was spent serving people other than herself. She knew and loved Jesus and others in a way that made you want to know and love Jesus and others more too.

She was safe, balanced, emotionally sturdy, and spiritually adventurous. She wanted her life to matter. She wanted to spend her energy and time helping others and serving everyone she came in contact with. There is not a person I know who interacted with her that wasn't impacted tremendously by her.

It feels impossible to reconcile how someone as selfless and giving as Amanda Blackburn could have had her life taken from her in a way that was so selfish, and demonic. It seems the epitome of unfair. Perhaps that is why this case captured people's attention all over the world. Perhaps it's because people were unwittingly drawn in by the very essence of a life well-lived that was cut way too short. Perhaps it's because we all want to believe that good like Amanda really does exist in this world, and we want to hope that it will ultimately triumph over evil. If there is one thing Amanda has taught me both in her life and her death, it's that even out of the worst of evils, good can come and tragic stories can be redeemed.

Diano, even if you didn't have a direct hand in the murder of Amanda Grace Blackburn, I want you to see how your self-centered, flippant, cowardly actions can lead to the most diabolical of events. Sure, you may not have pulled the trigger, Diano, but on November 10, 2015, you certainly contributed to robbing this world of quite possibly the most wonderfully purehearted person it has ever known.

But, Diano, as Amanda has taught us all, evil doesn't have to prevail ... even in your life. The worst of situations can be redeemed ... and so can the worst of people.

We're all here today to hear about punishment, indictment, charges, and counts ... but more than those things, my prayer today is that you feel conviction ... deep, deep, deep conviction ... in your heart. I'm not talking about the shallow, pitiful remorse you felt when you mouthed the words "I'm sorry" to Larry Taylor as you walked out of the courtroom last week. I'm not talking about the remorse you feel because people in the system now know you as a "snitch." I'm not even talking about remorse because you "hate how things turned out." But a deep, deep remorse that comes from knowing and admitting that you had something to do with this. A sorrow over knowing you absolutely destroyed a beautiful family's life. And you robbed a fifteen-month-old little boy of his mom and his sister. You took a wife and a daughter from a husband and a dad. You stole a daughter and a sister and a friend.

Yes, I'm talking about a different kind of remorse. I'm talking about a courageous sorrow, a strength from a broken and contrite heart, that would well up inside of you and compel you to look at a front row of people who loved Amanda and who desperately miss her and tell them you're sorry. And beg them for forgiveness.

I have to acknowledge that we are all grateful that you decided to do the right thing last Wednesday in testifying against Larry Taylor. No matter the reason why you did it, it gives me hope that there is still some good in you and that maybe that good can grow.

I can't begin to imagine what has occurred in your life that has made your heart so calloused and cold and evil, but I would beg you to see this moment as a turning point. I beg you to see this, right here, right now as a catalyst for change ... a line-in-the-sand type of moment where you decide to be less like Larry and more like Amanda. As I see it, Diano, you sit at a place where you still have a choice to make. A choice to walk away from what you used to be and step into what you could be. What would it look like for you to channel the energy, the ingenuity and craftiness you once used for evil, deplorable acts, and now use it for good?

Diano, I want you to know that inasmuch as I'm concerned, I have chosen to forgive you. And while this doesn't absolve you from the consequences you face because of what you have done, as for me, I have chosen not to carry bitterness against you. I have chosen not to hold this against you. I have chosen not to let my heart become cold and calloused as, somewhere along the line of your life, you have. I have chosen to trust God with my pain and let Him do something positive and constructive with it ...

And I'm hoping you do the same. I'm hoping you turn your life over to something much bigger than yourself. That you surrender to a power and authority and a friend that is grander than any you have ever experienced. Our entire family is praying that you surrender your life to Jesus and you let Him take this rotten, wretched life you've lived up to this point and, from here on out, turn it into something beautiful and life-giving to everyone you come in contact with. If Amanda has taught us anything in all of this, it's that if we'll let Him, God won't waste our pain ... or even the most destructive of decisions we can make.

Turning toward the bench, I continued.

Judge Hawkins, Your Honor. If I don't get another chance, I want to thank you for seeing this whole thing through. I know you've had weighty decisions resting on your shoulders your entire career, and I can't imagine the toll and distress this job must take on you. And I imagine this case has weighed on you over the last seven years as well. But I hope you see what I'm about to say as a humble petition. Please consider carefully the amount of time that would facilitate restorative justice for Diano. To the best of your ability and based on your experience, please discern the amount of time he would need to finally feel contrition, to have a true change of heart, and to resolve to live a more productive and fruitful life once he's served his time. I know that you'll hold both the severity and

gravity of his actions with the impact of his testimony as you
make this important decision.

Thank you.

When I finished, I folded my statement back up, nodded to Judge Hawkins, and returned to my seat.

Next, Diano's family was allowed a representative to speak. To my surprise, the only young man represented, Diano's brother, rose and walked confidently to the witness stand. He was well put together, neatly dressed, and carried a humble but self-controlled demeanor. For the next few minutes he spoke articulately, appealing to the judge that though this act Diano had committed was reprehensible, this was not *who* Diano was, nor had he wanted anyone to be harmed that day.

I was shockingly impressed with him. I would find out later when Diano's brother was about twelve years old, the family moved out of the inner city and into an area that would give him stronger opportunities to excel and escape the gravitational pull of urban gang life. No sooner was I moved by his monologue, however, did a twinge of fear pull me back to reality. Now it was Diano's turn.

What happened next I was not prepared for.

Diano stood, clad in the traditional orange jumpsuit, the shackles on his wrists and ankles constricting his attempts to brush his low-hanging dreadlocks away from his eyes. When he finally did, it revealed the tattoos on his neck and face and the gold-plated teeth protruding through his lips. But I did not expect what else it revealed. Streaming down his tattooed face were tears. As he scanned the room his eyes bypassed Judge Hawkins, skipped over his family on the front row, and locked directly with mine. Suddenly he burst into tears, thrusting his face into his open palms and sobbing uncontrollably. I couldn't believe it. I just froze. I didn't know what to do.

A female voice came from the group of his family members. "Look him in the eye, young man."

After several minutes he sucked it all in and regained his composure. "I'm so sorry," he said, looking directly toward me. "I could have stopped all of this from happening, and I didn't. And I don't know how I'm going to be able to live with myself for this." He paused for a moment to wipe tears from his cheek and brush his hair back, and then continued, "If I were you, I would *hate* me. But to hear you say that you've chosen to forgive me, I can't believe it. I don't know what to say to that. I'm just so, so very sorry." And then he sat down.

As he had spoken, all the tension that was seized up inside my body subsided, and I began to feel tears well up in my eyes. My heart felt a strange warmth. Here I was looking at the elder member of this criminal band, the one person who could have stopped this but who decidedly let Larry Taylor, whom he knew was deranged, stay with Amanda while he gallivanted off with Jalen to try to take money out of our account. I should have felt rage or callousness in the very least. But I didn't. I felt pity. I felt a deep compassion.

I want you to visit him in prison. It was the voice. The Whisper. The Prompt. The Nudge. I knew it was Him. And I knew that I had to lean into this even more. I couldn't walk away from this whole thing and try to forget about them and go on with my life. Instead, the words of the apostle Paul in Romans resounded in my heart:

Do not take revenge, my dear friends, but leave room for God's wrath, for it is written: "It is mine to avenge; I will repay," says the Lord. On the contrary: "If your enemy is hungry, feed him; if he is thirsty, give him something to drink. In doing this, you will heap burning coals on his head." Do not be overcome by evil, but overcome evil with good. (Romans 12:19–21 NIV)

The voice continued, *Remember, Davey, your healing isn't just for you. It's for many more people—and maybe even Amanda's killers.*

Diano was handed a thirty-year sentence that day. Both he and Jalen received abbreviated sentencing for their cooperation with the state, while Larry Taylor received eighty-six years. Later Larry would have another twenty years tacked on for a separate case of sexual assault and burglary, issuing to him more than one hundred years in the Indiana Department of Corrections. As Kristi and I walked out of the courtroom that day, something told us to wait behind and talk to Diano's family members. You see, it's easy to lump people into categories because of fear or hurt or disdain. But there is something so human and healing about turning and facing the hurt and making a demonstration that you're not holding it against anyone.

One by one, Diano's aunts and cousins stepped into the atrium from the courtroom, and one by one, Kristi and I embraced them, tears in all of our eyes. Kristi and I could have run into any one of these lovely ladies at a store or a restaurant over the last seven years, and we never would have given it a thought. Turns out our worlds aren't as divided as we tend to think they are. Diano's mom walked toward me and gave me a hug. Choking back tears, she just said, "Thank you." Finally, Diano's grandmother, the matriarch of this family with sparse male representation, embraced me and said, "Before your wife was killed, I had given up on humanity. But to see how you and your family have handled all of this has restored my hope, not only in humanity, but in Him." As she said "Him" she pointed to the sky, an unmistakable reference to God.

I left that day knowing that this wasn't over. We had now walked this road for just shy of seven years. Seven, the biblical number that signifies completion, perfection. It was so clear. This part of the story had found a sort of completion, but I knew a new chapter was beginning. A new challenge had been presented to me. A new *running toward the roar* would be required to continue in my healing. A new cup that I would ask to be taken from me, but in the end I would have to surrender my will to His.

But then, of course, there would be more cups to hold. More crosses to bear. More trials to go through. More tragedies to undergo. You see, friend, my story isn't over. There's more for me to do. And unfortunately, there will be more for me to endure. The same is true for you. At every turn of the page you'll find that pain and suffering is an inseparable and inescapable part of this life. And yet you'll also find that in every crisis, in every upending event, He's right there inviting you into a redemption story. One that heals you and leverages the work He's doing in your life to heal others. I mean, after all, He promises not to waste any part of our stories. Eventually He will work all things together for your good (Romans 8:28)—and for the good of those your story touches.

But what's even more pressing at this moment, as you put this book down, is for you to decide what you're going to do with *your* story. Will you waste it? Will you let yourself get stuck, paralyzed, floundering in hopelessness or self-pity or despair? Or will you take Him up on the offer He's presenting to you right now, to walk in healing, toward hope and wholeness? To turn your pain around into purpose. Will you embrace the truth that when you let Him take the lead in your healing, *nothing is wasted*?

ACKNOWLEDGMENTS

THEY SAY IT TAKES A VILLAGE TO RAISE A CHILD. I BELIEVE IT. IT also takes one to birth a book. This project would not have happened without the help of so many great people.

To King Jesus, who has made good on His promise that after we have suffered a little while He will "himself restore, confirm, strengthen, and establish" us (1 Peter 5:10 ESV). He will finish what He's started.

To Phil, Robin, Gavin, Amber, James, Angela, Mamaw, and Papa, who have been the dearest friends, nearest ministry partners, and will always be the closest of family.

To my mom and dad, Dave and Brenda, for vigilantly building a foundation of faith into every season of my life.

To my extended family for walking out a legacy of faith and modeling for me how to suffer well.

To my staff and volunteer leaders at Resonate for carrying Weston and me and walking with us through the fire.

To Megan, Jaime, Sallie, and "Sashy" (Ashley) for being surrogate moms to Weston for a season.

To Perry Noble, Shane Duffey, Kevin Myers, Brad Cooper, Howard Frist, and Clint Dupin for taking a chance on me and encouraging me to pursue God's call on my life.

To Ken Roberts, who helped me understand the subtle yet profound shifts of God's grace in leading us into convergence. Without him, I'm not sure there would be a *Nothing is Wasted Ministries* today.

To my other mentors and coaches who risked investing seeds of faith in me, never knowing if they would bear fruit.

To Ally Fallon, who coached me and celebrated with me through this whole writing process while in the midst of her own trials.

To my good friend Wes Yoder, who's more than just an agent but has quickly become a spiritual father.

To Clint, Andraea, and Karen for letting me use their vacation homes for writing retreats.

To Sleeping at Last, Dawn Golden, Andrew Belle, and Houses for providing my writing-zone music playlist.

To Kristi, who has picked up the baton and run with such grace. Thank you for bringing love and laughter back into my life.

To you, the reader, for picking up this book. I'm praying it ministers to you and that you will pass it on to someone else who needs hope and healing in the midst of their hurt.

NOTES

1 Elevation Worship. "Nothing is Wasted." Nothing is Wasted. Essential Music Publishing, LLC, 2011.

2 Lusko, Levi. *Through the Eyes of a Lion.* (Nashville: W Publishing, 2015), 157-158.

3 Tozer, A.W. *The Root of Righteousness*, 2015 ed. (Chicago: Moody Publishers, 2015), 165.

ABOUT THE AUTHOR

DAVEY BLACKBURN IS THE FOUNDER AND DIRECTOR OF NOTHING IS Wasted Ministries, which is a nonprofit organization that helps people in trauma, tragedy, and major life transition discover God's purpose out of their pain. Through the ministry of Nothing is Wasted and as a sought after speaker, Davey works with churches, college campuses, corporations, and correctional facilities to help people partner with God to take back their stories. Their seminal curriculum, Pain to Purpose, has helped thousands navigate their pain and trauma and find healing and wholeness. Davey hosts the *Nothing is Wasted Podcast* which now has over three hundred episodes and seen over three million downloads. Davey lives in Indianapolis, IN with his wife, Kristi, their three kids, Natalia, Weston, and Cohen, and their long-haired miniature dachshund, Henry.

Welcome to the
Nothing is Wasted
Ministry Compendium

In the following pages, you'll discover the heart and soul of our ministry, dedicated to bringing hope, healing, and purpose to those navigating trauma, tragedy, and major life transition.

Founded by Davey Blackburn, Nothing is Wasted Ministries was born out of personal tragedy. After the loss of his wife and unborn child, Davey embarked on a journey of healing, turning his pain into purpose by creating a ministry that offers support and resources to others facing similar struggles.

NOTHING IS WASTED

The Nothing is Wasted *Podcast*

Join the thousands finding solace and direction through our podcast. Tune in to listen and hold space for other stories of tragedy, redemption, and the reminder that God doesn't waste our pain.

With hundreds of episodes, you'll find inspiration by hearing from real people who are at various stages of their healing journey and experiencing God's redemption in their lives.

NOTHING IS WASTED

www.nothingiswasted.com

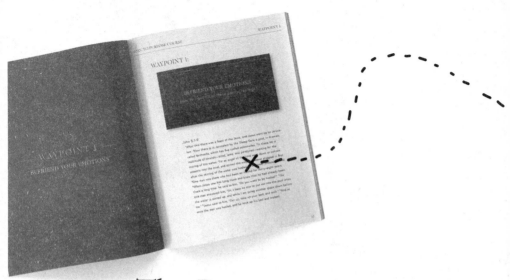

The *Pain to Purpose* Course

Ready to take action? Enroll in our on-demand Pain to Purpose Course, a comprehensive 11-part video series designed to help you rebuild and thrive after experiencing a crisis.

Gain practical tools and insights to move forward with renewed purpose and strength.

The *Pain to Purpose* 42-Day Devotional

Uncover the beauty in your brokenness with the 42-day Pain to Purpose Devotional.

Each day, explore scripture, reflection, and practical response questions designed to guide you toward healing and restoration.

NOTHING IS WASTED

www.nothingiswasted.com

Individualized
Coaching

Feeling stuck in your pain? Experience personalized support with a specialized coach.

Our network of coaches, matched based on your specific and unique pain point, will walk alongside you, providing guidance, encouragement, and accountability as you navigate your journey.

Start *Your Journey* Today

Your story isn't over. Life's darkest moments can become the catalyst for transformation. In Nothing is Wasted, Davey Blackburn shares his journey of loss and healing, inspiring others to find meaning in their own pain. Start your journey to healing and purpose with Nothing is Wasted Ministries today.

Every story of pain carries the potential for redemption. Let Nothing is Wasted Ministries help you discover yours.

NOTHING IS WASTED
www.nothingiswasted.com

Thank *You*

Thank you for allowing us to be a part of your journey. Remember, in the hands of a loving God, nothing is wasted.

We're here for you every step of the way with resources that can offer a roadmap for navigating trauma, tragedy, and life change. Visit www.nothingiswasted.com to learn more.